ENVIRONMENTAL ETHICS AND POLICY MAKING

Environmental issues raise crucial questions. What should we value? What is our place in nature? What kind of life should we live? How should we interact with other living things? Environmental management and policy-making is ultimately based on answers to these and similar questions, but do we need a new ethics to be able overcome the environmental crisis we face?

This book addresses these important questions and explores the values that decision-makers often presuppose in their environmental policy-making. Examining the content of the 'ethics of sustainable development' that the UN and the world's governments want us to embrace, this book examines alternatives to this kind of ethics, and the differences in basic values that these make in practice. Offering a detailed analysis of the ethics that lie behind current policy-making as it is expressed in documents such as *Agenda 21* and the *Rio Declaration*, this unique contribution to the field of environmental studies shows how different environmental ethical theories support different goals of environmental management and generate different policies when it comes to population growth, agriculture, and preservation and management of wilderness areas and endangered species.

Mikael Stenmark concludes that policy-makers must take more seriously the value assumptions and conflicts connected to environmental issues, and state explicitly on what values their own proposals and decisions are based and why these should be accepted. Those studying environmental issues or environmental philosophy will find this accessible text invaluable in presenting a clear understanding of environmental ethics and contemporary applications and policies.

Ashgate Translations in Philosophy, Theology and Religion

This new series presents the first English language translations of important contemporary and classic works in philosophy, theology and world religions.

Other titles in the series:

Philosophy and Revelation
A contribution to the debate on reason and faith
Vittorio Possenti, translated by Emanuel L. Paparella

The Natural Order and Other Texts
Asger Jorn, translated by Peter Shield

Environmental Ethics and Policy Making

MIKAEL STENMARK
Uppsala University, Sweden

Ashgate

Published by
Ashgate Publishing Limited
Gower House
Croft Road
Aldershot
Hants GU11 3HR
England

Ashgate Publishing Company
131 Main Street
Burlington, VT 05401–5600 USA

Ashgate website: http://www.ashgate.com

British Library Cataloguing in Publication Data
Stenmark, Mikael
  Environmental ethics and policy-making. – (Ashgate translations in philosophy, theology and religion)
  1. Envioronmental ethics 2. Environmental policy
  I. Title
  179.1

Library of Congress Cataloging-in-Publication Data
Stenmark, Mikael.
  Environmental ethics and policy-making / Mikael Stenmark.
  p. cm. -- (Ashgate new critical thinking in theology & biblical studies)
  Includes bibliographical references and indexes.
  1. Environmental ethics. 2. Environmental policy I. Title. II. Series.
  GE42.S74 2002
  179'.1--dc21   2001041343

ISBN 0 7546 0563 9

Printed and bound by Athenaeum Press, Ltd.,
Gateshead, Tyne & Wear.

Contents

Acknowledgments

I would like to extend my warm thanks to Carl-Henric Grenholm and David Kronlid for many valuable insights relating to the contents of the book and its presentation. I am also grateful to the Department of Theology at Uppsala University for providing a companionable working environment. This work was originally published in Swedish by Studentlitteratur in 2000, but a grant from the Swedish Research Council enabled it to be translated into English. I am very grateful to the Swedish Research Council for this grant and to Craig Graham McKay for his translation. Finally, it remains for me to thank the Swedish National Environment Protection Board and the Swedish Foundation for Strategic Environmental Research who financed the research project which resulted in this book.

M.S.

CHAPTER ONE

Introduction

It has often been observed that environmental problems have an ethical dimension. In her introductory address to the 1988 World Conference on the Changing Atmosphere, the Norwegian Prime Minister, Gro Harlem Brundtland, asserted that what was needed in getting to grips with environmental problems was 'a new holistic ethic in which economic growth and environmental protection go hand in hand around the world'.[1] Similarly, in the World Commission report, *Our Common Future*, the authors duly noted that they had 'tried to show how human survival and well-being could depend on success in elevating sustainable development to a global ethic' (World Commission 1987, p. 308).

The only trouble is that in *Our Common Future* and other core documents of environmental policy such as *Agenda 21* or the manifesto, *Ett miljöanpassat samhälle* (A Sustainable Society) issued by the Swedish National Environment Protection Board not much more is said on this subject apart from noting that values are relevant to environmental questions or that we need a new global ethic. No attempt is made to define more precisely how values are relevant to environmental issues or to determine the content of this new 'global' or 'holistic' ethic and to say how it differs from the 'old' or traditional ethic. In other words, the foregoing reports fail to give a clear answer to certain fundamental questions. For example, how exactly does one transform sustainable growth into a global ethic? Would such a new ethic imply, for example, that we had to respect the needs of other kinds of living beings or is it sufficient to take into account the needs of present and perhaps future generations of human beings? What kind of ethic is this really and to what basic values and principles is it committed?

I shall try to show that this lack of clarity is problematic. Before we can accept the notion of sustainable development as the embodiment of a new ethic and a new economic strategy, we have to know the values which underpin the proposal. We must also know which ethical perspectives are ruled out by such a proposal as well as the reasons for their exclusion.

My aim, therefore, is to try to identify more precisely the values on which the notion of sustainable development is based. I shall also attempt to determine the practical relevance of ethical theories for environmental policy making and management. The fundamental question for investigation is the significance of ethics for the creation of a sustainable society. This question in turn resolves itself into several subsidiary questions:

1. Do environmental issues have a moral dimension and, if so, in what sense?

---

[1] Brundtland, cited in Engel (1990, p. 1).

2. What values or ethical principles do environmental policy making and management rest upon?
3. Are there alternatives to the values or ethical principles which are fundamental to existing environmental policy making and management?
4. Would the choice of such alternative values or ethical principles as a rationale for decision making result in saliently different environmental policies and management?

The strategy I have chosen in trying to answer these questions is to begin with an examination of a number of basic documents of environmental policy, namely the World Commission's report, *Our Common Future* (1988), the United Nations' *Agenda 21* (1992), *The Rio Declaration* (1992) and *The Convention on Biological Diversity* (1992) and the Swedish National Environment Protection Board's *Ett miljöanpassat samhälle* (A Sustainable Society) (1993). I then try to identify, systematize and critically assess the ethical values underlying these documents and to present them within the context of a more comprehensive environmental ethic. Subsequently this 'ethic of sustainable development' is compared with other environmental ethical theories presented in studies such as Aldo Leopold's *A Sand County Almanac and Sketches Here and There* (1949), Tom Regan's *The Case for Animal Rights* (1983), Paul Taylor's *Respect for Nature* (1986), J. Baird Callicott's *In Defense of the Land Ethic* (1989a) and Holmes Rolston's *Conserving Natural Value* (1994a). This comparison will make clear how divergent convictions in environmental ethics affect the formation of environmental policies.

In the process of analysis, the nature of environmental ethics as an academic discipline will also become clearer. We shall gain more insight into the kind of questions treated in this discipline and why such a discipline is relevant to the analysis and solution of environmental problems. It is also hoped that the book will be able to provide decision makers at all levels with some of the knowledge of ethical theory, which is needed for thinking about the significance of moral convictions in discussions of environmental questions. Another hope is that the book will give people in general the means for identifying and critically analysing the moral positions – often concealed, unclearly formulated and, indeed, at times self-contradictory – on which current environmental policy making and management is based.

Our first question was *whether* environmental problems really have an ethical dimension. Are questions of value (not simply scientific, technical and economic questions of various kinds) of key significance in dealing with environmental problems? The answer appears to be obvious: clearly, values play an important role. It is therefore somewhat striking that, in most of the documents considered, no attempt is made to discuss values critically and systematically. A possible explanation for the absence of discussion can perhaps be traced to at least one of two assumptions: either that values are of little importance for work in environmental policy making or that it is self-evident what these values are and why they should be approved; no further discussion is therefore needed. A further explanation might be that the lack of discussion of values *per se* reflects the choice of experts. The possible failure to engage scholars normally concerned with the analysis of values or with ethical enquiry in the preparatory work resulted simply in these kinds of questions being overlooked. Whatever the real explanation is, it is clear that the question, 'Have environmental issues a moral dimension?' deserves serious consideration. I shall try to show that moral values crucially influence the development of environmental policy making. Indeed, it will be maintained that disagreements over the strategies to be adopted often derive from the conflicting moral values which the individual actors in this field associate with the environment. Basic concepts such as 'view of nature' and 'environmental ethics' will also be made more precise.

The next step in the analysis (the second question above) consists in a critical assessment of the views and values regarding nature which are most often presupposed in environmental research, policy making and management. What is the view of nature and the environmental ethic which serves as the starting point for governmental investigations, UN reports or research reports from the Environment Protection Board? What relevance do those working to create a sustainable society really ascribe to moral values? Do they share any unitary set of basic values? If not, what are the implications of this lack of agreement for the measures deemed necessary for attaining the goal of a 'sustainable development'? Do such people perhaps lack a common goal altogether? Do they each mean different things when they speak of a sustainable society? Finally, do the values held by environmental experts or decision makers differ from those accepted by people in general?

As I have already noted, the authors of the environmental documents analysed in this book are to some extent aware that values must play a central role in environmental questions and environmental management. At the same time, there is no real discussion of the values which underlie – or should inspire – a policy under consideration. It is therefore necessary first to reconstruct and identify the values and ethical principles which implicitly or explicitly underpin the environmental policies proposed in these documents. We shall find that these values and principles derive in great part from what philosophers call an *anthropocentric* (or *human-centred*) environmental ethic, namely the view that our attitudes to nature or to the various kinds of environmental policies adopted should ultimately be judged on the basis of how they affect human beings. Consequently, we do not have to take into consideration the well-being of other living creatures.

The ethic of sustainable development differs in one important sense, however, from traditional anthropocentrism, that is, from that ethic which the World Commission presumes to be the 'old' ethic. For the ethic of sustainable development includes the idea that we have moral obligations not only towards people now living but also towards *future* generations still unborn. We must consider the needs not only of people alive at the present time but also those of future generations. This means that the principle of equality as well as the principle of human dignity – that all human beings have the same moral worth and therefore the same basic rights – involve an extended temporal perspective which includes future human generations as well. In this sense the ethic of sustainable development is a genuinely new ethic. Never before, at least in the Western world, have we thought of ourselves as having moral responsibilities stretching five or ten generations ahead in time. It follows that the number of individuals we have to consider or respect in our actions has markedly increased.

The import of these intergenerational obligations has not, however, been precisely and fully explained. Are we obliged, for example, to try to enable future generations to attain the same standard of living that we enjoy or does it suffice to try to guarantee them a lower, but still acceptable quality of life? If we believe that future generations have the same right to the earth as we have, does this imply that we must compensate them for consuming non-renewable natural resources such as fossil fuels or minerals? Can we, for example, consume all the world's oil and still claim to fulfil our responsibilities towards future generations? Another important question which is left unanswered is whether the idea of an '*inter*generational' justice (justice with respect to generations at different points in time) differs saliently from the '*intra*generational' justice (justice with respect to all people living at the present time) which is also advocated. What difference does it make if we require that resources be distributed justly between people living at different times rather than between those living in different places?

Without an answer to these and similar questions, it remains unclear how advocates of sustainable development consider we should deal with situations where the interests of those living at the present time conflict with the interests of future generations. I shall therefore try to specify more exactly the values which guide and shape the environmental goals and measures proposed in these policy documents and to frame them in terms of a more explicit environmental ethical theory. I shall call this theory *intergenerational anthropocentrism*.

The third question was whether there are any alternatives to this anthropocentric ethic which forms the basis of existing environmental management and policy making. Where one system of values is adopted, alternative systems are indirectly rejected. The ethical positions thereby excluded may not merely be those of the 'old' ethic (that is, traditional anthropocentrism): other, 'new' or 'neotraditional' ethical theories may also be ruled out. I shall therefore try to sketch the possible contours of such an alternative, *non-anthropocentric*, environmental ethic. Quite a few scientists and philosophers clearly advocate such an alternative system of values. These non-anthropocentrists are critical of the way, within existing environmental policy making and management, natural products are treated merely as a resource for satisfying human needs and desires. In contrast, they believe that the intrinsic value of nature should be noted and respected. These critics think that in reality it is the exclusively human way of viewing nature that is ultimately responsible for our environmental problems.

A complicating factor in the analysis of a non-anthropocentric ethic is that environmentalists critical of the ethic of sustainable development may advocate different types of non-anthropocentrism among themselves. I shall therefore try to specify more precisely the meaning and content of some of these forms of environmental ethics. The most important division arises between 'biocentric' and 'ecocentric' ethics. Those advocating *biocentrism* claim that also other organisms than humans have an intrinsic value. On the other hand, because species and ecosystems are not in themselves living beings, they cannot be accorded any such value in themselves. Advocates of *ecocentrism*, by contrast, claim that individual beings are not alone in possessing intrinsic value: landscapes, water, air and ecosystems all possess an intrinsic value as well. In fact, according to ecocentrists, rightness or wrongness has to be judged on the basis of the well-being of the biotic community as a whole and not simply on the basis of the well-being of the human community. It is important to take heed of these differences in ethical theory since they lead to differing views about how to design an adequate environmental policy. What makes the analysis difficult, however, is that those advocating ecocentrism are often unclear about precisely which ethical principles should form the basis of environmental policy making and management. This means that I must first try to formulate these ecocentric principles before applying them to policy issues.

The fourth and last question to be analysed concerns those more practical differences in environmental policy making issues which arise from adopting anthropocentrism, biocentrism or ecocentrism, respectively. Where and why do these three ethical theories lead to different results when, supplemented by the appropriate scientific theories and data, they are used as a basis for environmental policies in shaping forestry or agriculture or in ensuring the preservation of biological diversity? And on what points is there agreement despite a divergence in the theoretical point of departure and consequently in the basic system of values underlying a programme or particular measures? My research shows that differing positions in environmental ethics generate differing conceptions of environmental policy making and that therefore ethical or moral disunity cannot be ignored. Where basic values differ, divergent policies arise.

I have chosen to concentrate upon a number of specific problems: population size; the proportion of land to be left uncultivated and how we should take care of such areas; how we should treat the problem of endangered species; and how to regulate the use of animals and plants in agriculture. Many other important fields of enquiry – patterns of consumption, energy use, transport issues and forestry management – are thus not analysed in detail. Nevertheless, it is hoped that the discussion will be sufficiently broad to show that our choice of environmental ethic is of central significance for the environmental policies which we undertake.

Ecocentrists, for example, think that the size of the human population should on occasion be considerably reduced so as to reach a level compatible with the well-being and integrity of other living beings, while representatives of the ethic of sustainable development find it sufficient to suggest that population size should be stabilized at a level compatible with the productive capacity of the supporting ecosystems. A very important policy question for biocentrists is how we treat animals in farming. For representatives of sustainable development, by contrast, the important question is whether land and animals are used efficiently and farsightedly, so that future generations of human beings will be able to satisfy their needs as well. Some biocentrists go so far as to assert that respect for the equal worth of animals implies that agriculture should be reformed in such a way that meat production is given up (or at least substantially curtailed).

In general, both ecocentrists and biocentrists question the assumption that human well-being should be the ultimate aim of all environmental and developmental policy making, whereas advocates of sustainable development presuppose it. These basic value commitments need to be motivated and justified.

Concerning current research in the field, there is surprisingly little material available. This assertion must not be misconstrued. Philosophers and theologians have obviously published a great number of monographs and articles about environmental issues and similarly there is no lack of works about aspects of environmental policy published by ecologists, economists, social scientists, politicians and other decision makers. The trouble with the former group, however, is that they often fail to display clearly the linkage between environmental ethics on the one hand and environmental policy and management on the other. The problem with the second group is the exact opposite. While they deal explicitly with environmental policy issues, the ethics and values which the policies are based on remain merely implicit or in certain cases are altogether absent. The present work is an attempt to bridge this gap. There are three monographs which have attempted – at least partially – to do something similar, namely Noel J. Brown (ed.), *Ethics and Agenda 21* (1994), Fredrick Ferré and Peter Hartel (eds), *Ethics and Environmental Policy* (1994) and the Swedish Council for Planning and Coordination of Research, *Miljöetik* (1994). But although these works provide certain important insights about ethics' relevance to environmental policy issues, a much deeper and comprehensive analysis is required if an ethically well-informed and structured environmental management is to be developed. My research is perhaps a first step in contributing to a more systematic approach of this kind.

Finally, I should emphasize that this book is not aimed primarily at philosophers and theologians but rather at decision makers at all levels who are working with environmental management issues, people engaged generally in environmental research and students whose education involves environmental courses of various kinds. It is hoped that it can also be read with enjoyment by others who are interested in environmental issues and environmental management. This means, first of all, that no knowledge of philosophy is presupposed and, secondly, that, although it is assumed that philosophers can have some use for the book, I have avoided deeper and more detailed arguments in ethics and have simplified certain ethical theories and distinctions.

The book is arranged as follows. In Chapter 2, I try to show, using concrete examples, that values inevitably play an important role in questions of environmental management and that science *per se* is unable to tackle these issues. We find that we cannot formulate any policy regarding environmental management without applying certain value judgments to the scientific information available to us: judgments as to what people should value, what kind of lives we should lead, what place we should assume within nature as a whole and how we should behave towards other living beings or even towards the earth's whole ecosystem. Key terms such as 'environmental ethics' and 'view of nature' are defined in this chapter.

In Chapter 3 I discuss the role and significance often given to values within environmental management and policy making and analyse some of the more important environment policy documents. We find, for example, that the values embodied in *Our Common Future* or *Agenda 21* mainly reflect an anthropocentric ethic. It also becomes clear what is characteristic of this type of environmental ethic and at what points intergenerational anthropocentrism differs from traditional anthropocentrism.

Nevertheless, the choice of an anthropocentric ethic as the basis for environmental management and policy making is controversial in so far as there exists a large group of environmentalists who reject this type of environmental ethics and advocate a non-anthropocentric ethic instead. The main features of such an alternative ethic are identified in Chapter 4. In this chapter we find that such an ethic can take at least two essentially different forms, biocentrism and ecocentrism. An analysis and comparison of these two forms of non-anthropocentric ethics follows.

Chapter 5 investigates how the choice of an ethic – anthropocentric, biocentric or ecocentric – has practical consequences for environmental management and policy making. In the final chapter, in line with *Agenda 21*'s directive (*Agenda 21*, 31.8) that increased ethical awareness in environmental decision making is desirable, the results of the present study and the relevance of ethics generally for environmental management, teaching and research are discussed.

CHAPTER TWO

The Ethical Dimension of Environmental Problems

It is not uncommon in political and scientific contexts to assume that science and technology form the key to the problem of environment. This basic assumption becomes clearer when we look at the people actually appointed to the various committees and authorities at a national and international level which have been set up to provide a basis for decision with regard to environmental and related issues. There are various reasons why this conscious or unconscious assumption is made. One explanation is that the ecological threats which confront us are often not immediately accessible to our ordinary senses. The risks involved can only be measured with the help of advanced technical equipment. Put quite simply, environmental problems often involve complex technical questions and therefore it seems reasonable to turn to the experts in the corresponding technical disciplines to solve the problems. Another underlying argument might be that, since science provides objective answers which are based on fact in a field where otherwise emotions and conflicts of interest abound, it is only natural that we should make use of science to guide us in this matter. However, I propose to argue that, although science and technology are of great significance in coming to terms with environmental problems, the latter are not exclusively – indeed not even primarily – of a scientific or technical nature.

The Limitations of Science

In order to grasp the nature of the limitations of science and technology as far as environmental issues are concerned, let us consider what science can tell us about the environment. It can provide us with the information, for example that the ozone layer has become thinner, that biological diversity is decreasing, that the lakes of the world suffer from increasing acidification and that there is an increase in air pollution. At the same time, it can provide a causal explanation of these changes. In addition, it can often tell us the measures we can take to change the prevailing state of affairs. In other words, science can tell us *what* is the case, *why* it is the case and what *can* be done to change things. Finally, technology provides us with the *practical means* required to carry out these changes.

Observe, however, that we are unable to develop an environmental policy or carry out certain environmental measures purely on the basis of this scientific information. Let us consider a rather trivial example to show why this is so.[1]

---

[1] The example, somewhat modified, is taken from Ariansen (1993, p. 96).

From the assertions

(1) River R can deliver an energy output of X gigawatt,
(2) there is a profitable way of damming River R, and
(3) flora and fauna in the region will be placed at risk if River R is dammed,[2]

it is impossible to derive any conclusion as to whether we ought to dam River R or not or more generally determine what attitude we should adopt to River R and its flora and fauna. In order for such a conclusion to be drawn, we must supply one or more value statements as additional premises to our argument. A value statement is one which does not merely say what is or is not the case or merely specifies what can be done but says something about what *ought* to be done. The assertion

(4) All rivers which can be dammed profitably ought to be dammed

serves as an example of such a value premise. (The underlying argument might be, for example, that economic growth ought to be considered more important for human beings than the preservation of flora and fauna.) It is only after such a premise has been appended that any conclusion, such as

(5) We ought to dam River R

can be drawn. Ecologists or other natural scientists are therefore unable to reach a conclusion in matters of policy purely on the basis of scientific information.

Let us consider a further example which illustrates why it is impossible. Suppose someone were to argue as follows:

(1) There are certain species of flora and fauna which are endangered because of x, y and z,
(2) we can save these species by countermeasures A, B and C,
(3) therefore we ought to preserve these endangered species.

It is correct that ecology can give us knowledge of the kind expressed in premises (1) and (2). However, ecologists cannot derive (3) from premises of this type. Logically, the argument is invalid. Conclusion (3) is only derivable if we add a premise which expresses a value judgment of some kind, such as in the following:

(1) There are certain species of flora and fauna which are endangered because of x, y and z,
(2) we can save these species by countermeasures A, B and C,
(3) *the species in question are of great value to human beings (for example, they possess a recreational value, a genetic value or a value linked to our culture or history) and such a value ought to be protected,*

---

[2] These assertions can be assumed to depend on available scientific information.

(4) therefore we ought to preserve these endangered species.

There is also another kind of value judgment, different from that expressed in premise (3) above, which could instead serve as the basis of a policy for the preservation of species and which we shall discuss more fully later on:

(3*) *The species in question have a value in themselves: that is, an intrinsic value quite independent of their potential utility for human beings (their instrumental value) and we have no right to violate such values.*

Premise (3*) expresses perhaps even more clearly than (3) a value judgment which we perceive lies beyond the competence of science. Science alone cannot derive it or justify it. Ecology cannot reasonably be expected to determine what in the environment has or has not intrinsic value. Today we ascribe to all human beings an intrinsic value and thereby certain fundamental rights. But there is scarcely anyone who would maintain that ecology or any other science could have yielded us this insight. All environmental measures and all environmental policy are based on similar, explicitly – or more often implicitly – stated attitudes and judgments about what is valuable, what should be encouraged and about whose interests should be satisfied.

   The idea that ecology (or some other science) can tell us what attitude we ought to have towards nature is therefore unfounded. Naturally, this is not to say that ecology cannot give us empirical knowledge which is relevant to the decisions we have to make. It is not possible, however, purely on the basis of ecological theories to deduce how we as human beings ought to relate to ecosystems of various kinds. As Per Ariansen has pointed out:

> It is undoubtedly true that ecologists share with everyone else the view that we ought not to unleash processes which can destroy the very basis of our lives but ecologists do not have any special ethical system as ecologists *per se*. It is not a specifically ecological value that an increased greenhouse effect (global warming) is undesirable. The climate in the Sahara is not an ecological evil. Ecology as a science has revealed complex dependencies within the ecosystem whereby apparently small, humdrum factors can bring about dramatic changes. But ecology cannot as a science impose views upon us about what is morally dubious – for example that using nuclear power as a source of energy, exterminating the stock of whales or contributing to the spread of deserts are evil things. The premises for such conclusions must be fetched from elsewhere. (Ariansen, 1993, p. 58)

If the survival of a species, indeed of human beings, is desirable, it must be so for reasons which go *beyond* ecology, biology and other sciences. However the mistaken view that this is not the case is by no means uncommon in political and scientific discussions. For example, in the report *Ekologisk grundsyn* (From an Ecological Perspective), produced by the Swedish Committee on the Environment and Natural Resources, we read that 'ecology studies the relationship between organisms and the environment and on this basis makes more or less far-reaching attempts to explain and *guide* us in adapting to nature'.[3] This normative view of ecology appears also when 'an ecologically based view' is defined as 'the view regarding the relationship between human beings and nature and of nature's importance for human beings – for their survival and the provision of their needs, for their health and welfare'.[4] However, a more reasonable position is that ecology is a scientific discipline akin to any other scientific discipline and one therefore which makes no direct moral claims. Consequently, ecology cannot serve as a moral guide in any adaptation to nature (although it can naturally propose possible measures for adoption), nor is it within its competence to decide what value human beings should assign to nature.

It is customary in philosophy to refer to this failure to distinguish *questions of fact* from *questions of value* as 'the naturalistic fallacy'. We commit this fallacy whenever we argue that because something *is* the case, it *ought* therefore to be the case. The point being made here is that, whenever we maintain that something is right or wrong, valuable or worthless, we must do more than simply refer to what is normal or natural. Naturally, this does not entail that we cannot support moral positions by citing empirical facts. But what is good or evil, worthwhile or objectionable cannot be deduced automatically from a description of what constitutes a natural (or artificial) process or state of affairs in nature.

If the above line of argument is correct, it follows that science *per se* is at a loss for a reply in ultimately deciding how we should act in regard to environmental matters. If Göran Sundqvist is correct when he says that it 'is obvious that environmental questions in contemporary Western democracies are largely defined as scientific matters', this conclusion must appear somewhat shocking for many decision makers and natural scientists (Sundqvist, 1996, p. 100). Science cannot tell us what we should do, only what we can do. It can tell us how the world 'is' but not how it 'ought' to be. Max Weber hit the nail on the head when he once observed: 'Science is like a map that can tell us how to get to many places but not where to go.'[5] There is no direct inference from how nature actually is to how it ought to be or, above all, to how we should relate to it. From the biological fact (if fact it be) that it is the fittest who survive, it does not follow, as the social Darwinists believed, that society ought to mirror this scheme of things. Nor does it follow from the biological fact that human beings form an inevitable part of an ecological system that we should try to imitate nature in what we do.

In order to come to terms with the environmental problem, we naturally require to know a number of things, such as how industry and commerce, the broader economy and indeed the entire structure of our society influence the environment and how, conversely, various environmental measures affect commerce, industry and the economy as a whole. This knowledge requires, *inter alia*, ecological, economic and sociological research. In all this, science can provide an important and, indeed, decisive contribution. This implies that the causal diagnosis and treatment of environmental problems is also dependent on science.

---

[3] Naturresurs- och miljökommitténs rapport (1982, p. 4) (emphasis added).

[4] Ibid., p. 1 (original emphasis removed).

[5] Weber, quoted in Stevenson and Byerly (1995, p. 35).

The point that I am making, however, is that we must not believe that it is sufficient merely to gather empirical facts. We also have to *evaluate* them, deciding what *importance* is to be attached to them. For example, are the consequences of pollution and their strict regulation good or bad? Obviously, we can regard such pollution as bad, but the question is *how* bad. What negative consequences does the strict regulation of pollution have for trade and industry or for that matter for animal life? Should we in general be concerned at all about what is good or bad for the well-being of animals? Why or why not? What moral rights does a company have to pursue its business in order to generate profit and what are the limits of such rights? Have companies also certain responsibilities in this context? Let us consider a concrete, present-day example. We do not simply require to know how the flow of water between the Baltic and North Sea is affected by building a bridge between Sweden and Denmark. We also have to know what importance is to be attached to a possible deterioration in this flow. Is our concern for animal life in the Baltic of greater value than the fostering of trade between Sweden and the rest of Europe? More generally, should we sacrifice certain endangered plant and animal species in order to increase global food production so that all human beings can eat their fill? Which goal has the higher moral value? Promoting one particular goal and the moral value we attach to it means, not infrequently, that we are forced to sacrifice some other desirable goal.[6]

The environmental problem therefore inevitably raises a number of questions. What should we as human beings value? What kind of beings are we and what do we wish to be? What lives ought we to live? How should we as human beings behave towards other living organisms? Environmental decisions and policies are ultimately determined by our answers to these and similar questions. Our relation to nature is determined by what we consider to be a good life for ourselves and other living beings.

If my argument is correct, we must recognize that environmental problems have three dimensions: a *scientific*, a *social* and a *normative* (that is to say, a moral or ethical) one. If we wish to deal effectively with environmental problems, we have to pay attention to all three of them. We must know, for example, if the ozone layer is indeed in danger and what the causes of ozone depletion are. Similarly, scientific data are required about biological diversity, the acidification of lakes, air pollution and so on. Quite simply, how does the biological cycle function? At the same time, however, we need to know the behaviour of the social cycle. What are the priorities which shape people's lives and mould their various lifestyles? What about consumption patterns? What is the connection between economic growth and environmental destruction? Can we make worthwhile use of economic measures within environmental policy? However, we cannot confine ourselves merely to considering environmental problems from scientific and social perspectives. We also have to form some view of how the relationship between the biological and

---

[6] My treatment naturally does not do full justice to the complex relationship between science and value, between 'is' and 'ought'. For a more detailed treatment of the problem, see, *inter alia*, Taylor (1986, ch. 1), O'Neill (1993, ch. 9) and Stenmark (1999).

social cycles *ought* to be. How should nature and culture relate to each other? How ought we as human beings to behave towards each other and to surrounding nature? Should we, for example, try to preserve animals and plants which are threatened with extinction or should we limit population growth, or indeed even reduce the number of human beings on the earth? If so, why?

Traditionally, two academic disciplines, namely theology and philosophy, have had the opportunity to present the type of normative reasoning which is essential if the ethical dimension of the environmental problem is to be analysed and treated adequately. They form domains within the academic world where questions such as 'What is morally right and wrong?', 'What constitutes a good human being or a good society?' and 'How should human beings relate to other living organisms?' can be studied. They are academic disciplines which discuss what moral views human beings should hold about the environment, what values ought to be given priority in ethical terms and what values or value judgments should inspire and lead us in dealing with the environment and in social planning. In other words, theology and philosophy can provide decision makers at all levels with knowledge of ethical theory and world views which are needed in order to reflect self-consciously and critically about the importance which their own and other people's moral and political values and views have for environmental issues. Moreover, they provide people in general with tools which allow them to discover and critically analyse the often hidden value judgments and assumptions linked to some world views which crop up with environmental issues.

It is when we try, for example, to resolve conflicts that arise between economic, cultural and environmental interests that some of the most difficult moral questions arise. However, without some (explicit or implicit) ethical position with regard to these problems, no environmental strategies can be devised and no practical environmental work can be carried out. If our aim is to deal adequately with environmental problems, we require at least two things, namely

(a) scientific and social studies of the relationship between human beings and nature, and
(b) a critical and constructive analysis of people's various ethical judgments, their views of nature, their world views and of the consequences that all these different positions have for the creation of a sustainable society.

These different types of academic study can then, it is hoped, form the basis for environmental decisions and measures.

Environmental Ethics and Views of Nature

Value judgments are therefore decisive when it comes to dealing with environmental problems and, without them, it is impossible to make any decision whatsoever about environmental issues. But what are value judgments? When it comes to broader or more specific aspects of environmental management, what are the value judgments which guide society and what are those which ought to guide it? The answers to these and similar questions are studied in the academic discipline called ethics or moral philosophy. Within ethics, we try systematically to make explicit and precise the norms which regulate our actions and discuss their justification. Let us cite two examples of such norms. The first is the utilitarian principle, 'the greatest possible happiness of the greatest possible number of people'. The second is the principle of autonomy: 'all human beings have the right to determine their own lives'.

We can say that *ethics* is the systematic and critical study of our moral attitudes, actions and beliefs about how we ought to live and about what sort of people we ought to be. This sense of the word 'ethics' does not mean, however, that all human beings have an ethic: not everyone after all has reflected systematically upon the values which guide their actions. Nonetheless, all human beings have a *morality*, in the sense that they possess views about what is good or bad and about what constitutes right and wrong actions.[7] All human beings have a morality whether they are conscious of it or not, but far fewer have systematically analysed and reflected upon the content of their morality. Morality in the sense we are using it thus designates our value judgments about what is right or wrong, about the nature of a good person, a good society and a good relationship to other living beings, whereas ethics denotes our conscious and systematic reflections upon these judgments.

In distinguishing between morality and ethics in this way, it should be noted that we can be good at the one without necessarily being good at the other. We can be skilled in ethics but exhibit shortcomings in our morality, and vice versa. Just as I can be an excellent teacher without having consciously thought much about educational theories, so too I can be a good person without having reflected much upon morality. Conversely, just because I know a lot about educational theories and principles, it does not necessarily follow that I am a good teacher. In short, there are no 'moral experts' (or, to put it more exactly, we are all on a par when it comes to moral expertise). On the other hand, we can, if we wish, speak of 'ethical experts', 'experts in ethics' or, in a word, of *ethicists*. An *ethicist* (or, to use a more old-fashioned expression, a moral philosopher) is a person who has detailed knowledge of ethical theories and the critical analysis of such theories and who, as a rule, carries out research into certain moral questions. Just as it is prudent for a teacher to take account of the insights which educational research provides, it is also wise for decision makers and people in general to make use of the insights of the ethicists and the ways in which they analyse and test moral views.

In making the general distinction between morality and ethics, we can also naturally apply this more specifically to the case of environment, thus distinguishing between environmental morality and environmental ethics. Environmental morality would thus consist of those moral attitudes to nature and the environment which actually occur. Environmental ethics, by contrast, refers to the systematic analysis of, and reflection upon our relationship and attitudes to

---

[7] An alternative approach is naturally to treat 'morality' and 'ethics' as entirely synonymous.

nature. All human beings therefore, consciously or unconsciously, have an environmental morality but not everyone has an environmental ethics. We can define environmental ethics more precisely in the following way:

> *Environmental ethics* is the systematic and critical study of the moral judgments and attitudes which (consciously or unconsciously) guide human beings in the way they behave towards nature.[8]

The basic question in environmental ethics is thus not how human beings ought to behave towards other human beings but how they ought to behave with regard to nature – animals, plants, species and ecosystems. We can thus distinguish between an environmental and what we might call a 'human' ethic (that is, an ethic centred on human beings).[9] In contrast to environmental ethics, *human ethics* is the systematic and critical study of the moral judgments and attitudes which (consciously or unconsciously) guide human beings in the way they behave towards each other. The object of human ethics is interpersonal relations, while the object of environmental ethics is human beings' relationship to their natural environment, in other words to nature. Human ethics has existed, in the Western world, from the days of antiquity when Socrates, Plato and Aristotle discussed such matters. This is not true of environmental ethics. While human beings in all ages have had certain moral attitudes to the environment, the academic study of environmental ethics did not exist before the 1960s and 1970s.[10]

Environmental ethics or more far-reaching attempts to construct a theory of environmental ethics began first when a number of people began to realize that we faced an environmental crisis of global proportions. Philosophers, ecologists and others could see that we had treated nature as an inexhaustible resource which is able to absorb and neutralize our waste. In so doing, we had overestimated the earth's resources and acquired habits which threatened the welfare and continued existence of ourselves and other living creatures. Faced with this situation, these thinkers 'discovered' environmental morality – both their own and that of other people – and began consciously to think about different moral attitudes towards nature. It was not until 1974, however, that the first systematic book on the subject of environmental ethics appeared and received international attention. This was John Passmore's *Man's responsibility for nature: Ecological problems and Western*

---

[8] Note, however, that the term 'environmental ethics' is sometimes given a more limited meaning. In certain connections, it is used to denote more specifically the ethical system which maintains that human beings have direct moral responsibilities to nature or to other living creatures and not merely responsibilities to other human beings. John O'Neill, for example, writes as follows: 'To hold an environmental ethic is to hold that non-human beings and states of affairs in the natural world have intrinsic value' (O'Neill, 1993, p. 8). I contend that such a narrow definition must be rejected because it is tendentious and has the absurd consequence that the ethical approach represented by advocates of sustainable development cannot be classified as an environmental ethic.

[9] The plural form, 'ethics' in general denotes the study as a whole, whereas the singular form 'ethic' denotes one specific form of study or approach within ethics. The distinction is rather fluid and my choice has been determined mainly by the accepted terminological practice of the thinkers discussed.

[10] For a historical account of the development of environmental ethics, see above all Nash (1988) but also Eckersley (1992) and Sörlin (1991).

traditions. A couple of years later, *Environmental Ethics*, the first academic journal devoted to the subject, began publication. Today the situation is quite different. There are several journals dealing with environmental ethics and every year sees the publication of a relatively large number of monographs and anthologies. However, in research terms, environmental ethics is still in its infancy.

Every value system which sets out to guide us in our intercourse with nature constitutes a form of environmental ethic. Among other things, this implies that a theory of environmental ethics identifies, makes precise and justifies certain ethical norms or principles which its proponents believe could and should guide us in our relations with other living beings or with nature as a whole. A theory of environmental ethics thus ought to explain in what sense, if any, human beings have or ought to have moral obligations towards other living beings; it should identify what these conceivable obligations might be and the possible consequences of their acceptance for the lives and life styles of human beings. Yet another vital question for environmental ethicists is naturally how what we have called human ethics relates to environmental ethics. Which ethical principle is to have priority if a principle of human ethics conflicts with a principle of environmental ethics? What do we do, for example, if the principle of ownership, namely that people have a right to decide over their own property, which forms part of some systems of human ethics, conflicts with a principle of environmental ethics which says that, in the case of animal species threatened with extinction, the animals and their habitat must be protected? Indeed, is it possible to speak of moral rights both in human ethics and environmental ethics? We usually agree that all human beings have certain fundamental rights, but do animals and plants also have rights? As we shall discover, environmental ethicists give different answers to these questions.

Another important distinction, in addition to the one between environmental and human ethics, is that between *descriptive* and *normative* ethics. Sometimes, in speaking of 'ethics', we mean simply the actual description of the value judgments which people pass about a certain phenomenon, such as abortion, recycling or nuclear power. In this context, environmental ethics means simply the study of the values which people actually express in their relationship to nature or the values which steer their possible involvement in environmental issues or environmental work. Here the task of environmental ethics is to try to discover, describe and classify those values which directly or indirectly shape environmental research, environmental education and environmental policy. The task is to lay bare and analyse the value judgments, whether explicit or implicit, which steer our patterns of thought and our attitudes in environmental issues. This type of ethics is what ethicists normally call 'descriptive ethics'.

Within 'normative ethics', we go a stage further and try to *analyse critically* people's values and to suggest constructive proposals concerning the values upon which environmental measures and policies *ought* to be based. What measures are morally defensible if our goal is to achieve sustainable development? Should we, indeed, approve of such a goal? Have we moral obligations to future generations of human beings? Do such intergenerational obligations diminish with time? How should intergenerational justice, that is to say, the moral obligations of now living

individuals to future generations, be weighed against the duties we have to other
now living human beings, such as those to be found in the developing countries (so-
called 'intragenerational justice')? Should we also take the view that human beings
have moral obligations to animals and plants? If we do, what has priority when the
interests of human society conflict with the interests of the biotic community?
These and similar questions belong to normative environmental ethics. The latter
discipline thus considers the various arguments and tries to establish what views on
right and wrong, on good and evil, are acceptable or reasonable.

Because the concept of the environment or nature plays a central role in the
foregoing definition of environmental ethics as well as in general discussions about
the environment, it is important to try, at least to some extent, to give it a little more
precision. (I shall treat the terms 'environment' and 'nature' as synonyms.) When
we examine things more closely, we discover that the idea of nature is used in
various differing senses. Very often the word 'nature' is a term to describe, animals,
plants and inorganic matter, in other words the sum of things making up the
material world. In this context, the concept of nature often has a descriptive use,
namely it is meant to denote a specific phenomenon or set of specific phenomena
without directly assigning them any special value, be it positive or negative. This
descriptive use of the concept of nature can either, as above, embrace everything
that exists in the natural world or it can have a more restricted sense in excluding
human beings and possibly their artefacts. The concept can also have a still more
restricted sense whereby it denotes only that which is largely uninfluenced or
changed by human beings, namely undisturbed nature or wilderness.

In the arguments we are about to meet, human beings are also sometimes
included in the concept of nature. This wider notion is used above all when there is
a wish to emphasize that human beings should not be perceived as something
independent of nature but rather as an integral part of it. In the definition of
environmental ethics above, it is clear, however, that the concept of nature is
defined more narrowly. It does not embrace human beings and their artefacts. The
concept of nature represents the whole surrounding world and perhaps also
primarily that part of this world which is not directly influenced by human beings.
Nature is defined as something apart from human beings.

The above definition of environmental ethics also assumes that human beings differ
from nature (or the rest of nature) in a fundamental way. Firstly, they can view
themselves as standing in a relationship to nature and thereby view nature as something
other than themselves. Human beings are self-conscious beings. For example, they are
able to realize that they are dependent on nature for their existence. Secondly, they can
decide how they should relate to nature, by for example acknowledging (or not
acknowledging) their obligations to animals. Human beings can impose moral
restrictions upon themselves. As a result, they are *moral agents*. They are, as far as is
known, the only creatures on this earth which are capable of right or wrong actions.
They alone have a responsibility for their actions. Other organisms are looked upon as
'amoral' creatures: that is, creatures whose actions can be neither right nor wrong.

In the environmental context, the concept of nature does not merely have a
descriptive function; it also has a normative one. 'Nature' is something which coincides

with 'what is natural', something given by nature and uninfluenced by man. In this way, nature acquires a positive value. The concept conjures up an association with a desirable state worth striving for. Nature is seen as an ideal, something to be close to and something to be in harmony with. Nature is something 'good' because it is 'the natural' or 'the original'. The concept of nature in this sense has clearly a very positive sense.

Thus to sum up, the concept of nature can be defined in a wider or narrower sense, depending on whether we exclude or include human beings and their artefacts. It can also be defined in a descriptive or normative way, where the latter involves various moral judgments. In my analysis, I shall try to specify what meaning is being assigned to the concept where this is not evident from the context. The meaning of 'view of nature' naturally depends on which of the foregoing meanings we attach to the concept of nature. However, I shall primarily mean by 'view of nature' the way in which an individual, group or society looks upon the elements and structure of nature. Thus a view of nature contains a *metaphysics*, a view about the essence of nature, such as whether it is dynamic or static, or whether it is fragile (with a low level of tolerance) or robust (with a high level of tolerance).[11] A view of nature also involves certain epistemological views. For example, what Barry Commoner has called 'the third law of ecology' (Nature knows best) is often justified on the basis of certain epistemological assumptions. This law entails that 'any major man-made change in a natural system is likely to be *detrimental* to that system' (Commoner, 1971, p. 41). For that reason Commoner considers that it is better not to try and manipulate an ecosystem but instead leave it to find its own equilibrium. This view seems a reasonable one, if we accept that nature is an immensely complex and interdependent system about which we know very little. In other words, epistemological scepticism forms at least part of the reason why we should accept ecology's 'third law'. A third component in a view of nature is a system of values (or an *axiology*) which tells which values are ascribed to nature in various circumstances. This axiology is often evident, for example, when nature is described figuratively as an enemy who has to be defeated or as a friend and brother or as a resource to be exploited or as an entity whose moral standing must be respected. Environmental moral attitudes thus go to make up a view of nature.

Although these various theoretical components can be distinguished in a view of nature, it is important to point out that people are often unaware of the view of nature they hold. Furthermore, a view of nature is not something that we lightly choose and discard. On the contrary, we are often brought up according to some definite view of nature. It forms part of our cultural and social inheritance.[12] In spite of that, it is reasonable to assume that all human beings embrace a view of nature in some sense or other. Everyone has some view about what nature is, how it functions, what we are able to know about it and how we ought to relate to it.

---

[11] Stig Waldén holds that the difference in views about whether nature is fragile or robust forms an important ideological demarcation line which is not always noted in environmental discussions (see Wandén, 1993, pp. 12–19).

[12] For a discussion of various views of nature in the Western world, see for example Merchant (1980), Hargrove (1989, chs 1–4), Anderberg (1994, ch. 2), Des Jardins (1997, ch. 8). See also Callicott (1994) for a cultural and geographically more comprehensive account.

CHAPTER THREE

Anthropocentric Environmental Ethics

I shall now try to identify the values and ethical principles which form the basis of existing environmental management and policy. My approach is to examine a number of core national and international documents on environmental policy. The aim is to identify, systematize and critically review the values which are presupposed in these documents and to use them to construct a more comprehensive environmental ethic. The primary documents for examination are the World Commission's Report Our *Common Future* (1988), the UN *Agenda 21* (1992), *The Rio Declaration* (1992) and the *Convention on Biological Diversity* (1992), and the Swedish National Environment Protection Board's report *Ett miljöanpassat samhälle* (A Sustainable Society) (1993).

Basic Values in the Ethic of Sustainable Development

As has been already suggested in Chapter 1, the decision makers who are dedicated to creating a sustainable environment are less than clear about the importance they ascribe to values and ethics. At the same time they duly observe that environmental problems have an ethical dimension. In her opening speech at the 1988 World Conference on the Changing Atmosphere, the Norwegian Prime Minister, Gro Harlem Brundtland, asserted that success in tackling environmental problems requires us to develop 'a new holistic ethic in which economic growth and environmental protection go hand-in-hand around the world'.[1] Brundtland believes that the successful solution of environmental problems is not simply a matter of various technologies and methods of dealing with pollution and the waste of resources: it also means that people have to rethink their relationship to nature.

The Brundtland Commission's report, *Our Common Future*, also stresses the importance of ethics and morality in coping with environmental problems. The report sums up as follows: 'We have tried to show how human survival and well-being could depend on success in elevating sustainable development to a global ethic' (World Commission, 1987, p. 308). The problem, however, is that all that is said is that values are relevant to environmental issues and that we need a new global ethic. No real attempt is made to explain more specifically the exact relevance of values or to say what precisely this new ethic is and how it differs from the 'old' one. If we are to make 'sustainable development' into a global ethic, which values do we accept and which do we reject?

---

[1] Brundtland, quoted in Engel (1990, p. 1).

The same is true of the Swedish follow-up to the UN Rio Conference which is summed up in the government report, *Our Task following Rio, The Swedish programme of action for the 21st Century* (1992). In the introduction, something is said about the values upon which the document is based. The authors proceed from the assumption that we ought 'as a long-term goal [to] strive for a sustainable development – one which is based upon an adaptation to biogeochemical cycles' (Working Committee on the Environment, 1992, p. 3). They further write on the same page that a 'transition to sustainable development must in the future permeate every aspect of social activity'. However, there is no discussion or analysis of the ethical dimension of environmental problems. Does the idea of a sustainable development not entail specific ethical viewpoints? Or is it assumed that science can provide us with a descriptive, non-normative definition of the concept 'sustainable development'.

In the Swedish National Environment Protection Board's policy programme, *A Sustainable Society*, it is emphasized that it 'is in social organization, our values and our way of life that we must seek the ultimate causes of environmental problems' (Naturvårdsverket, 1993, p. 27). But in the programme of action, attention is almost exclusively concentrated on technical measures, improvements and adjustments which are necessary in the present social system in order to create a sustainable society. Such a society is achieved mainly through environmental taxes, environmental labelling, consumer responsibility and similar measures. Thus, in spite of the fact that moral values are considered to form one of the ultimate causes of environmental problems, the report fails to discuss what our moral values are, what ethical system they are based on or what values we ought to have and why.

However, the authors of *Agenda 21* seem to a certain extent to be aware of this lack of ethical analysis because they write that it is necessary 'to develop codes of practice and guidelines regarding environmentally sound and sustainable development' and that one measure which ought to be taken is 'strengthening and establishing national advisory groups on environmental and developmental ethics' (*Agenda 21*, 31.10).

Despite the fact that a discussion or analysis of the values and ethic which should shape environmental management is lacking, there are at the same time certain values which are presupposed in these environmental policy documents. I shall try to indicate some of these and thereby identify certain basic values of this new global ethic.

All the environmental policy documents accept the aim that the development of society must be *sustainable*. By 'sustainable development' the World Commission means 'development that meets the needs of the present without compromising the ability of future generations to meet their own needs' (World Commission, 1987, p. 43). It can naturally be asked whose needs are being considered, but later on the same page it is made clear that it is human needs and interests that are meant. This fundamental view is expressed still more clearly when the concept of sustainable development is defined in Världsstrategin för miljövård, *Omsorg om jorden* (Global strategy for environmental management, *Caring for the Earth*) as 'improving human quality of life while at the same time living within the scope of the supporting ecosystems' (1993, p. 13). Thus a core value component of what we may call the 'ethic of sustainable development' is that *it is human needs which ought to take pride of place in shaping environmental management.*

The central importance of this value is underlined also by the fact that according to the report of the World Commission, the aim of environmental management is 'to begin managing environmental resources to ensure both sustainable human progress and human survival' (World Commission, 1987, p. 1). It is human well-being which is 'the ultimate goal of all environment and development policies' (p. xiv). This fundamental view is also expressed in the Rio Declaration.[2] Its first principle is as follows: 'Human beings are at the centre of concerns for sustainable development. They are entitled to a healthy and productive life in harmony with nature.'

Observe, however, that environmental management must not merely take note of people who are alive at present: it must also show consideration for future generations of human beings. The World Commission writes:

> We borrow environmental capital from future generations with no intention or prospect of repaying. They may damn us for our spendthrift ways, but they can never collect on our debt to them. We act as we do because we can get away with it: future generations do not vote; they have no political or financial power; they cannot challenge our decisions. But the results of the present profligacy are rapidly closing the options for future generations. Most of today's decision makers will be dead before the planet feels the heavier effects of acid precipitation, global warming, ozone depletion, or widespread desertification and species loss. (World Commission, 1987, p. 8)

Thus another basic value component of the ethic of sustainable development is that *it is not simply the needs of people who are alive now who should be considered but also those of future generations.* In other words, if we accept the idea of sustainable development, we must also accept that we have a moral obligation to future generations. It is thus a question of a temporally extended principle of justice and equality. The fundamental norm is that the lives of all human beings – those alive now and those still to be born – are equally valuable. We are therefore not free to exhaust natural resources because in so doing we would diminish the range of choice and the well-being of future generations.

What exactly, then, are the needs of present and future generations which we must consider in shaping environmental management and in the creation of a sustainable society? They are primarily made up of fundamental human needs such as the need for food, water, security, basic medical care and education: 'The Commission believes that widespread poverty is no longer inevitable. Poverty is not only an evil in itself, but sustainable development requires meeting the basic needs of all' (ibid.).

A sustainable development entails that the basic needs of *all* human beings are satisfied because poor people are often forced to live in a way which threatens the

---

[2] The Rio Declaration is the official document which the countries participating in the UN conference on environment and development (UNCED) (Rio de Janeiro, 1992) recognized as a long-term goal for the development of human society.

viability of the ecosystems on which they depend for their survival. 'Meeting essential needs requires not only a new era of economic growth for nations in which the majority are poor, but an assurance that those poor get their fair share of the resources required to sustain that growth' (ibid.). The Commission thus does not consider that the present distribution of resources or welfare should be passed on to future generations. Instead there must be a more just distribution in the future. The same fundamental view is present also in the Rio Declaration: 'All States and all people shall cooperate in the essential task of eradicating poverty as an indispensable requirement for sustainable development, in order to decrease the disparities in standards of living and better meet the needs of the majority of the people of the world' (Rio Declaration, 1992, principle 5). The basic moral position which is expressed here is that all human beings have a moral right to have at least their most basic needs satisfied and that at the same time the rich countries have an obligation to try actively to eliminate mass poverty (see World Commission, 1987, p. 11).

The documents on environmental policy are also unanimous about the desirability of economic growth. Such growth is not merely compatible with a sustainable society but is indeed necessary if it is to be achieved. In her foreword to *Our Common Future*, Brundtland writes that what is required to solve the problems of the environment is 'a new era of economic growth – growth that is forceful and at the same time socially and environmentally sustainable' (ibid., p. xii). For economic growth to be socially and ecologically sustainable, it must be based upon qualitative improvements rather than the increased consumption of resources. In general, according to the report of the Swedish Environmental Advisory Council, the guiding principle should be 'to administer rather than consume nature's capital' (Miljövårdsberedningen, 1992, p. 63). Economic growth which is based on increased exploitation of natural resources is thus incompatible with long-term sustainable development. A sustainable society can only be created through economic growth within the framework of sustainable development. Thus a further central value assumption in these reports becomes clear, namely that *we ought to strive for economic growth in so far as it can be achieved in a socially and an ecologically sustainable way.* The concepts of sustainability and economic growth are compatible.

It is important, however, to note that the word 'development' in the key phrase 'a sustainable development' must not be identified with economic growth. Although economic growth is assumed to be important, the concept of development involves much more than simply an increase in gross national product (GNP). The World Commission writes as follows: 'We came to see [development] not in its restricted context of economic growth in developing countries' (World Commission, 1987, p. 4). 'Sustainability requires views of human needs and well-being that incorporate such non-economic variables as education and health enjoyed for their own sake' (ibid., p. 53). Other kinds of non-material values which are mentioned in the various policy documents include peace, security, aesthetic enjoyment, recreation and outdoor activities, self-determination and psychological and spiritual well-being. 'Development' thus entails an enhanced *quality of life*. The development promoted by advocates of sustainable development thus entails more than merely improvement in the material conditions of people's lives. Commenting on the Swedish situation, the National Environment Protection Board writes

> Quality of life or well-being can depend on the existence of areas of unspoiled nature in the immediate vicinity of towns, shore access, bathing water standards and so on. A deterioration in quality of life can consist in the fact that mushrooms, berries, game and fish cannot be used as food in some part of the country. Living in an area disturbed by noise can entail a deterioration in quality of life as can noise in recreational areas. (Naturvårdsverket, 1993, p. 31)

The idea of sustainable development also implies an acceptance of certain *limits* on economic growth. The World Commission writes that these limits are 'not absolute limits but limitations imposed by the present state of technology and social organization on environmental resources and by the ability of the biosphere to absorb the effects of human activities' (World Commission, 1987, p. 8). Thus a sustainable development is limited by the following factors: (a) technology, that is the technical means currently at our disposal together with such improvements as may be developed in the future, (b) social institutions and the economy, viz. the present social and economic structures along with those improvements to them which may be possible in the future, and (c) the earth's biosphere, that is, the sustainability or productive potential of ecosystems.

It is the latter limitation, the productive potential of ecosystems, which constitutes the new and distinctive feature of the notion of sustainable development. Our individual actions, as well as national and international environmental programmes must be based on an awareness that the biosphere's capacity to withstand the effects of human activities is limited. A *holistic* approach, deriving mainly from ecology, is accepted. This approach is characterized by an emphasis on the connection or interdependence which exists between different natural entities or processes and by the view that human beings form an integral part of an ecological system on which their existence and well-being depends. The World Commission writes, for example, 'The environment does not exist as a sphere separate from human actions, ambitions and needs' (ibid., p. xi). William D. Ruckelshaus considers this approach to be characteristic of what he calls a 'sustainable consciousness'. 'The human species is a part of nature. Its existence depends on its ability to draw sustenance from a finite natural world; its continuance depends on its ability to abstain from destroying the natural systems that regenerate this world' (Ruckelshaus, 1994, p. 350).

According to these documents on the environment, what we must try to achieve is a sustainable development or a sustainable society. For a society to be sustainable, it requires, according to the authors of the report from the Swedish Environmental Advisory Council, to be adapted to the biogeochemical cycles (Miljövårdsberedningen, 1992, p. 3). Thus an alternative name for society which is characterized by a sustainable development, is a 'biogeochemical recycling society', a society where the processing of material – from the extraction of raw materials to the depositing of waste – is cyclical. Our society must therefore be transformed, from one which uses up and creates indebtedness, to one which conforms to the biogeochemical cycles. In the so-called 'Biogeochemical cycle Bill', the Swedish government asserted that all decisions in environmental policy should be aimed at bring about a society based on biogeochemical cycles:

> Whatever is extracted from nature must in a sustainable way be used, reused, recycled or finally disposed of with the minimal use of resources and without injury to nature. A society which applies the principle of biogeochemical cycles may be called a *biogeochemical recycling society*. (Regeringens proposition, 1992/93: 180, p. 14).

An alternative term for such a society is used in the Swedish National Environment Protection Board's policy programme. There a society which develops in a sustainable way is called a 'sustainable society': 'It means that the combined environmental effect of activities within different parts of society must be accommodated within the framework of what human beings and nature can withstand' (Naturvårdsverket, 1993, p. 11).

Social development thus ought to be technologically, economically and ecologically sustainable. It is naturally reasonable to assume that at least one additional limitation on social development is assumed in these environmental documents: a sustainable development must be limited also by *moral* considerations. The significance of such a limitation is evident when we consider the following extremely radical solution of the environmental problem. Suppose that someone suggested that we should exterminate the majority of Europeans and North Americans because we would thus very effectively limit the unnecessary wastage of natural resources and thereby achieve sustainable development. This mode of proceeding seems technologically possible, ecologically sustainable and so on, but despite that, it would not be compatible with the notion of sustainable development which is expressed in the above environmental documents. Why? Because an advocate of sustainable development tacitly assumes that we ought to respect the basic rights assigned to every human being. If the above solution to the environmental problem were to be accepted, human rights would be violated. For this reason, social development must also be 'morally' sustainable. Members of the World Commission seem implicitly to note this because their statement that 'sustainable development requires meeting the basic needs of all' presupposes that human life ought to be respected (World Commission, 1987, p. 8).

On the basis of this discussion, we can try to provide a definition of the expression 'a sustainable development' which is more informative than the one suggested by the World Commission: A development is *sustainable* if the social changes which take place satisfy the needs of present and future generations without either endangering the productive potential of supporting ecosystems or violating basic human rights.

The *view of nature* which emerges in the environmental policy documents is one where nature is exclusively seen as a resource. There is talk of 'the productive potential of ecosystems', 'natural resources', 'the wild living resources', 'biological resources', 'shared utilities', 'genetic resources', and so on. These resources can either be *renewable* (that is, like trees, solar radiation and water they are replaced within a reasonable period of time) or *non-renewable*, such as minerals and fossil fuels. Thus yet another value of key importance is that *nature must be seen above all as a resource, as something we human beings have the right to use as long as the productive potential of the ecosystems remains unthreatened.*

Usually by 'natural resource' is meant that nature constitutes a material or economic resource. However, given that the concept of 'sustainable development' embraces more than simply economic growth, it is reasonable also to allow the concept of 'natural resource' to cover more than the material and economic goods which nature supplies. If a person needs to relax and a visit to an area of natural beauty satisfies this need, then the area in question becomes a natural resource for this person. The person in question uses nature as a means of reducing stress, anxiety or a feeling of panic. Thus nature can be used not simply to secure instrumental values of an economic kind but also to secure instrumental values of a non-material kind.

An example of this extended use of the concept of resource would seem to lie behind the words of the Swedish National Environment Protection Board:

> That the protection of natural and cultural landscapes is given as a special aim would seem to give expression to the view that the aesthetic and historical values of a landscape together with those aspects of a landscape which give every district its special character are worth preserving. The protection of the landscape also creates opportunities for recreation and open-air activities. (Naturvårdsverket, 1993, p. 32)

According to the National Environment Protection Board, the landscape is not simply an economic resource but also a cultural and historical resource, an aesthetic resource and a recreational resource and one of environmental management's aims is also to ensure this kind of resource use and satisfaction of needs. We could say that a 'natural resource' is *everything which human beings can make use of in nature to satisfy their needs.* In this way, utility in itself and not the type of utility is what is decisive in determining whether we consider something in nature as a resource or not.

Given that these policy documents assume that nature ought to be considered as a resource, our relationship to nature is limited only by what nature can withstand, in other words by the robustness or productive potential of the ecosystems. No other limitation in our attitude and relationship to nature is discussed. When the World Commission report speaks of 'the ecosystem's overall integrity'[3] and the Rio Declaration speaks of 'the integrity of the Earth's ecosystem',[4] it is unreasonable to suppose that ecosystems possess integrity in the same sense that human beings possess integrity, namely that other people have a duty to respect us for what we are and to respect our needs and wishes irrespective of our intellectual or physical

[3] 'Sustainable development requires that the adverse impacts on the quality of air, water, and other natural elements are minimized so as to sustain the ecosystem's overall integrity' (World Commission, 1987, p. 46).
[4] 'states shall cooperate in a spirit of global partnership to conserve, protect and restore the health and integrity of the Earth's ecosystem' (*The Rio Declaration*, 1992).

capacity. Integrity therefore is linked in some way to our human dignity. For example, in medicine a clinical measure or treatment which is carried out contrary to a person's wishes is considered to be a violation of their integrity. For this reason, we require patients to give their consent to the treatment. If patients are for some reason incapable of maintaining their integrity by exercising their power to decide, they have the right to have it safeguarded by another person, usually some near relation (so-called 'consent via deputy').[5]

To say that a person ought to be considered as a 'resource', as something which other people have a right to 'use' for their own ends, or to maintain that our use of a person is limited by what this person can 'withstand', that is their sustainability, is to employ utterances which do not express respect for the person's integrity but rather constitute violations of it. It is reasonable to assume that this is also true in speaking about nature in a similar way. In these documents, 'ecosystem's integrity' must therefore mean something other than that nature is defended and respected.[6] One suggestion is that the concept of integrity is used as a symbolic decoration for the concept of robustness. If this interpretation is correct, we can substitute the word 'robustness' for the word 'integrity' in the following quotation from the World Commission report without any essential loss of meaning: 'Sustainable development requires that the adverse impacts on the quality of air, water, and other natural elements are minimized so as to sustain the ecosystem's overall integrity' (World Commission, 1987, p. 46).

We have seen that the environmental measures put forward in these environmental policy documents are based upon certain ethical principles. These principles coincide largely with the opinions of so-called 'conservationists'.[7] Conservationists wish to demonstrate the value of the products of nature as a human resource but stress that these resources have been exploited in a far too short-sighted and inefficient way. What is needed instead is a well-considered and carefully planned management of nature so that the resources will last longer and be used more efficiently. Gifford Pinchot, the founder of 'the conservation movement' in the USA, writes as follows:

> The central idea of the Forester, in handling the forest, is to promote and perpetuate its greatest use to men. His purpose is to make it serve the greatest good of the greatest number for the longest time ... The idea of applying foresight and common sense to the other natural resources as well as to the forest was natural and inevitable ... It was foreseen from the beginning by those who were responsible for inaugurating the Conservation movement that its natural development would in time work out into a planned and orderly scheme for national efficiency, based on the elimination of waste, and directed towards the best use of all we have for the greatest good of the greatest number for the longest time. (Pinchot, 1914, pp. 23–5)

---

[5] See, for example, Chapter 1 in Tranöy (1993) and Chapter 3 in Beauchamp and Childress (1989).

[6] It is important to note this, since there is a crucial difference of opinion on this point between the ethic of sustainable development and an ecocentric environmental ethic.

[7] See, for example, Norton (1987, pp. 234–5), Sörlin (1991, p. 170 and Des Jardins (1997, pp. 39–46).

Forest management is concerned with extracting from the forests those resources needed by human beings without destroying or impoverishing them.

The basic idea behind a conservationist approach is that we are required to deal with natural resources in an orderly and far-sighted way. Otherwise the resources will be exhausted and ultimately human beings will be the victims. For this reason, conservationists support the commercial exploitation of nature and they impose no limitation on how nature should be utilized apart from the requirement that it should be efficient and far-sighted. Human beings are thereby assumed to have the right to extract as much as possible from nature, provided that the sustainability of natural ecosystems is not threatened. Human beings are allowed to take what they want from nature. However they must not take more than nature can recreate.

Holistic and Intergenerational Anthropocentrism

Let us now try to specify in a more systematic and integrated fashion the various value components which form the core of the ethic of sustainable development and then compare this new ethic with the 'old' ethic which proponents of sustainable development want us to abandon. On the basis of the arguments in the previous section, the basic value components in an ethic of sustainable development are as follows.

(B1) *The principle of human superiority*: it is human needs which ought to be central in our dealings with nature. In other words, the normative starting point is that an environmental policy is to be judged on the basis of its effect on human beings.

(B2) *The principle of nature as a resource*: nature ought to be seen exclusively as a resource which we as human beings have a right to use for our own ends.

(B3) *The principle of intragenerational justice*: within each generation, we ought to try and achieve a more just distribution of resources between rich and poor.

(B4) *The principle of intergenerational justice*: we have moral obligations to future generations of human beings and therefore, in making use of natural resources, we ought to be concerned not simply with the needs of people who are alive at present but also with the needs of future generations.

Three important ecological insights should also be noted. Together with the basic values above, they form, I hold, the innermost core of the idea of sustainable development. They are:

(A) *The thesis on interdependence (or ecological holism)*: there is an interaction and interdependence between human beings and all other organisms in the system of nature; human beings form an integrated part of nature.

(B) *The thesis on limited natural resources*: the natural resources which are available to human beings are not inexhaustible and furthermore we have not made use of these resources in an efficient and far-sighted manner.

(C)   *The thesis on nature's vulnerability*: there is a limit to the ecosystem's capacity
to absorb human waste, and in several areas we have reached this limit.

Sometimes it is supposed that the value judgment that we ought to strive after
economic growth is an important constituent of the idea of sustainable
development: otherwise what would the word 'development' mean in this context?
Ought we therefore not to classify this line of thought as a basic value component?
It is quite clear that the idea of economic growth is assigned an important
significance in these environmental policy documents, but this value judgment is
nevertheless one that is derived and is therefore not on the same normative level as
the principles (B1)–(B4). The reason for this is that the aim behind sustainable
development is ultimately to satisfy the basic needs of human beings who are alive
at present, as well as of future generations. It is only to the extent that economic
growth is an efficient means to achieving this goal that such growth is compatible
with the notion of sustainable development or of a sustainable society.
Consequently, if economic growth does not show itself to be an efficient means in
this respect, we ought not to pursue it. In other words, it is appropriate to formulate
the normative principle regarding economic growth as a conditional statement:

(D1)   *The principle of economic growth*: we ought to strive after economic growth
provided (a) that such growth contributes to ensuring that the basic needs of
all human beings are satisfied and (b) that such growth takes place in an
ecologically sustainable way.

The desirability of economic growth is motivated and also limited by an
acceptance of the more basic normative principles (B1) and (B2) together with the
ecological insights (A) and (B). Note also that the concept of 'development' is not
automatically redundant, even if it subsequently emerges that economic growth is
undesirable, since the concept can also mean that a more equitable distribution of
resources in society is achieved or that a cultural or spiritual development is
achieved rather than an economic one.

What kind of environmental ethic does the idea of sustainable development
express? The group of environmental ethical theories which are most closely
related are those which usually go under the philosophical heading of
'anthropocentrism'. The basic normative idea in anthropocentrism is that human
beings alone have an intrinsic value and that as a result nature only has an
instrumental value. (For a discussion of the terms 'intrinsic' and 'instrumental'
value, see the next section.) Bryan Norton writes that 'the thesis of
anthropocentrism... [is that] only humans are the locus of intrinsic value, and the
value of all other objects derives from their contribution to human values' (Norton,
1987, p. 135). Baird Callicott describes an anthropocentric environmental ethic in
a similar way when he writes that such an ethic 'grants moral standing exclusively
to human beings and considers nonhuman natural entities and nature as a whole to
be only a means to human ends' (Callicott, 1995a, p. 276). Finally, Joseph Des
Jardins writes: 'Some philosophers argue that our responsibilities to the natural

environment are only indirect, that the responsibility to preserve resources, for example, is best understood in terms of the responsibilities that we owe to other humans. Anthropocentric ('human-centred') ethics hold that only human beings have moral value' (Des Jardins, 1997, pp. 9–10).[8]

Although it is not expressly said in the environmental documents studied that nature merely has an instrumental value, it is reasonable to suppose that the ethic of sustainable development indirectly implies such a normative assumption. The principle of human superiority (B1), together with the principle of nature as a resource (B2), give rise to an anthropocentric environmental ethic. From the assumption that human needs ought to be central to environmental policy and management, it certainly does not follow that only human beings can have an intrinsic value. Even if other living beings are assigned a value in themselves, it is still possible for human interests to be considered of central concern and for the value of human beings to be judged superior to that of other living organisms. But when this principle of human superiority is combined with the assumption that nature ought to be valued as a resource or as a means which we human beings can make use of as we like (on condition that the productive potential of the ecosystems is not threatened), it is implicitly assumed that nature does not have a value in itself. If nature were to be assigned an intrinsic value, it would imply that, in addition to the requirement that our use of nature must be efficient and far-sighted, there are *other* limitations which would apply to the way human beings may make use of nature. These limitations would be a direct consequence of an acceptance of nature's dignity or integrity. This would be analogous to the situation in human ethics where the acceptance of the proposition that other people have an intrinsic value means that, in making use of human beings for our own ends, it is no longer sufficient merely to require that our use is efficient and long-term. Additional limitations on our actions are required. (See the next section for what this entails more specifically.)

Given that advocates of sustainable development suppose that environmental measures and environmental policies should only be judged on the basis of how they affect present and future generations of human beings, it is assumed that human beings are the only beings on the earth which demand our *moral consideration*: in other words, only human beings have an intrinsic value. The characteristic aspect of anthropocentrism is this idea that non-human species as well as natural objects only possess a value to the extent that they in some sense benefit human beings. Nature has only an instrumental value.

---

[8] Observe, however, that the concept of anthropocentrism is in certain contexts given a somewhat different meaning. Sverker Sörlin writes that anthropocentrism is the view 'that nature is there to serve human beings' (Sörlin, 1991, p. 91) and Stig Wandén holds that anthropocentrism is the same as answering yes to the question, 'Should human beings and their development be accorded greater importance than other courses of events and forms of life in nature ...?' (Wandén, 1993, p. 12). Here I shall instead have recourse to the traditional philosophical way of defining anthropocentrism. This entails that, according to my terminology, certain formulations of non-anthropocentrism (notably weak biocentrism and weak ecocentrism) are compatible with anthropocentrism in the senses used by Sörlin and Wandén.

Since the view that only human beings have an intrinsic value is not directly formulated in the environmental documents which are considered in this study, we can describe this standpoint as an *implicit* basic value component:

(IB5) *Anthropocentrism*: only human beings ought to be assigned an intrinsic value while, by contrast, nature has only an instrumental value.

Instrumental Value, Intrinsic Value and Inherent Worth

What does it more exactly mean to assign to an object or a being an intrinsic value or an instrumental value? An answer to this question is crucial, since these terms are used in various senses and as a result there is some confusion about what it means to affirm or deny that certain beings other than human beings have an intrinsic value when we are discussing environmental ethics.[9] Let us begin by examining the term 'instrumental value'. We can say that an object has an instrumental value (or resource value) if it has a value as a means for attaining something else which is considered of value. The value of the object depends on the use it has for the person making use of it. Money is one example of something to which we ascribe an instrumental value. It is valuable to the extent that we can use it as a means of achieving something else which we consider valuable, such as health, security or happiness. Usually, we conceive of money as something which only has an instrumental value, that is, it has a value for us only as far as we can make use of it, and nothing else. When its utility ceases, it becomes worthless.

On the other hand, when we claim that something has an intrinsic value, we deny that the object in question has merely an instrumental value. 'Intrinsic value' is then used as a synonym for 'non-instrumental value'. We can say that an object has an intrinsic value if it is valuable in itself irrespective of whether it has a value in attaining something else of value. In the majority of ethical theories, it is taken for granted that human beings have an intrinsic value in this sense. In other words, all human beings are valuable in themselves, irrespective of the use that other people or society can derive from them. The so-called 'principle of human dignity' (that all human beings have a value in themselves and that all human beings have an equal value and have therefore the same basic rights) which is of central importance in human ethics, is based upon such an assumption. As the philosopher Immanuel Kant would have said: you must always treat your fellow human being as an end and never merely as a means.

Naturally, however, it has not always been the case that all human beings have been recognized to possess an intrinsic value. It was not so very long ago that slaves only possessed an instrumental value. They were a resource or asset which their owners could make use of, and nothing more. Let me give two examples of the way the concept of intrinsic value is used in this sense in environmental ethics:

---

[9] For a discussion of these terms, see, for example, Callicott (1989f), Norton (1987, pp. 138–9, 151–2, O'Neill (1993, ch. 2), Taylor (1986, chs 3–4) and Marietta (1995, ch. 7).

Moral concern for individual animals follows from the hitherto ignored presence of morally relevant characteristics, primarily sentience, in animals. As a result, I am comfortable in attributing what Immanuel Kant calls 'intrinsic value', not merely use value [or instrumental value], to animals if we attribute it to people. (Rollin, 1995, p. 116)

The well-being of non-human life on Earth has value in itself. This value is independent of any instrumental usefulness for limited human purposes. (Næss, 1984, p. 266)

Sometimes, however, intrinsic value has a sense which goes beyond the value that an object has in itself, independently of its value as a resource or its utility to something else. The object is assumed to have a value which exists independently of human valuations. According to this view, we do not *assign* to an object an intrinsic value: we *discover* its value. Intrinsic values exist independently of us. An intrinsic value is something which exists irrespective of whether there is any evaluator who can value it or not. We can say that an object has an intrinsic value if it has a value independently of an evaluator's evaluation or judgment. 'Intrinsic value' is then synonymous with 'objective value' and not with 'non-instrumental value'.

As a rule, human beings are considered to be the only beings on earth who are capable of making value judgments. If someone therefore were to maintain that other non-human living organisms have an intrinsic value in this second sense, it would be equivalent to asserting that, even if no humans remained on earth, these beings would be valuable and have a value in themselves. In such a situation, given that only human beings are capable of making value judgments, it would be the case that no-one had the capacity to discover and respect the intrinsic value of these organisms. As an example of an attempt to argue that nature has an objective intrinsic value, consider the following:

Do not humans value Earth because it is valuable, and not the other way around? Is the value in this life-support system really just a matter of late-coming human interests, or is Earth not historically a remarkable, valuable place prior to the human arrival and even now valuable antecedently to the human uses of it? The human part in the drama is perhaps the most valuable event of all. But it seems parochial, as well as uninformed ecologically, to say that our part alone in the drama establishes all its worth. (Rolston, 1988, p. 4)

These two meanings of intrinsic value must, however, be carefully distinguished because we can grant that non-human living organisms have an intrinsic value in the first sense but not in the second sense. It can be maintained that there are no values independent of people making value judgments and that, as a result, other living organisms cannot have any value if human beings did not exist while at the same holding that *we* ought to assign to them a non-instrumental value. The same argument can naturally be employed within human ethics. To say that human beings have intrinsic value then means that we as people making value judgments assign to every human being a value which is independent of the utility which other people or society can derive from them, while at the same time it is denied that such a human value exists independently of us as arbiters of value.

A confusion of these two senses of intrinsic value is not uncommon. As John O'Neill points out,[10] Donald Worster, in *Nature's economy*, is guilty of such a conceptual confusion when he writes:

> One of the most important ethical issues raised anywhere in the past few decades has been whether nature has an order, a pattern, that we humans are bound to understand and respect and preserve. It is the essential question prompting the environmentalist movement in many countries. Generally those who have answered 'yes' to the question have also believed that such an order has an intrinsic value, which is to say that not all value comes from humans, that value can exist independently of us: it is not something we bestow. On the other hand, those who have answered 'no' have tended to be in an instrumentalist camp. They look on nature as a storehouse of 'resources' to be organized and used by people, as having no other value than the value some human gives it. (Worster, 1985, p. xi)

When Worster characterizes the environmentalists who believe in respect for nature, he uses the term 'intrinsic value' in the second sense. But when he refers to the other group of environmentalists, those who do not, when he is speaking about nature as a resource, he begins by relying upon the notion of intrinsic value in the first sense and then goes on – in claiming that nature has no value other than the one assigned to it by human beings – to rely on a concept of intrinsic value in the second sense.

In order, therefore, to avoid misunderstanding and unnecessary confusion, let us use the term 'inherent worth' when we are speaking of intrinsic value in the second sense and reserve the expression 'intrinsic value' for the first sense. We thus make the following distinction:

- *Instrumental value*: the value which an object has as a means of attaining something else which is assigned intrinsic value; in other words, an object's resource value.
- *Intrinsic value*: the value that an object has independently of its utility to other individuals; in other words, an object's non-instrumental value.
- *Inherent worth*: the value which an object possesses independently of human beings; in other words, a value which is independent of the values ascribed to it by us.[11]

Yet another conceptual relationship which requires to be clarified is that between instrumental value and intrinsic value. In discussions about the environment, one

---

[10] See O'Neill (1993, p. 10).

[11] Note, however, that this tripartite division involves the answer to two separate questions. The first question is of a normative ethical nature. Does nature have a value in itself? Those who answer 'yes' to this ascribe an intrinsic value to nature, while those who say 'no' assign it a merely instrumental value. The second question is of a metaethical nature: does the value of nature exist independently of human valuations? Those who answer 'yes' (the value objectivists) assign to nature a value in itself while those who answer 'no' (the value subjectivists) deny quite generally that inherent worth exists. Note also that my categorization is put forward as a suggestion since there is, unfortunately, no standard established usage for these terms among environmental ethicists.

sometimes gets the impression that we have to choose between either assigning an intrinsic value to nature or assigning an instrumental value.[12] However, note that an object can simultaneously have both an instrumental value and an intrinsic value. Human beings can be valuable in themselves and at the same time be of use to other people or to society. For example, I can value a carpenter for the use I derive from him and still not deny his intrinsic value or his moral dignity. By ascribing an intrinsic value to the carpenter, I impose a limit on the ways in which I can make use of him as a resource for my own ends. To accept that nature has an intrinsic value therefore does not imply that it may not be used as a resource; it entails only that there are limits to the ways in which we human beings may make use of nature. We shall return to consider the nature of these limitations in the next chapter.

According to anthropocentrists, human beings are not merely the only 'moral agents' (that is to say, beings who can treat others in a right or wrong way); they are also the only 'moral subjects' (that is to say, beings who can be treated in a right or wrong way). Human beings are *moral agents* because they have a capacity to reflect about their existence, to make choices on the basis of these reflections and can therefore be held morally responsible for their actions. Humans are the only beings that we know of on earth who can act either morally or immorally and in this respect they differ from other natural phenomena such as rivers, trees and tigers. Consequently, it is not meaningful to maintain that a tiger is morally responsible for its actions or that the way in which it treats other animals is morally praiseworthy or worthy of moral condemnation. In contrast to human beings, tigers are *amoral* beings.

A 'moral subject', on the other hand, is something which can be treated rightly or wrongly and towards which moral agents have certain responsibilities. According to anthropocentrists, the class of moral agents is coextensive with the class of 'moral subjects'. Human beings are the only 'moral subjects' which exist on earth. They are the only beings which can be treated rightly or wrongly. As a result, while human actions towards other human beings can be moral or immoral, human action with respect to nature can never be other than amoral. For example, R.D. Guthrie writes that 'a human's act toward other organisms is, in and of itself, an amoral one. It becomes a moral act only when humans are affected' (Guthrie, 1995, p. 74).

This means that our moral obligations, such as to refrain from unnecessary pollution or from the wanton extermination of animal and plant species, are obligations *concerning* the environment but not obligations *to* the environment. The only things to which we have direct obligations are human beings, whether those alive at present or future generations. Since animals, plants and ecosystems are not 'moral subjects' according to anthropocentrists, they do not enjoy 'moral standing' – we are not obliged to consider them in our actions. To say that 'nature is under threat' thus implies that its value is diminished in relation *to us* as users of nature

---

[12] The biologist David Ehrenfeld seems to proceed from such an assumption when he maintains, in *The arrogance of humanism*, that we ascribe either a resource value (that is, an instrumental value) to species and ecosystems or an intrinsic value (Ehrenfeld, 1978, p. 201).

and that its instrumental value decreases. Only human beings can possess intrinsic value and the value of all other (natural or artificial) objects derives from their contribution to human values. Nature thus should be preserved for our sake and not for its own sake because nature lacks intrinsic value. In the same way, we do not need to defend money or cars for their own sake. If they are to be preserved, it is for our sake or the sake of other people.

Dualistic and Holistic Anthropocentrism

Does the anthropocentrism which the idea of sustainable development presupposes differ from earlier forms of anthropocentrism? I hold that it does. That there is an important difference between 'traditional' anthropocentrism and the anthropocentrism associated with 'sustainable development' is partly due to a change in certain basic factual assumptions about the relationship of human beings to nature and the availability of natural resources. The traditional anthropocentric view of nature is not based on the ecological insights (A), (B) and (C) above (see pp. 27–8) but rather on the following assumptions:

(D) *The thesis on the separation of human beings from nature*: human beings differ so radically from all other forms of life on earth that they cannot be seen as part of nature.

(E) *The thesis on unlimited natural resources*: the assets which nature bestows on human beings are so great that they are in practice inexhaustible.

(F) *The thesis on nature's robustness*: nature has a capacity which always allows it to absorb human waste.

Let me comment briefly on the meaning of these theses in order to provide a background for the ecological insights (A), (B) and (C) which form the foundation of the ethic of sustainable development and the way this change in the theoretical content of the Western world view has also led to a shift in values. Thesis (D) expresses an anthropological–biological view of the nature of human beings and of that which sets them apart from nature. Don E. Marietta writes, 'For roughly two thousand years [within] the mainstream of Western thought ... [the] human person was looked upon as separate and different from the rest of living things and the lands and water that sustained them. Until this century very few people thought of humans as a part of nature' (Marietta, 1995, p. 2).[13] The thesis on separation of human beings from nature thus says something about human nature. Human beings differ ontologically from all other living creatures on the earth and the difference is so great that human beings cannot be seen as a part of nature. In other words, thesis (D) formulates a pre-Darwinian view of the nature of human beings and their

---

[13] In his presentation, Marietta does not, regarding this point, distinguish, as I do, between the normative and factual (descriptive) content of the modernist Western world view, which he calls 'the man-apart-from-nature view' (Marietta, 1995, p. 2).

relation to nature. Ian Barbour sums up this viewpoint in the following way: 'the Newtonian world view perpetuated a sharp separation of *humanity* from *the nonhuman world*. It was claimed that apart from the human mind, the world consists of particles in motion. Newton accepted the Cartesian dualism of mind and matter' (Barbour, 1993, p. 58).

I shall not, however, commit myself as to how this thesis should exactly be interpreted. The important thing to see is that the thesis implies a denial of – or rather the ignoring of or the lack of knowledge of – the fact that human beings are, like other organisms, part of an ecological context and, like them, human beings are dependent on fully functioning ecosystems, in other words on the factual thesis (A) of sustainable development.

The anthropocentrism associated with sustainable development can therefore as I have mentioned earlier, be classified as 'holistic'. Marietta expresses this viewpoint when he writes:

> Of course, a human-centered ethic must not be short-sighted and must take account of ecological knowledge to be an adequate ethical stance. I believe this includes the adoption of a moderate holistic view of humanity that recognizes that humans are truly a part of nature, even if being part of nature is not all that humans are. Only a holistic anthropocentrism can be a scientifically credible and morally adequate humanism. (Marietta, 1995, p. 7)

Let us call this form of holism *ecological holism*: the view that there is an interaction and interdependence between human beings and all other organisms in natural systems and between different natural systems. Ecological holism is the view that the biosphere forms an interrelated and interdependent whole (in other words thesis (A) above). Stig Wandén describes a similar position when he writes as follows:

> *Holism* implies that one has to view nature as a whole, since all life depends on the physical surroundings (the sun, the nourishment of the soil, the climate, the sea) and on other life, while at the same time life in its turn influences the environment. It is impossible to study individual elements of an ecosystem without taking into account how the system itself functions since the elements are very much dependent on it. (Wandén, 1997, p. 42)

The holism which Wandén describes, however, is not quite the same because he describes not only an ecological holism but also another type of holism of a more methodological character, a holism which should perhaps instead be contrasted with 'atomism' rather than dualism. To simplify somewhat, we can say that the characteristic feature of an *atomistic view* is that there is a consistent tendency to distinguish one thing from another and that everything is seen as a separate entity which is more or less randomly a mere part of other things. In an atomistic viewpoint, the interrelations between things are minimized and emphasis is placed instead on what is unique and individual in every thing. The *holistic view*, by contrast, characteristically emphasizes the connections between different things and beings and, as Wandén writes, it is impossible to 'study individual elements of an ecosystem without taking into account how the system itself functions since the elements are very much dependent on it'. What is unique and individual in every thing is minimized; instead, emphasis is placed on the interrelations between things. Let us call this form of holism *methodological holism*, since it is not primarily concerned with the content of certain scientific theories but with the choice of approach in carrying out a scientific or some other type of inquiry.

This distinction between ecological holism and methodological holism is important since, as Wandén maintains, it is 'scarcely possible to be always holistic [that is, methodologically holistic] in practical environmental management. We are forced to limit the field studied in order to be able to grapple with practical problems: recycling in suburbs, agricultural and forest management, the installation of chimney filters and so on' (ibid., pp. 43–4). In other words, the choice of a holistic or a more atomistic approach in the analysis of a phenomenon or in developing a policy is something which has to be decided in each individual case. There is no general answer to such an issue. However it does not rule out an adoption of ecological holism. Thus we must distinguish between holism of type 1 – the view that the biosphere (including human beings) forms an interrelated and interdependent whole – and holism of type 2 – the view that in the study of a given phenomenon, more emphasis should be given to the phenomenon as a whole than to its parts. Holism of type 1 should be contrasted with dualism, while holism of type 2 should be contrasted with atomism.

In a discussion of anthropocentrism, there is an important dividing line between dualistic anthropocentrism on the one hand and holistic anthropocentrism on the other (where, in the latter, the word 'holistic' is being used in the sense of holism of type 2):

> *Dualistic anthropocentrism*: the view that human beings alone have intrinsic value and that they differ so radically from all other terrestrial forms of life that they cannot be seen as part of nature.

> *Holistic anthropocentrism*: the view that human beings alone have intrinsic value but that they are intimately related to the rest of nature and, like all other organisms form part of an ecological framework and depend on fully functioning ecosystems.

Note, however, that the words 'dualistic' and 'holistic' in this context are being used only to describe certain factual positions. They are not being employed in a normative way. Acceptance of (D) together with (B1)–(B4) yields dualistic anthropocentrism, while acceptance of (A) together with (B1)–(B4) yields holistic anthropocentrism.

How, then, should we interpret Brundtland's statement, cited earlier, that what is needed to deal with environmental problems is 'a new holistic ethic in which economic growth and environmental protection go hand-in-hand around the world'? A reasonable interpretation which is not directly related to the above discussion, is to take the word 'holistic' as a synonym for the world 'global' (cf.

World Commission, 1987, p. 18). A holistic ethic would then mean an ethic which embraces all human beings on the earth and extending to future generations. (Holism in this sense would then be contrasted neither with dualism nor with atomism but with *particularism* or *contextualism*.) Another interpretation would be to take her pronouncement as directly expressing holistic anthropocentrism as specifically defined above, namely an ethic viewpoint which takes into account the fact that the biosphere (including human beings) forms an interrelated and interdependent whole.[14]

Let us proceed further and briefly indicate the substance of the two factual theses (E) and (F) of traditional anthropocentrism. Their meaning first becomes clear when one notes the fact that advocates of sustainable development reject them. Thesis (E) expresses the view that a shortage of natural resources for human processing will never occur. Natural resources are so plentiful that there are no limits to the extent to which human beings can make use of them. It is not denied that a certain raw material which is used to manufacture a certain product can be used up, but it will always be possible to replace natural resources with other raw materials so that a substitute can be produced.[15] The resources which nature offers to human beings are so large that in practice they can never be exhausted. Nature can be seen as a store where people are able to go in and fetch what they require without any risk that it will end up empty. Traditional anthropocentrism assumes not only that nature's resources in practice are inexhaustible but also that nature has a capacity of always being able to absorb human waste. The thesis on nature's robustness (F) says that we shall never approach a limit to nature's capacity to take care of the waste which our exploitation of nature entails.

The Anthropocentrism of Sustainable Development

The shift in basic factual assumptions, from (D), (E) and (F) to (A), (B) and (C), has helped to make the normative content in the anthropocentrism of sustainable development diverge from traditional anthropocentrism on at least one central issue. It embodies the idea that we have moral obligations not merely to people now alive but also to future generations. This means that the principle of justice or the principle of human dignity – that all human beings have the same value and therefore the same basic rights – have been extended in time to embrace both present and future generations. In this respect, the ethic of sustainable development is a genuinely new ethic.

In general, anthropocentrists have never before considered that we human beings had moral obligations which go beyond those we have to our children and grandchildren, even extending to distant generations. As Des Jardins points out, the same is true of philosophers: 'some of the most pressing environmental challenges

---

[14] A third reading of the word 'holism' which is of central importance in environmental ethics will be analysed in Chapter 4. Given this reading, the speech on 'a holistic ethic' would have a quite different meaning from the one we have discussed (see p. 80).

[15] See Ariansen (1993, p. 130) and Norton (1991, pp. 76–7, 112).

force us to consider in detail the ethical effects of our actions upon people of the future. Yet this issue was often ignored in much traditional philosophy, and groundbreaking work was required. Philosophical ethics needed to be extended beyond traditional boundaries' (Des Jardins, 1997, p. 85). Having studied traditional (utilitarian and deontological) ethical theories, John Passmore, for example, draws the following conclusion:

> So whether we approach the problem of obligations to posterity by way of Bentham and Sidgwick, Rawls or Golding, we are led to something like the same conclusion: Our obligations are to immediate posterity, we ought to try to improve the world so that we shall be able to hand it over to our immediate successors in a better condition [than we found it in] and that is all. (Passmore, 1974, p. 91)

The *principle of intergenerational justice* – that, in making use of natural resources, we ought to consider not only people alive at present but also future generations – is thus nowhere to be found in traditional anthropocentrism. With the acceptance of the ethic of sustainable development, the number of individuals we must morally consider in our actions has been very much increased. Their number is not simply made up of persons alive at present but also includes the set of future human beings. In the context of environmental policy this means that we must not merely speak of '*intra*generational' justice (justice between different groups of people living at the same time) but also of '*inter*generational' justice (justice between different generations).

If the resources which we derive from nature are so great that in practice they are inexhaustible, and if nature has a capacity always to absorb human waste, there is no real reason to reflect on whether we have any moral obligations to future generations (such as the people who will be alive in a hundred or two hundred years' time). But when our perceptions about the structure and composition of nature and its robustness change and we see that natural resources are not inexhaustible, that we have not used these resources efficiently and far-sightedly and that there is a limit to ecosystems' capacity to absorb human waste, the issue of a just distribution of resources between present and future generations arises. Moreover, when we become aware that never before have human activities so directly and powerfully affected the earth's atmosphere, climate and biological diversity as they do today, and realize that certain human resources are not renewable, the problem becomes acute. Thus the thesis on limited natural resources (B) and the thesis on nature's vulnerability (C) decisively persuade advocates of the ethic of sustainable development not simply to make use of the *principle of intragenerational justice* – that within every generation of human beings, we should try to achieve a just distribution of resources between rich and poor – but also to assume the *principle of intergenerational justice*.

We can thus distinguish between at least two forms of anthropocentrism:

> *Traditional* or *intergenerational anthropocentrism:* the view that individual behaviour and environmental policy making should only be judged on the basis of how they affect people who are alive at present, and

The ethic of sustainable development or *intergenerational anthropocentrism*: the view that individual behaviour and environmental policy making should be judged on the basis of how they affect both people who are alive now and future generations.

The principle of intergenerational justice together with the ecological insights (B) and (C), provide in turn a reason for yet another central normative principle in the ethic of sustainable development:

(D2) *The principle of efficiency and far-sightedness*: human use of natural resources should be efficient and far-sighted.

Because nature's capacity to absorb our waste is limited, we must try to find some way of altering our utilization of nature so that the needs of future generations are not put at risk. We must try to manage natural resources in an adequate way. In general, according to proponents of sustainable development, management of resources is adequate in so far as it is efficient and far-sighted. (B2) is thus derived from, or subsidiary to, (B4), the principle of intergenerational justice. This is because the reason why natural resources should be used in an efficient and far-sighted way derives from the assumption that we would otherwise be unable to fulfil our obligations to future generations. If we accept the principle of intergenerational justice, we also ought to accept the principle of efficiency and far-sightedness as an ethical and practical guide.

When is the utilization of nature efficient and far-sighted? In connection with the subject of renewable resources, the Swedish National Environment Protection Board writes: 'Adequate management of resources ... can be defined as utilization which preserves the resources' productive potential also in the long term. It means *inter alia* that the productive potential of wooded areas has to be preserved and that arable and potentially arable land must be kept in a condition which will allow it in the long term to be used for food production' (Naturvårdsverket, 1993, p. 31). In other words, the utilization of renewable resources is morally acceptable as long as we live off the 'return' on nature's capital and not on the capital itself.

The authors of the Board's report are less certain when it comes to non-renewable resources. They write that this issue is concerned with the implications we attach to the just distribution of resources between present and future generations: 'It is impossible to give an unequivocal answer to this. What constitutes the responsible management of a resource depends upon how easily the resource can be recycled and how easily it can be replaced by other material or by other types of production and consumption' (ibid., pp. 31–2). They hold, however, that scarcity of, for example, energy or mineral resources is not imminent and that the key issue instead is how waste from non-renewable resources should be dealt with. We shall have reason to return to this question in the next section. The more concrete policy proposals generated by the principle of efficiency and far-sightedness will be discussed in Chapter 5, when we deal with the implications of the various theories of environmental ethics for policy issues and practical environmental management.

Our Responsibility to Future Generations

The advocates of sustainable development are well aware that the effects of the depletion of the ozone layer, global warming and acid rain above all threaten future generations. They consequently advocate acceptance of the principle of intergenerational justice (B4). In utilizing the earth's natural resources, we should consider not only the needs of people who are alive today but also those of future generations. However, the content of this intergenerational obligation is not specified, nor are we given any real guidance about how we are to deal with situations where the interests of people alive at present conflict with those of future generations. What, surprisingly, is lacking in the policy documents based on the concept of 'a sustainable development' is an adequate treatment of the elements which *de facto* make the ethic of sustainable development a new ethic. One of the cornerstones of the whole idea of sustainable development is thus left unanalysed and imprecise.

A thorough analysis of the moral obligations we have to future generations lies outside the scope of the present work. At the same time it is desirable to try briefly to specify more exactly the possible implications of intergenerational justice. Which norm or norms should we use to decide how far there is a just distribution of resources between the present and future generations? Are there any significant differences between intragenerational justice and intergenerational justice, given that in one case the distribution is concerned with people living at different times while in the other it concerns people living in different places at the same time? How far should we consider future generations if by so doing we impair the possibility of improving the well-being of people alive at present?

Note, however, that our responsibility to the future does not merely concern our *obligations to* future human beings (that is, those who in fact will exist) but also involves the issue of the *number* of people who ought to be born in the future. As Avner de-Shalit writes:

> a policy of ours can affect someone who is not yet born in two ways. It can affect people's very existence i.e. it may determine whether they are going to exist or not, and, more generally, our acts may affect the number of future generations ... Or a policy may affect people's lives: that is to say, their standard of living or quality of life. (de-Shalit, 1995, p. 69)

The principle of intergenerational justice arises partly, as we have seen, from the ecological insights (B) and (C), namely that natural resources are limited and that there is a limit to the ecosystem's capacity to absorb our waste. It is therefore possible that the issue of our responsibility to future generations can partly be resolved, or indeed avoided altogether, by limiting the number of people who are born in the future. The solution of environmental problems does not then consist primarily of an alteration in our utilization of nature but in a radical reduction in world population. If a rapid increase in population increases the pressure on natural resources then a rapid population reduction ought to be able, *mutatis mutandis*, to reduce the pressure. But even if a programme for a drastic reduction in population were to be adopted, this would not mean that all talk of intergenerational justice would become superfluous. Various environmentally toxic substances, such as radioactive waste, could still constitute a serious threat to this reduced number of people in the future. As long as the ways in which people alive now use nature can threaten future human beings, the issue of our obligations to future generations remains.

We must thus distinguish between two quite different problems concerning our responsibility with respect to future generations:

> *The problem of population*: what should be the population size in the future if the aim is a sustainable development of society; and
> *The problem of obligation*: what are our moral obligations to future generations? How do we achieve a just distribution of resources (and distribution of risks) between people alive now and future generations?

The proponents of sustainable development as a rule do not advocate any radical measures with respect to the problem of population. The World Commission maintains, however, that it is important at least 'to limit extreme rates of population growth' (World Commission, 1987, p. 11). According to the World Commission 'sustainable development can only be pursued if population size and growth are in harmony with the changing productive potential of the ecosystem' (ibid., p. 9). It is therefore asserted that it is important to provide people with the opportunity of education and thereby increase their capacity for self-determination on the assumption that self-determination would lead to fewer children being born. The World Commission furthermore encourages governments lacking 'long-term, multifaceted population policies' to develop one 'to strengthen social, cultural, and economic motivations for family planning, and to provide to all who want them the education, contraceptives, and services required' (ibid., p. 11).

One of the aims which stems from the concept of sustainable development and which receives special mention is the securing of a sustainable level of population (ibid.). An indication of what constitutes a sustainable level of population emerges when three alternative UN calculations of long-term population growth are presented:

> – if replacement-level fertility [i.e. with somewhat more than two children born to each couple] is reached in 2010, global population will stabilize at 7.7 billion by 2060;
> – if this rate is reached in 2035, population will stabilize at 10.2 billion by 2095;
> – if, however, the rate is reached only in 2065, global population in 2100 would be 14.2 billion. (ibid., p. 102)

The tone of the argument suggests that the World Commission favours the first alternative as a basis for a population policy programme. Thus a further important value component in the ethic of sustainable development is:

(D3) *The principle of population growth*: an increase in population should only take place if such an increase is in harmony with the changes in the productive potential of supporting ecosystems.

Since too drastic an increase in population threatens nature's capacity to produce sufficient food and other requirements for the earth's population, measures have to be taken so that it will be possible for future generations to satisfy their needs in an ecologically sustainable way. We therefore have a moral obligation to future generations as well as to children and grandchildren alive at present to try to ensure that population growth is in balance with changes in the productive potential of supporting ecosystems. (D3) is thus motivated ultimately by the basic value components (B3) and (B4), together with the ecological insights (A), (B) and (C).

Given that no radical reduction in the size or growth of the population is proposed, the solution to environmental problems must consist above all in changes in the utilization of renewable and non-renewable natural resources. As a result, the problem of obligation, and not the problem of population, becomes of central importance. To what extent should we in our actions be concerned with the interests of future generations? How should we proceed in order to ensure that our way of dealing with the resources which nature supplies entails that both people alive at present and future generations are treated in a just way?

Let us try to answer these questions, using the World Commission's definition of sustainable development as our starting point: 'Sustainable development is development that meets the needs of the present without compromising the ability of future generations to meet their own needs' (World Commission, 1987, p. 43). If we flesh out this line of thought, it implies that, when I make use of a certain natural resource, say a watercourse, I am morally bound to use it in such a way that people who are alive at present, as well as future generations, also have the possibility of using the watercourse in order to satisfy their needs. In other words, 'sustainable development demands a more cyclical processing of material' (Naturvårdsverket, 1993, p. 30). Thus we are morally justified in making use of natural resources – genes, species and ecosystems – in order to satisfy all our needs whatever they might be, on condition that coming generations also have the possibility of utilizing them for their needs.

My example, however, clarifies an obscurity which may arise at this point. In utilizing the watercourse, I perhaps create a pumping system in order to use the water more efficiently. However, the watercourse is still there for others to use. Imagine instead that I utilize it in such a way that I drain the waterway by means of ditches in order to create arable land. Do I not put at risk the possibilities of future generations to use the watercourse in order to satisfy their needs? Obviously I do. They can in fact no longer make use of the watercourse because it is no longer there. However, the World Commission naturally does not consider that by acting in such a way I am breaking my intragenerational and intergenerational obligations.

> Every ecosystem everywhere cannot be preserved intact. A forest may be depleted in one part of a watershed and extended elsewhere, which is not a bad thing if the exploitation has been planned and the effects on soil erosion rates, water regimes, and genetic losses have been taken into account. In general, renewable resources like forests and fish stocks need not be depleted provided the rate of use is within the limits of regeneration and natural growth. (World Commission, 1987, p. 45)

The people of today are assumed not merely to have the right to consume the products of nature; they also have the right to alter existing natural areas without their moral obligations to future generations being set aside. We are thus not required to live with minimal influence on nature. Moreover, we have the right to make use of non-renewable resources such as fossil fuels and minerals even if, by so doing, we reduce future generations' access to these products. The condition which must be fulfilled, however, is that 'the rate of depletion and the emphasis on recycling and economy of use should be calibrated to ensure that the [non-renewable] resource does not run out before acceptable substitutes are available' and that we should 'foreclose as few future options as possible' (ibid., p. 46). Intergenerational justice therefore does not imply that the same type or set of natural resources is to be distributed equally between the generations. Thus the following principle of justice is rejected:

> *The static intergenerational principle of justice*: we have a moral obligation to bequeath to the next generations the same set and kinds of natural resource which we inherited from previous generations.

But which specific principle of justice forms the basis of the discussion about sustainable development? What ethical requirements must be satisfied in using renewable and non-renewable natural resources, so that there is a just distribution of resources between present and future generations of human beings? What we require to know more precisely is whether the resources we leave behind us will suffice to satisfy their needs to the same extent that we today are able to satisfy our needs or whether it is sufficient if they are at least able to satisfy their basic needs. Are we obliged to try and enable them to achieve the same quality of life as we have or is it sufficient that that we try to guarantee future generations a lower, but still acceptable, level? No answer, or at least no unequivocal answer, is given to these questions.

Let us consider the alternatives we are faced with. Compare the following two pronouncements of James P. Sterba and Andrew C. Kadak:

> a right to life applied to future generations would be a right of a person whom we can definitely expect to exist to receive the goods and resources necessary to satisfy their basic needs or to noninterference with their attempts to acquire the goods and resources necessary to satisfy their basic needs. (Sterba, 1981, p. 107)

> no generation should (needlessly), now or in the future, deprive its successors of the opportunity to enjoy a quality of life equivalent to its own. (Kadak, 1997, p. 50)

Sterba and Kadak appear to represent two divergent views about what intergenerational justice is, and one is considerably more demanding than the other. The question which we must try to answer is which of these two principles of justice or alternatively which other principle of justice, is presupposed in the environmental policy documents we are examining. However, let us approach the question by first clarifying the content of (B3), that is to say the principle of intragenerational justice, since it is somewhat simpler to determine.

How should we try to arrange the distribution of natural resources between people alive at present? According to the World Commission, a sustainable development requires that there is both between human beings and between nations 'equitable access to the constrained resource' (World Commission, 1987, p. 45). This requires at least 'meeting the basic needs of all and extending to all the opportunity to satisfy their aspirations for a better life' (ibid., p. 44). By 'basic needs', however, is meant something more than merely that certain rudimentary needs are satisfied. Besides needs such as the supply of food and water as well as protection against the weather and wind, there are also such things as access to work, health care and education (ibid., pp. 49, 54). The need for education means more precisely that we should aim to give all people throughout the world an opportunity to read and write (ibid., p. 112).[16]

The most important task consists in satisfying the needs and interests of the growing populations of the developing countries. Our aim must be to 'enable poor households to meet minimum consumption standards' (ibid., p. 54). According to advocates of sustained development, this is not merely desirable but also our moral obligation. This means that we have not merely *negative* obligations to people alive today but also certain *positive* ones. We must not merely avoid causing distress or suffering through our actions. In addition we must help others to satisfy their fundamental needs. We are morally obliged to try to some extent to even out differences in standards of living between people. However, we would appear to have no duty to try to see to it that all people can achieve the same standard of living or quality of life. A principle of equality which says that all people have a right to an equal share of resources is thus rejected, as is also a principle of need which implies that those people who are most in need should receive the greatest share of resources.

The principle of intragenerational justice which the argument about a sustainable development seems to presuppose could thus be formulated more precisely as follows:

(B3) *The principle of intragenerational justice**: we have a moral obligation to utilize natural resources in such a way that at least the basic needs of all people who are alive at present can be satisfied.[17]

The environmental policy documents do not explain how a just distribution of the natural resources which remain after an application of (B3) is to be effected. It is perhaps reasonable to suppose that such a distribution is just or not, depending on how the people who now possess the natural resources acquired them. If someone takes possession of, or utilizes, a natural resource which no-one previously has owned or utilized and which is not needed to satisfy basic human needs, it is a case of *rightful acquisition*. If someone's ownership or right of utilization of a natural resource is acquired from another person, it is a case of *rightful transfer*, providing

---

[16] Note that what constitutes a basic need can to some extent vary from culture to culture (see Stenmark, 1997, pp. 8f).

[17] Actions which go beyond the need to satisfy the basic needs of all people who are alive at present would in this case be praiseworthy but not morally obligatory.

this latter person is responsible and gives his or her voluntary consent. On the other hand, if someone acquires this type of natural resource in some other way, for example through theft, deception or force, it is not morally acceptable and a correction of the injustice in possession ought to take place. An otherwise unequal distribution of resources beyond that required by (B3) is thus just if the conditions for rightful acquisition and rightful transfer are fulfilled.[18]

However, it is assumed in many countries that it is morally permissible to reduce too unequal a distribution on the grounds of the general good (or quite simply on the basis of a majority decision on wealth taxes, progressive income taxation and so on). Certain national governments would argue that people's right to welfare go beyond the satisfaction of their basic needs and comprise the right to higher education, free medical care, public transport, a state pension and unemployment allowance. I therefore view the demand for an intragenerationally just distribution of natural resources as an expression of an ethical minimal standard: *at the very least* we have a moral obligation to try to satisfy the basic needs of all people who are alive at present.

The intragenerational distribution principle which is assumed in *Our Common Future* and *Agenda 21* could therefore be formulated as follows:

An *intragenerational distribution of natural resources is just* if it implies that as far as possible the basic needs of all people who are alive at present are satisfied and at the same time the acquisition or transfer of other natural resources between people takes place in an ethically acceptable way (for example, in accordance with the principles of rightful acquisition and rightful transfer).

Let us now return to the question of how the intergenerational principle of justice which is presupposed in the concept of sustainable development is best formulated. Is it perhaps reasonable to suppose that there is a direct parallelism between intragenerational and intergenerational justice? If the answer is 'yes' to this question, (B4) could be formulated as follows:

We have a moral obligation to utilize natural resources in such a way that not only people who are living at present but also future human beings can satisfy their basic needs.

Let us call this particular formulation of B4 *the weak principle of intergenerational justice*. A problem with this way of drawing a direct parallel between

---

[18] Here I am applying Robert Nozick's entitlement theory of justice (Nozick, 1974, ch. 7). However, this theory is *only* applied to the question of the form of a just distribution of natural resources which are not needed to satisfy the basic needs of people who are alive at present. It is important to note that this is the case since there is a considerable difference between the formulation of the view of intragenerational justice in the theory of sustainable development and in Nozick's neoliberal theory of justice. According to Nozick, we have in general no moral obligation to concern ourselves with the improvement of the conditions pertaining to the health, education and diet of other human beings. Thus Nozick would not accept (B3).

intragenerational and intergenerational justice is that the emphasis in the World Commission report and other environmental policy documents rests more on the collective, as opposed to the individual, level when questions relating to justice between generations are discussed. In the case of intergenerational justice, it is not a question (as it is when intragenerational justice is discussed) of whether we violate the rights of individual people if we do not try to satisfy their basic needs. Rather than supposing that we have a responsibility to every now living and future human being, it is assumed (consciously or unconsciously) that we have a responsibility to a certain collective unit, namely future human *generations.*

Nothing is said about the reasoning behind this shift in perspective, but it is perhaps reasonable to suppose that it is due to the fact that an identification problem arises in the case of intergenerational justice which does not arise in the discussion of intragenerational justice.[19] We know which people are alive at present. But we know neither who the people of the future are, nor how many they will be, nor what interests and needs they will have. In order to avoid the identification problem, we therefore ought to interpret our intergenerational obligations as obligations to a collective – coming generations – and not to certain determinate future individuals.

Thus it seems as if the *individualism* (the view that individual rights are basic and that it is primarily to individual human beings that we have moral obligations) which in fact permeates major parts of these environmental policy documents, and which ultimately can be traced to the UN Declaration on Human Rights, is replaced by a *collectivism* or *communitarianism* when we come to issues which touch upon our responsibility with respect to the future. (Collectivism or communitarianism is the view that individual rights are not basic and that we can have moral obligations with respect to collective entities such as a society, a country, an institution, a moral community or to humanity as a whole, which are independent of and occasionally also contrary to the rights of individuals.)[20] Individualism is given up because it is impossible for us to identify future human beings.

If this argument is correct, (B4) ought to be formulated somewhat differently from our earlier version:

> *The weak principle of intergenerational justice**: we have a moral obligation to utilize natural resources in such a way that not only people who are alive at present but also future generations can satisfy their basic needs.

This formulation of the weak principle of justice expresses somewhat more lucidly than before (see above) the idea that our intergenerational obligations are to a

---

[19] According to Norton, the identification problem involves, among other things, the question: 'How can unknown and unknowable interests, rights and values of the future be taken into account if the individuals who will experience and express those values cannot be identified?' (Norton, 1995, p. 894).

[20] Note, however, that these three terms can be given another meaning. For example, we can mean by communitarianism the view which seeks to free itself from the picture where individualism and collectivism are seen at opposite poles (see Murphy and McClendon, 1989). This also gives us yet another possible meaning of the term 'holism': it can be taken to be synonymous with communitarianism (see, for example, Norton, 1991, p. 218).

definite entity (one or several generations) and not to particular future individuals. The ethic of sustainable development can thus be assumed to contain a collective, rather than an individual, principle of intergenerational justice.

More concretely, the weak principle of justice implies that we have a moral duty not to place at risk future generations' possibilities of achieving at least a minimal standard with respect to food, water, housing, energy, health care and education. We have a responsibility to future generations to see to it that there is productive agricultural land so they can eat adequately, that there are productive woodlands so that they can build houses and that the pollution of air and water does not threaten their well-being, and so on. On the other hand, we have no responsibility to ensure that they can achieve a standard of living or a quality of life which is equal to our own.

What are the consequences when we apply this interpretation of (B4) also in the case of non-renewable natural resources? It must reasonably mean that we are free to make use of these as much as we wish, provided that we do not put at risk future generations' possibilities of satisfying their basic needs. If we suppose that the population principle implies that a sustainable population ought to reach a level where births match deaths and that the population thereby stabilizes at 7.7 thousand million in 2060, it is permissible for people alive at present, say, to use up all fossil fuels on condition that the remaining energy resources are sufficient to satisfy the basic needs of these people. The energy resources which we leave after us must at least suffice for the needs of future generations with respect to food and protection against the elements, and allow the maintenance of a minimum level of health care and education. Just as our intragenerational obligations imply that all human beings alive at present have a right to a certain minimum standard of living, so future generations should have a right to a certain minimum quality of life. Succeeding generations should at least be guaranteed a quality of life which is comparable to that which today we (rich people) ought to guarantee the poor of the earth. Our obligations to future generations can in this respect be placed on a par with the obligations which we (rich people) have to the world's poor.

It is, however, doubtful whether it is possible to interpret the view of intergenerational justice which is to be found among advocates of sustainable development in terms of the notion of the weak principle of intergenerational justice sketched above. The first indication that our obligations to future generations are more demanding than this is to be found in the key phrase which figures in this form of anthropocentric environmental ethic: 'sustainable development'. This notion of development plausibly incorporates the view that those who come after us (and not merely we ourselves during our lifetimes) should enjoy a better existence. The World Commission writes that it 'came to see that a new development path was required, one that sustained human progress not just in a few places for a few years, but for the entire planet into the distant future' (World Commission, 1987, p. 4). This is not in itself a sufficient support for a stronger interpretation of (B4) since it is possible to put forward the notion of intergenerational justice without asserting that it is our moral duty to bring it to realization. The pronouncement of the World Commission can simply be treated as an expression of general developmental optimism.

However, if we once more examine the pronouncements on how non-renewable resources should be used, we must, in my view, see that the World Commission at least on occasions implicitly seems to subscribe to a stronger principle of justice than that given above. The Commission writes that, when it concerns 'minerals and fossil fuels, the rate of depletion and the emphasis on recycling and economy of use should be calibrated to ensure that the resource does not run out before acceptable substitutes are available' (ibid., p. 46). Here it is explicitly stated that we have no right to completely exhaust non-renewable resources before we have developed an acceptable substitute. Why? No explanation is given, but it is not enough merely to refer to the weak principle of justice. Instead, a normative assumption to the effect that future generations have the same rights in principle to enjoy the earth's natural resources as people who are alive today, is required. We must compensate succeeding generations if we exhaust a resource by developing 'acceptable substitutes' in order that they – by assumption – do not have an inferior situation to that of our own generation. Thus we may not exhaust a non-renewable resource without providing compensation because future generations have a moral right to enjoy the same level of quality of life as that of the present generations.

This implicit principle of justice can be formulated more precisely as follows:

> *The strong principle of intergenerational justice*: we have a moral obligation to utilize or consume natural resources in such a way that future generations can expect to achieve a quality of life which is equal in value to that enjoyed by us.

When people who are alive at present consume non-renewable natural resources such as fossil fuels, future generations are denied the possibility of utilizing these resources. Since we cannot repay them for the loss of the energy source by, so to speak, returning the energy after we have used it, according to the strong principle of justice we must in some sense compensate them for this loss. We can do this by developing substitute products in the form of alternative energy sources which will allow succeeding generations to expect a standard of living equal to that of our generation. Brian Barry is an ethicist who advocates just such a strong principle of intergenerational justice. He writes: 'future generations are owed compensation in other ways for our reducing their access to easily extracted and conveniently located natural resources. In practice, this entails that the combination of improved technology and increased capital investment should be such as to offset the effects of depletion ... So the choice is not between reducing the resource base for future generations and keeping it intact but between depletion with compensation and depletion without compensation' (Barry, 1989, pp. 511–12, 516).

It is naturally difficult to know exactly how one is to apply this more demanding view about intergenerational justice and its implications. Barry is aware of this difficulty: 'I imagine that few would really want to say that we would be beyond criticism on grounds of justice if we ran down capital and used up natural resources in whatever way best suited us, as long as we left our successors somewhat better equipped than people were in the Stone Age. But it is hard to come up with a clear-cut principle to say exactly how far the bounds of justice extend' (ibid., p. 518). He means, however, that this view of intergenerational justice at a more concrete level could imply that, if our generation consumes 10 per cent of the world's oil, we have a moral obligation to future generations to develop a technology which makes it possible to extract 10 per cent more oil from every drilling. Alternatively, one could say that if we consume 50 per cent of the oil, we ought to develop, for example, a technology which allows us to make use of solar energy to the same extent. My proposal is thus that we should (or at least could) interpret the World Commission's pronouncement on our obligation to develop acceptable substitutes in a similar way.

What, then, would explain this difference between intragenerational and intergenerational justice? Why is it assumed in the environmental policy documents which are associated with the idea of sustainable development that our moral obligations to people alive at present are in this respect less extensive or less demanding than those to future generations? My hypothesis is that this difference can at least partially be explained in terms of the asymmetry which, as we have seen earlier, constitutes the solution to the problem of identification. The intergenerational principle of justice is to be interpreted in collective or communitarian terms, unlike the intragenerational principle which is interpreted in individualist terms. The idea would then be that there is no real reason why we as a collective entity should enjoy a better situation than succeeding generations viewed as one or several collectives. The justification for a difference in resources between human beings is not applicable between generations. In other words, the reason why a human being is morally justified in having access to more resources than some other individual existing at the same time can be explained in terms of how the acquisition of resources took place.

If, for example, I succeed in writing a book which many people buy voluntarily and which thereby allows me to acquire a larger piece of land and build a bigger house than my neighbour (who has not been able to earn a similar sum of money), there is a difference in achievement which we assume, *ceteris paribus*, justifies an unequal distribution of resources between us. But we cannot assume in a corresponding way that there is this kind of difference between present and future generations which would justify our enjoyment of a superior quality of life or a greater amount of natural resources. For this reason, an equality principle should be assumed in arguments involving intergenerational justice which is not required when intragenerational justice is discussed.

I have chosen to argue that it is most reasonable to assume that the ethic of sustainable development contains a strong principle of intergenerational justice. But it is worth noting that some of the proponents of sustainable development oscillate in their arguments about our responsibility towards succeeding generations between a weaker and stronger principle of justice. An example of this kind of swinging back and forth can be found in Andrew Kadak's article, 'An intergenerational approach to high-level waste disposal' (1997). In the article, Kadak presents certain ethical guidelines which are intended to regulate, among other things, dealing with, and disposing of, nuclear waste. These guidelines were proposed by a working group of which Kadak himself was a member and which was appointed by the NAPA.[21] He writes that 'the objective was that no generation should (needlessly), now or in the future, deprive its successors of the opportunity to enjoy a quality of life equivalent to its own' (ibid., p. 50). This overall goal is supplemented by six principles of implementation of which one is the following: 'There is an obligation to protect future generations provided the interests of the present generations and its immediate offspring are not jeopardized' (ibid.). Kadak also maintains that these principles imply that 'the priority for today is the present population, although considerations of future generations must be factored into presentday decisions' (ibid.).

The problem with Kadak's reasoning is that, on the one hand, he maintains that future generations have a right to the same quality of life as we have, while, on the other hand, he also holds that we should place the interests of people alive now before those of future generations. These two statements, as they stand, are incompatible. I maintain that in the first quotation he seems to accept the strong principle of justice, whereas in the two following quotations it is at best the weak principle of justice which is assumed. The weak principle of justice allows us to give priority to our own interests irrespective of whether they are basic or not, provided we do not put at risk future generations' possibilities of satisfying their basic needs. This does not entail that we can unconditionally give priority to *all* of our interests. According to the weak principle of justice, the basic needs of future generations have priority over those of our interests which go beyond our basic need for work, food, energy, housing, health care and education. It is only when our interests conflict with the non-basic interests of future generations that we can unconditionally give priority to our interests. Even if one made do with the weak principle of justice, it would be impossible to write, as Kadak does, that 'there is an obligation to protect future generations provided the interests of the present generations and its immediate offspring are not jeopardized'.

Kadak's unqualified assertion about the present generation's priority becomes even more problematic if the strong principle of justice is assumed, namely that we have a moral obligation to utilize or consume natural resources in such a way that future generations of human beings can expect to achieve a quality of life that is equal to that which we enjoy. This implies that we cannot even assume that our own non-basic needs always come before the non-basic needs of future generations. Suppose that we put forward the view that foreign immigrants living in a given country should have the right to the same quality of life as the native citizens of that country. Then we would inevitably be inconsistent in our reasoning if we simultaneously maintained that, in a distribution of various resources in order to satisfy the non-basic interests of these two groups, we should always give priority to native citizens. It is reasonable to suppose that the same must hold in a discussion of the distribution of resources between generations.

If we assume, as Kadak initially does, that 'no generation should (needlessly),

---

[21] NAPA is the acronym for National Academy of Public Administration. According to Kadak, it is 'a nonprofit, nonpartisan organization chartered by the U.S. Congress to improve the effectiveness and performance of government at all levels' (Kadak, 1997, p. 49).

now or in the future, deprive its successors of the opportunity to enjoy a quality of life equivalent to its own', we must, given the condition expressed by the word 'needlessly' in this statement, hold that we have the right to deprive our successors of the opportunity to an equivalent standard of life to our own *only* if our own basic needs are threatened. In Kadak's own words: 'There is an obligation to protect future generations provided the [*basic!*] interests of the present generation and its immediate offspring are not jeopardized.' On the basis of the strong principle of justice, we can exclusively speak about the 'priority of people alive today' only if the basic needs of people alive just now conflict with the needs of future generations.

Thus we can reformulate this principle of justice a little more clearly, as follows:

> *The strong principle of intergenerational justice**: on condition that our own basic needs are not threatened, we have a moral obligation to utilize or consume natural resources in such a way that future generations can expect to attain a quality of life equal to that which we enjoy.

Let me also formulate this principle of justice in which the difference between how we ought to deal in the respective cases of renewable and non-renewable natural resources becomes clearer:

> *The strong principle of intergenerational justice***: on condition that our own basic needs are not threatened, we have a moral obligation (a) to utilize renewable natural resources in such a way that such utilization does not threaten the long-term productive potential of the ecosystems and (b) to consume non-renewable natural resources in such a way that future generations are compensated so that they will not have a quality of life inferior to that which we enjoy.

To summarize, two main types of problem arise in dealing with the question of our responsibility to future generations: the population problem (what should be the future population size if our aim is that of developing a sustainable society?) and the problem of obligation (what are our moral obligations to future generations and how do we achieve a just distribution of resources between present and future generations?). Given that a radical reduction in population has not been proposed, the solution of environmental problems must primarily consist of a change in our utilization of renewable and non-renewable natural resources. As a result, the problem of obligation becomes of central importance.

The problem of obligation can in turn be broken down into a number of important subsidiary problems. The first, namely the *identification problem* (we know neither who the future people are nor how many they will be, nor what their interests will be), is avoided at least partially by giving up the individualism which characterizes the intragenerational discussion and adopting instead a collectivist or communitarian view of intergenerational justice. Our responsibility is not considered ultimately to be to certain particular individuals in the future but to a collective, namely future generations. The second subsidiary problem which we have devoted the larger part of this section to analysing, we can call *the problem of extent*: exactly how extensive are our obligations to future generations? Here I have contented myself in mainly presenting two plausible alternative answers. According to the weak principle of justice, we have a moral obligation to utilize natural resources in such a way that not only people who are living at present but also future generations can satisfy their basic needs. According to the strong principle of intergenerational justice, we have a moral obligation to utilize natural resources in such a way that future generations can be expected to attain a standard of living equivalent to that of the present generations.

A third subsidiary problem involved in the problem of obligation and one with which we must now deal, can be called *the problem of remote generations*. As we have seen, the advocates of sustainable development indirectly reject what Norton calls 'presentism', viz. the view that our obligations can only apply to our immediate descendants (Norton, 1995, p. 894). But how far into the future do our moral obligations really extend? Have we the same type of obligations to immediately following generations that we have to more distant generations? This question is left untouched in the policy documents we have analysed but it is an important issue since, in certain cases, our use of natural resources has an effect far into the future. For example, radioactive waste from our nuclear power stations will continue after tens of thousands of years to be a danger to those who are in its vicinity if the waste is not stored in the proper way. Avner de-Shalit has recently touched on this issue:

> We have, I believe, positive and negative obligations to close and immediate future generations. That is, we should consider them when deciding on environmental policies; we should not overburden them; furthermore, we should supply them with goods, especially those goods that we believe are and will be necessary to cope with the challenges of life, as well as other, more non-essential goods. The case is different with the very remote future generations: there, our 'positive' obligations (those beyond merely preventing damage, e.g. providing resources) 'fade away', so to speak. To people of the very remove future we have a strong 'negative' obligation – namely, to avoid causing them enormous harm or bringing them death, and to try and relieve any potential and foreseeable distress. (de-Shalit, 1995, p. 13)

I imagine that de-Shalit's view is intuitively shared by many people, but at the same time let us stop to think a little more about the arguments which can be advanced in its defence. One argument which de-Shalit himself gives, is based on a principle which is frequently assumed in ethical contexts: ought implies can. He writes that

> a theory of morality, or of applied philosophy (as environmental philosophy is) should not demand what is absolutely impossible. If people are told that they should share natural resources, e.g. coal, with people who will be alive six or twelve generations from now, they will at least listen and may even tend to agree. But if they are told that they should share access to coal with someone living in the year 2993 or 3993, the response will probably be, 'To hell with morality and intergenerational justice! This is ridiculous; such policies do not make any sense because they are inconceivable!' (de-Shalit, 1995, p. 14)

Another argument for our moral obligations to more immediately succeeding generations being stronger than those to distant ones quite simply cites our inability to know what needs people living some 20, 40 or 60 generations after us will have with respect to energy, transport, housing, education and so on. However we would still have certain obligations to these distant generations since we can reasonably assume that they will need to protect themselves from radioactive waste, skin cancer or starvation and at the same time have access to fully functioning ecosystems, fresh air, food and pure water. However, although we can assume that these distant generations have an interest in being protected from radioactive waste for example, it is implausible to suggest that we know what sources of energy or means of transport they will require.

Because our abilities to know what needs distant generations will have are much less than our capacity to judge the needs of generations closer to us, it is reasonable to suppose that our moral obligations diminish with time. We can therefore assume, as de-Shalit does, that we have only certain *negative* obligations to distant generations of human beings. It can thus be argued that we should, for their sake, ensure that radioactive waste is safely stored and perhaps also reduce its amount, limit the use of those gases which cause the greenhouse effect, avoid putting the long-term productive potential of ecosystems at risk and refrain from causing severe natural catastrophes or alterations in climate, and so on. It would thereby be morally acceptable, for example, to leave behind radioactive waste without these distant generations being in any way compensated by our contributing actively to their welfare. This would be permissible provided we did not threaten their health and safety. If we accept the strong principle of intergenerational justice then generations which are closer to us in time must receive compensation in the form of money, technology or knowledge for being compelled to shoulder the task of storing our radioactive waste.

Note, however, that if we accept this argument it implies that our obligations to distant generations are less extensive than what is specified according to both the strong and the weak principles of justice. If for the moment we refrain from specifying exactly which future generations are to be reckoned as 'distant', this principle could be formulated as follows:

> *The minimal principle of intergenerational justice*: we have a moral obligation to utilize or consume natural resources in such a way that we do not threaten the life opportunities of distant generations of human beings.

Thus we have identified a spectrum of principles of intergenerational justice, ranging from the static principle of justice at one end to the minimal principle of justice at the other. The strong and weak principles of justice form two intermediate positions. As we have seen, the static principle is scarcely adequate. It remains to decide when a transition from the strong or weak principle to the minimal principle would be justifiable. Where is the dividing line between what I have chosen to call generations 'nearer to' us and those who are to be termed 'distant'? Obviously, it is impossible to draw any sharp and fixed boundary. Nevertheless, it would still be desirable if we were at least able to indicate in some way possible arguments for such a tentative dividing line. In order to find an answer to this difficult question, I suspect that one must return to the original reason for this distinction between different generations. The reason is that, when we go sufficiently far into the future, we lack the ability to judge reliably what these generations will require by way of energy, transport, housing, education and so on.

A certain guidance can perhaps be derived by glancing backwards into history and asking, 'How far were people in Europe in the Middle Ages able to form a view about the needs of our own generation?' Is there any difference in the answer if we raise the same question with respect to the people who lived at the end of the nineteenth century? One thing at least is clear and that is that those who lived at the end of the nineteenth century were in a much better position to judge than those who lived during the sixteenth century. If we are justified in blaming any of these generations for today's environmental situation, this blame is more justly given to those who lived in the nineteenth century than to those who lived in the sixteenth. There are, however, certain important differences between them and us which reasonably make our responsibility greater and cause it to extend further in time. One such difference is the fact that we have ecological knowledge which they lacked. I am thinking primarily of the content of theses (A), (B) and (C). It will be recalled that, according to (A), there is an interaction and interdependence between human beings and all other living beings while, according to (B), the natural resources available to human beings are limited; finally, according to (C), there is a limit to the capacity of ecosystems to absorb human waste. With the help of statistics and computers, we are in addition much better placed to make predictions about future population size, the spread of deserts, the depletion of the ozone layer and the extent of the earth's non-renewable resources and the rate at which they are being consumed.

I would therefore suggest, although I have not really been able to substantiate this line of thought, that as a rough guideline we could think of the strong principle of justice as expressing our obligations to succeeding generations living some 150 years in the future. The weak principle of justice specifies our obligations from this point to a point still further in the future, say by another 150 years or so. Finally, the minimal principle of justice covers the remaining time from this latter point onwards for as long as we assume that human beings will live upon the earth. But, irrespective of this, there remains with regard to these points a task of clarifying the idea of intergenerational justice for ethicists and decision makers who embrace a holistic and intergenerational anthropocentrism. This is a task which, naturally, the exponents of the 'old' ethic, namely traditional anthropocentrism, do not need to address. On the other hand, such an environmental ethic lacks the capacity to be ecologically sustainable in the long term and ought for that reason to be rejected.

Although the authors of the policy documents which we have examined draw attention to the fact that environmental problems have a normative dimension and that there is even a need for a new ethic, they do not explain or analyse the normative foundations of their own environmental policy making.[22] It is possible to

---

[22] The report of the Swedish National Environment Protection Board, *Ren luft och gröna skogar*, is something of an exception (see Naturvårdsverket 1997, pp. 13–21).

some extent to excuse the World Commission and the authors of *Agenda 21* and say that their work was only conceived as a starting point for a more exhaustive discussion of the meaning of the concept of sustainable development, including its normative implications. Since the end of the 1980s, the United Nations has continued to appoint committees of enquiry and launch research into environmental questions and it might be thought that these decision makers had anticipated tackling a detailed treatment of the ethical issues only at a later stage of the UN project. The only problem is that any such declarations are hard – if not impossible – to find. The only publication which explicitly deals with environmental ethics produced by the UN that I have been able to find is *Ethics and Agenda 21* (UNEP, 1994). In the first part of the book, a number of philosophers and theologians are given four to five pages to discuss the ethical questions which they believe are raised by *Agenda 21*, while the second part of the book consists of a summary of *Agenda 21*.[23] The World Bank has published the booklet, *Ethics and spiritual values* (1996) which has a similar format to that of *Ethics and Agenda 21*. Naturally, there is reason to suspect that there are several other works on environmental ethics which the UN has sponsored, but it is worth noting that I was able to find without any difficulty hundreds of publications dealing with economic questions.

When we consider the economic resources which are available within the framework of the United Nations Environmental Programme (UNEP), we are somewhat surprised (or horrified) about how little has been achieved since the World Commission's exhortation to transmute 'the practical principles needed for a sustainable growth into a global ethic' and Gro Harlem Brundtland's inspiring speech on the development of 'a new holistic ethic in which economic growth and environmental protection go hand-in-hand around the world'. Reference to both these pronouncements was made at the beginning of this chapter. Noel J. Brown, the director of UNEP, seems to some extent to be aware of this shortcoming. He observes, in the introduction to, *Ethics and Agenda 21*: 'Still to begin, however, is the ethical debate on the moral implications of Agenda 21' (UNEP, 1994, p. 2). Thus we have to hope that in the future the UN will seriously consider setting aside resources for the development and analysis of the content of the ethic of sustainable growth and that similar measures are taken at a national level. It is a matter of some importance because, as Ronald Engel writes, 'Ethical clarity cannot be generated casually, but requires the same kind of rigorous intellectual attention as that given scientific, technological, and legal considerations' (Engel, 1990, p. 7).

The normative component which above all must be clarified is that which *de facto* makes the ethic of sustainable development into a new ethic, more specifically the idea that we have moral obligations to future generations. My attempt to sketch various alternative interpretations of what the talk about intergenerational justice implies must not be seen as more than a sketch. Nonetheless, it is to be hoped that

---

[23] It would therefore seem that the UN has not initiated any research into environmental ethics, although this has not prevented a number of philosophers and ethicists from developing an anthropocentric environmental ethic. (We have already made the acquaintance of some of these in this chapter.) See, for example, Brennan (1988), de-Shalit (1995), Ferry (1995), Hargrove (1989), Marietta (1995), Norton (1987, 1991) and Passmore (1974).

my discussion has led to some of the principal alternatives being identified: are future generations morally entitled to a quality of life that is equivalent to the one we ourselves enjoy (*the strong principle of justice*) or is it sufficient if we bequeath them natural resources which allow them to satisfy their basic needs? In other words, can they at least attain a standard of living which we ought today to guarantee the world's poorest people (*the weak principle of justice*)? Or should we instead apply a neoliberal approach to our relationship to future generations and assume that we are in no way obliged to help future generations to secure their well-being (*the minimal principle of justice*)? We have only negative obligations to our descendants, namely not to threaten their future opportunities in life by placing at risk the long-term productive potential of ecosystems.

In other words, the World Commission's definition of 'sustainable development' whereby 'sustainable development is development that meets the needs of the present without compromising the ability of future generations to meet their own needs' (World Commission, 1987, p. 43) can be interpreted in at least three different ways. 'Without compromising the ability of future generations to meet their own needs' can imply that they should be so equipped (a) that they can attain the same quality of life as that which we (well-off members of the Western world) enjoy; or (b) that at the least they should be able to secure a reasonable and tolerable standard of living which does not merely cover food for the day and a roof over one's head but also such things as elementary school education, medical care and employment opportunities; or lastly (c) that at least they can ensure their survival: in other words, we do not expose them to radioactive radiation or radioactive waste, dramatic natural catastrophes or severe alterations in climate.

CHAPTER FOUR

Non-anthropocentric
Environmental Ethics

Are any of the core values which form the basis of the reports from the United Nations or the Swedish National Environment Protection Board, or which are embraced by the advocates of the ethic of sustainable development, in any sense contestable or controversial? What is clear is that there exists another important group of environmentalists, usually called 'preservationists'.[1] David Ehrenfeld maintains, for example, that 'There is no true protection for Nature within the humanist system – the very idea is a contradiction in terms' (Ehrenfeld, 1978, p. 202). He means that it is a contradiction because how could such humanist values and attitudes constitute a solution to the problems that they themselves have created? It is the anthropocentric way of looking at nature which ultimately is the cause of our environmental problems. We find ourselves in the situation we are because we have looked upon nature merely as a resource which we can utilize for our own ends.

The fundamental mistake which so-called 'conservationists' (that is, anthropocentrists) make, according to the preservationists, is thus to consider nature's products simply as a resource for satisfying human needs and interests. Instead, there is reason for affirming that nature has an intrinsic value. Preservationists aim at preserving nature for its own sake and not for our sake. While advocates of sustainable development seek to defend nature *for the sake of* human beings, preservationists seek to defend nature *against* human beings. As one of their critics formulates it: 'It is no longer a matter of defending man, considered as the center of the world, from himself, but rather of defending the *cosmos* from him' (Ferry, 1995, pp. xxiv). Preservationists thus place nature's integrity before any human forms of utilization. It is therefore important for them, as Paul Taylor writes, that 'we sharply distinguish conservation (saving in the present for future consumption) from preservation (protecting from both present and future consumption)' (Taylor, 1986, p. 185).

The solution to environmental problems does not consist in using natural resources more efficiently and more far-sightedly but quite simply in our learning to respect nature. Modern human beings must radically rethink their relationship to nature. However, preservationists disagree about how far this process of rethinking should be taken and about the consequences it has for the structure of our society. Respect for nature means that there are limits to the way nature may be exploited which are quite different from the requirement that our use of resources must be efficient and far-sighted. Human beings do not have the right to

---

[1] See, for example, Norton (1987, pp. 234–5), Sörlin (1991, p. 70) and Des Jardins (1997, pp. 39–46).

extract as much as possible from nature. Instead, we human beings have a duty to preserve nature, not because some particular process yields a profit or is in our own interest, but because plants and animals have moral standing and therefore cannot be treated in any way we like.

Thus, behind the arguments of the preservationists, there is hidden an environmental ethic which differs from both traditional and intergenerational anthropocentrism. It is not simply human beings and their needs which must be respected; in addition, respect is due to nature or non-human life. Aldo Leopold, one of the most important representatives of the preservationist movement in the United States, gives voice to such an ethic when he writes: 'A thing is right when it tends to preserve the integrity, stability and beauty of the biotic community. It is wrong when it tends otherwise' (Leopold, 1949, pp. 224–5). It is not simply human actions directed towards other human beings that can be moral or immoral but also human actions towards other living things – indeed, even towards the whole ecosystem.

The type of environmental ethic which also assigns a value-in-itself to nature and to other living beings is usually called a 'non-anthropocentric ethic'. The starting point of such an ethic is that every influence exerted on nature should be judged on the basis of the effect it has on all living beings and not simply on the basis of its effects on humans. To speak of nature being threatened thus primarily implies that its value is diminished in relation to itself and not primarily in relation to us as persons making use of nature. Non-anthropocentrists are naturally themselves seriously concerned about environmental pollution and the exhaustion of our natural resources, but it is not only – and perhaps indeed not even primarily – due to the fact that human well-being is threatened: it is because nature itself is put at risk. Nature must be seen as something which is valuable in itself. It must be preserved for its own sake.

Some non-anthropocentrists not only maintain that nature has an intrinsic value; they go on to say that everything in nature (including human beings) is equally valuable. In such a formulation of a non-anthropocentric ethic, it is not simply a matter of the principle of justice (as in the case of intergenerational anthropocentrism) being extended in temporal terms; the range of things to which it applies is also extended. All living things and not merely human beings have an equal value. Paul Taylor, who represents this radical version of non-anthropocentrism, consequently writes: 'The killing of a wild flower, then, when taken in and of itself, is just as much a wrong, other-things-being-equal, as the killing of a human' (Taylor, 1983, p. 242) .

Are there no passages in the reports from the World Commission, *Agenda 21* or the Swedish National Environment Protection Board which lean towards a non-anthropocentric ethic? In the World Commission report, there are some which can be interpreted in this way. Thus, among other things, we find the following:

> The diversity of species is necessary for the normal functioning of ecosystems and the biosphere as a whole. The genetic material in wild species contributes billions of dollars yearly to the world economy in the form of improved crop species, new drugs and medicines, and raw materials for industry. But utility aside, there are also moral, ethical, cultural, aesthetic, and purely scientific reasons for conserving wild beings. (World Commission, 1987, p.13)

In the first part of the quotation, an anthropocentric justification is clearly given for the conservation of the diversity of species. In the final sentence, however, it is suggested that there are other justifications for this biological diversity in terms of what are called moral, ethical, cultural, aesthetic and purely scientific reasons. At the same time, nothing concrete is said about the implications of these reasons, or about what it is that distinguishes moral and ethical reasons. It follows that the reasons for conserving the diversity of the species can be given both an anthropocentric and a non-anthropocentric interpretation.

Another indication that there are non-anthropocentric reasons for protecting and conserving wild species appears most clearly in the following passage from the World Commission report: 'the case for the conservation of nature should not rest only with development goals. It is part of our moral obligations to other living beings and future generations' (ibid., p. 57). Thus we not only have a moral responsibility for future generations of human beings but also for other living beings. However, it is not explained what this moral duty consists in or how it limits our utilization of nature.[2] It never seems to have entered the minds of the authors of the report that a recognition of moral responsibility for other living beings would constitute a further – and perhaps even decisive – limitation on how 'natural resources' can be utilized, beyond those included within the framework of sustainable development.

In the Rio Declaration, as we have see, it is stated that 'Human beings are at the centre of concern for sustainable development' (article 1). This evaluation is also underlined in the third principle where it is said that the 'right to development must be fulfilled so as to equitably meet developmental and environmental needs of present and future [human] generations'. At the same time, however, it is stated in the seventh principle that 'States shall cooperate in a spirit of global partnership to conserve, protect and restore the health and integrity of the Earth's ecosystem.' But the same type of problem arises with respect to such pronouncements as those which arose with respect to the statements of the World Commission. As I have already tried to show in the previous chapter, it is hard to see how nature's integrity (in the sense of dignity or worth) can be respected if human present and future needs always occupy the centre of attention.[3] If human needs are always to be given priority, what does the talk about the integrity of ecosystems really mean? There is a failure to note that there is a potential conflict between human interests and the 'interests' of ecosystems.

Also, in the case of *Agenda 21*, there is at least one occasion where nature's intrinsic value would appear to be affirmed. In the discussion about how to make it possible for the technological and scientific community to provide a more open and effective contribution to the decision process in environmental issues, it is stated:

---

[2] The above quotation contains the only proncouncement from the Commission about a moral responsibility for other living beings. By contrast, our responsibility for future generations of human beings is touched on in every chapter.

[3] See Chapter 3.

> Increased ethical awareness in environmental and developmental decision-
> making should help to place appropriate priorities for the maintenance and
> enhancement of life-support systems for their own sake, and in so doing ensure
> that the functioning of viable natural processes is properly valued by present and
> future societies. (*Agenda 21*, 31.8)

The phrase 'for their own sake' would seem to indicate that the authors of *Agenda 21* recognize that life-sustaining systems have a value independent of the the utility (instrumental value) which we human beings derive from them and that we ought to let our recognition of such an intrinsic value influence how we set priorities in the decision-making pprocess in the area of environment and development. However, nothing else is said about this. Here, as in other parts of *Agenda 21*, there is no discussion about how relative priorities should be set in weighing the worth and dignity of human beings against that of other living beings. Such a discussion ought to be important if the other living beings or life-sustaining systems are assigned intrinsic value.

It is possible that the following pronouncement of the Swedish National Environment Protection Board can also be interpreted along non-anthropocentric lines: 'Making the protection of the natural and cultural landscape a special aim can be seen as an acknowledgment that the aesthetic and historical values, together with those elements of landscape which give every district its own special character , are worth preserving' (Naturvårdsverket, 1993, p. 32). However, once more it is possible to give both anthropocentric and non-anthropocentric arguments for preserving the natural landscape.[4]

In short, we can distinguish between an environmental ethic which puts *human beings* at the centre and those which put *nature* at the centre. We can then choose one of at least two different ways of tackling the ethical dimension of the environmental problem. On the one hand, it can be maintained that all we ought and need to be concerned with is what human beings themselves would win or lose in a conflict between self-interest and environmental considerations. On the other hand, it can be argued that environmental problems can only be solved if attention is paid not only to what is in the interest of human beings, but to what is in the 'interest' of plants and animals. According to non-anthropocentrists or preservationists, we need a non-anthropocentric system of values to be able to solve the ecological crisis which threatens the earth. People in general and decision makers in particular must adopt a non-anthropocentric ethic. It is not enough simply to revise our anthropocentric values. We must radically re-evaluate our relationship to nature.

Thus, in principle, one could choose between two different types of environmental ethic as a basis for decision making in enviromental management and policy. The question which we must ask ourselves is what practical significance this choice – anthropocentric or non-anthropocentric – has for the actual form given to environmental management. However, it requires first that we identify and analyse the various value components which a non-anthropocentric ethic contains.

---

[4] See Gillespie (1997) for a more thorough discussion of anthropocentric and non-anthropocentric value assumptions in legal and policy texts, at a national and international level.

As we have seen, all non-anthropocentrists share the view that nature in addition to human beings has an intrinsic value. It follows that they all agree that there are limitations to the way in which human beings may utilize nature which are quite different from those advanced by proponents of sustainable dvelopment, namely that such utilization has to be efficient and far-sighted. These limitations are of a moral character and follow from the fact that we assign moral standing to nature. Thus we can define this form of environmental ethics as follows:

> A *non-anthropocentric ethic* holds that living beings or natural things other than human beings have an intrinsic value or have moral standing;

alternatively,

> A *non-anthropocentric ethic* holds that individual behaviour as well as proposed environmental policies must be judged on the basis of how they affect the whole of nature and not simply present or future generations of human beings.[5]

The basic idea of non-anthropocentric ethics is thus that, when we are deciding how to act, we should always pay attention to the effects our actions have upon nature. We can act morally rightly or wrongly not only towards other human beings but also towards other beings on earth. For that reason, we cannot ignore the well-being of other living creatures and exclusively focus on what is useful to or promotes human society.

However, a complication in the analysis of non-anthropocentric ethics arises from the fact that environmentalists who are criticical of anthropocentrism and the ethic of sustainable development often (consciously or unconsciously) formulate the alternative ethic which they themselves embrace, in different ways. It is important to note these differences in basic ethical assumptions since, as we shall see in the next chapter, they often lead to differing views about the form an environmental policy programme should take.

What then are these differences? All non-anthropocentrists agree that objects other than human beings have moral standing. But they differ from one another on this point since some of them assign moral standing only to living individuals, whereas others entertain the idea that species and ecosystems also have moral

---

[5] In my attempt to avoid making the ethical theory too complex and inaccessible, I have chosen not to distinguish between deontological and consequentialist versions of anthropocentrism and non-anthropocentrism. I would point out, however, that our choice between a deontological or consequentialist normative ethic determines to some extent our choice of these two definitions of non-anthropocentrism. Put very briefly, the difference between these two ethical theories is that, whereas according to a consequentialist (very often a utilitarian) an action is morally right or wrong depending on its consequences, the deontologist holds that there are several properties of an action besides its consequences which must be taken into account in judging whether it is right or wrong. For example, deontologists may maintain that there are certain general moral rules which human beings are always obliged to follow. For a discussion of the difference between deontological and consequentialist theories, see, for example, Ashmore (1987) or some other introductory book on ethics.

standing. Because of the use of the ambiguous and vague word 'nature', this distinction has been hidden in the above. In other words, non-anthropocentrists give different answers to the question: what is it, more precisely, which has intrinsic value in nature? In addition to human beings, the things which can be assigned moral standing may comprise particular individuals of non-human species or biological wholes such as species or ecosystems.

The most important dividing line between non-anthropocentrists separates 'biocentric' and 'ecocentric' environmental ethics.[6] Those who advocate biocentrism maintain that all life (and not simply human life) has an intrinsic value but, since species and ecosystems are not in themselves living beings, they cannot have moral standing. Paul Taylor writes, 'Not only is it intelligible to speak of owing duties to animals and plants, but it is the case that we humans who are moral agents do have such duties, just as we have duties to our fellow humans' (Taylor, 1986, p. 20).[7] Proponents of *ecocentrism*, on the other hand, insist that land, water and air together with ecosystems have moral standing and not merely living things. In fact, according to many ecocentrists right and wrong are a function of – in other words are determined by – the well-being of the whole biotic community and not simply by that of the human community. Baird Callicott describes this group of non-anthropocentrists in the following way:

> [They] saw in the environmental crisis a profound repudiation by the environment itself of modern Western civilization's attitudes and values toward nature. Thus, nothing less than a sweeping philosophical overhaul – not just of ethics, but of the whole Western world view – is mandated. These philosophers, among whom I count myself, have been called 'ecocentrists' since we have advocated a shift in the locus of intrinsic value from individuals (whether individual human beings or individual higher 'lower animals') to terrestial nature – the ecosystem – as a whole. (Callicott, 1989a, pp. 3–4)

The complexity of the situation, however, does not end with the fact that non-anthropocentrists differ in their views about how far we should show concern for nature in our actions. The answer depends partly on how highly they value the various objects in nature (including human beings) which have moral standing. Are they all equally valuable or have some a higher value than others? Taylor is clear about where he stands on the issue. He rejects 'the idea of human superiority' and maintains that 'every species counts as having the same value in the sense that, regardless of what species a living thing belongs to, it is deemed to be prima facie deserving of equal concern and consideration on the part of moral agents' (Taylor, 1986, p. 155). Callicott, on the other hand, holds the opposite opinion. He writes: 'The Land ethic manifestly does not accord equal moral worth to each and every member of the biotic community; the moral worth of individuals (including, take

---

6 There is unfortunately a lack of a uniform and accepted terminology with regard to this point. Sometimes 'biocentrism' and 'ecocentrism' are used as synonyms for 'non-anthropocentrism'. Other terms which have been used in this connection include 'ecosophy', 'deep ecology' and 'the land ethic'.

7 See Taylor (1986, pp. 118–19), for a discussion of why he rejects ecocentrism.

note, human individuals) is relative, to be assessed in accordance with the particular relation of each to the collective entity which Leopold called "land" ' (Callicott, 1989b, p. 28).

Non-anthropocentrists thus give different answers also to another question: are the objects which are assigned intrinsic value equally valuable? This leads to a further distinction between two types of non-anthropocentrism:

Value-undifferentiated non-anthropocentrism: the view that living beings or natural objects other than human beings also have an intrinsic value and that everything with intrinsic value is equally valuable.

Value-differentiated non-anthropocentrism: the view that living beings or natural objects other than human beings also have an intrinsic value but that not everything with intrinsic value is equally valuable.

Certain forms of non-anthropocentric ethic thus permit a differentiation of values in nature. Note, however, that it is not necessarily the case that human beings are considered the most valuable beings. Certain ecocentrists believe, for example, that the preservation of key ecosystems can be of greater importance than the preservation of a large number of human beings. Looking at things from such a perspective, human beings are therefore not always – perhaps are never – at the centre of environmental management, as we can read in the report of the World Commission or in the Rio Declaration.

The environmental ethical discussion is not only about the question of which natural objects have intrinsic as opposed to instrumental value but also about the relative intrinsic values possessed by natural objects or processes in relation to one another. Further on we shall see more clearly what this entails and what practical consequences it has for environmental issues. Yet in principle it is no harder to understand than the comparable discussion within human ethics. A question much discussed at one time in the Western world was whether slaves have an intrinsic value or merely an instrumental value. The majority of people today believe that there are strong reasons for maintaining that all human beings have an intrinsic value. However, just because we accept such a viewpoint this does not mean that we in practice assign to all human beings an equally high value. On the contrary, women have often been assigned a lower value than men. If we maintain that it is morally right that women do not have the right to inherit property or to vote in political elections, this indicates that we *de facto* embrace a moral view according to which women and men are assigned different values.

Non-anthropocentrism thus contains both biocentrists and ecocentrists, while biocentrism and ecocentrism in turn can either be value-differentiated or value-undifferentiated. But although it is important to note these differences, we must not, as Bernard Rollin has pointed out, allow them to 'cloud the dramatic nature of this common attempt to break out of a moral tradition that finds the loci of value in human beings and derivatively, in human institutions' (Rollin, 1995, p. 114). The fact that there are two main types of non-anthropocentric ethic (biocentrism and ecocentrism) entails, as we shall see, that it is also possible to formulate two different types of 'preservationist' environmental management in contrast to the 'efficient' management associated with sustainable development. In the next section, I shall try to analyse and formulate more precisely these two approaches to non-anthropocentric ethics.

Biocentric Ethics

What is characteristic of advocates of a *biocentric* (or *life-centred*) *ethic* is that they maintain that the lives of organisms other than human beings have moral standing. However, because species and ecosystems are not in themselves living beings, they cannot be assigned any intrinsic value. One of the earliest and best known Western proponents of a biocentric ethic was Albert Schweitzer (1875–1965). He writes:

> The great fault of all ethics hitherto has been that they believed themselves to have to deal only with the relations of man to man. In reality, however, the question is what is his attitude to the world and all life that comes within his reach. A man is ethical only when life, as such, is sacred to him, that of plants and animals as that of his fellow men, and when he devotes himself helpfully to all life that is in need of help ... The ethic of the relation of man to man is not something apart by itself: it is only a particular relation which results from the universal one. (Schweitzer, 1949, pp. 158–9)

The mistake that is made in ethics is that that we look upon morality as a question of relations between human beings. According to Schweitzer, we must instead recognize that we stand in a relationship to the sum total of living things. Our behaviour and attitudes are morally acceptable only when life as such is sacred for us. Thus we can formulate biocentrism or a biocentric ethic as follows:

> *Biocentric ethic* is the view that living creatures, and only they, have an intrinsic value or have moral standing (that is, they can be treated in a morally right or wrong way and are beings to which humans have obligations);

> *Biocentric ethic* is the view that individual behaviour as well as proposed environmental policies must be judged on the basis of how they affect other living beings and not merely present and future generations of human beings.

Perhaps the best known advocate of biocentric ethics today is Paul Taylor. Because of this, I propose to take his environmental ethic as my chief example of what is characteristic of a biocentric ethic. However, we must bear in mind that there is also room for important variations within biocentrism. At the end of this section, I shall therefore identify and distinguish three different versions of biocentrism.

According to Taylor, the central thesis of biocentric ethics is that 'actions are right and character traits are morally good in virtue of their expressing or embodying a certain ultimate moral attitude, which I call respect for nature' (Taylor,

1986, p. 80). This implies among other things that all living things are assigned an intrinsic value and are thereby treated as an object for moral concern. But why should we take the view that all living beings have moral standing? According to Taylor, we must do so because the characteristic feature of all life is that the conditions regulating its existence can be threatened or promoted. It is meaningful to say that all living things strive (consciously or unconsciously) to attain some good for themselves or that it is in the interest of a living being that certain things are present or occur:

> Concerning a butterfly, for example, we may hesitate to speak of its interests or preferences, and we would probably deny outright that it values anything in the sense of considering it good or desirable. But once we come to understand its cycle and know the environmental conditions it needs to survive in a healthy state, we have no difficulty in speaking about what is beneficial to it and what might be harmful to it ... Even when we consider such simple animal organisms as one-celled protozoa, it makes perfectly good sense to a biologically informed person to speak of what benefits or harms them, what environmental changes are to their advantage or disadvantage, and what physical circumstances are favorable or unfavorable to them. The more knowledge we gain concerning these organisms, the better are we able to make sound judgements about what is in their interest or contrary to their interest. (Taylor, 1986, pp. 66–7)

In contrast to stones, ecosystems and machines, living organisms are 'ends-in-themselves' or 'teleological centers of life'. They strive to achieve a certain maturity and to reproduce themselves.

Taylor holds, however, that the fact that all living organisms strive for something beneficial to themselves is a necessary but insufficient reason for ascribing to them an intrinsic value. To say that a being has an intrinsic value is identical to making a *normative* statement that this being is an object of moral concern and therefore is one to which human beings have moral obligations. Taylor maintains, nevertheless, that when we understand and accept what he calls a 'biocentric outlook on life', it becomes natural for us to pass from the *descriptive–biological* statement that all life strives for something beneficial to the *normative–ethical* view that all life has an intrinsic value.

The biocentric outlook on nature consists of a number of beliefs about nature and the place of human beings within it. There are four core beliefs:

(a) that human beings are members of a global living community in the same sense and on the same conditions as all other living beings;
(b) that all living beings, including humans, are integral elements in a system of interdependence in the sense that the survival of every being depends not simply on its surroundings but also on its relation to all other living beings;
(c) that every organism is a teleological centre of life in the sense that the organism is able to strive for what is beneficial to itself;
(d) that human beings do not have certain inherent rights to set themselves over other living things and in other words, they do not constitute a higher form of existence than other living things (see Taylor, 1986, pp. 99–100).

The last point is, according to Taylor, the most important one and entails a rejection of a hierarchical view of nature, namely that terrestial forms of life can be divided in value terms into higher and lower categories. A person who accepts the biocentric view rejects the idea that human beings have a value or a dignity which is to be found either not at all or to a very little degree among lower forms of life. Instead, one accepts *the principle of species–impartiality*. This principle implies that all living beings are treated as if they had equal value in the sense that, irrespective of the species they belong to, they ought to be assigned equal weight and moral consideration by a moral agent (in other words, a human being), provided that no more weighty consideration is overriding in the circumstances (ibid., p. 155).

Taylor holds that when we accept the belief system which forms the biocentric outlook on nature, we immediately understand how and why human beings must embrace an attitude of respect for nature. In the same way that we insist that others must not interfere or prevent our own striving, we ought to respect the striving of other teleological centres of life. These views are thus what explains and justifies the attitude. According to Taylor, people who embrace an attitude of 'respect for life' will subject themselves to certain ethical rules. These rules tell us which general types of actions we are morally bound to carry out or refrain from. The rules are, however, merely *prima facie* rules: in other words, they hold on condition that there are no other ethical rules which carry more weight. (Compare the discussion of this point in human ethics. The rule that it is wrong to lie is a *prima facie* rule. In certain cases, it does not hold since some weightier rule is applicable. Suppose that I have hidden a Jew in the attic of my house. If agents of the Gestapo knock on my door and ask if there are any Jews in my house, I act in a morally right way if I lie. This is because the rule that one should not endanger the lives of others overrides the rule not to lie.)

Four Biocentric Ethical Rules

Taylor holds that there are at least four fundamental rules which ought to determine how human beings should behave morally with respect to other living beings forming part of the world's natural ecosystem. Our most fundamental duty to nature is as far as possible to do nothing to cause other living beings injury or suffering. Taylor calls this rule 'the rule of nonmaleficence' (Taylor, 1986, p. 172). We can define it as follows:

(1)   *The rule of non-maleficence*: we have a duty not to cause other living beings injury or suffering.

The rule of non-maleficence expresses a prohibition or *negative* duty by demanding that human beings should refrain from certain actions. It does not require that human beings should do certain things, such as preventing some evil from befalling an animal or plant, or providing care in the event of sickness. The rule does not say that we have a duty to do something good for other living beings or help them in any way. Instead, the rule sets out to morally forbid people to carry out injurious or destructive acts against other living beings. In the same way that we do not have a right to injure human beings (because human beings have intrinsic value) so too we have not the right to injure other living beings.

The second ethical rule (the 'rule of non-interference') which Taylor puts forward also expresses a prohibition or negative duty:

(2) *The rule of non-interference*: we have a duty not to limit or violate the freedom of other living creatures.

Since human beings can limit organisms in many different ways, the rule of non-interference contains several more specific duties. It requires us, among other things, to refrain from preventing other living beings from striving to attain that which is beneficial to them as individuals. We must also refrain from capturing and moving them from their natural habitat, irrespective of how we treat them:

> When we take young trees or wildflowers from a natural ecosystem, for example, and transplant them in landscaped grounds, we break the Rule of Noninterference whether or not we then take good care of them and so enable them to live longer, healthier lives than they would have enjoyed in the wild. We have done a wrong by not letting them live out their lives in freedom. In all situations like these we intrude into the domain of the natural world and terminate an organism's existence as a wild creature ... By destroying their status as wild animals or plants, our interference in their lives amounts to an absolute negation of their natural freedom. Thus, however 'benign' our actions may seem, we are doing what the Rule of Noninterference forbids us to do. (Ibid., pp. 174–5)

The rule of non-interference leads therefore to a radical 'hands off policy' with respect to all living things and their habitat. We can already now see that biocentrism has concrete consequences for environmental management and policy making which means that it comes into conflict with a great many of the policies discussed in the environmental documents we have examined. For example, the rule of non-interference implies that, even in cases where there is an immediate risk of a species being exterminated on account of some natural chain of events, we are not morally bound to take any action to prevent this process (ibid., p. 177). The rule, however, is restricted by the fact that it applies only to natural courses of events. Attempts to save endangered species which are threatened by some previous human intervention in nature can be morally justified if they fall under another ethical rule, namely *the rule of restitutive justice*.

Before we investigate what this rule implies, let us look more closely at the relation between the rule of non-interference and the principle of species impartiality. Taylor would seem to hold that the latter rule is a logical consequence of the former (ibid., p. 178). This is because the principle of species impartiality implies that, by intervening in the natural chain of events, we must not promote the good of one organism at the cost of another organism. When it is a case of living beings which are useful to us, it is particularly important that we see that it is our moral duty not to intervene in such a way. The question is, however, whether Taylor has not given another interpretation to the principle of species impartiality than he previously presented. In its original formulation, the principle says merely that the interests of members of different species are to be assigned equal importance. But, from this, it does not follow that we would not be able to intervene in the natural course of events. All that the principle of species impartiality requires of us is that we do this in such a way that we do not promote the good of one organism at the cost of another. Thus we can say that the rule of non-interference comprehends the principle of species impartiality but nevertheless it is possible to embrace the latter and at the same time reject the former rule. This is something Taylor would seem to deny.

Taylor's third principle, the 'rule of fidelity', is only applicable to wild animals and only those which can be tricked or betrayed by moral agents:

(3)   *The rule of fidelity*: we have a duty not to deceive wild animals or to abuse the trust they have in us.

The most common transgression of the rule of fidelity is hunting and fishing. In order for these pursuits to be successful, it is in fact necessary that animals be systematically deceived. The human deception of animals demonstrates that human beings assign to the deceived animal a lower value than that they assign to themselves (the same is true when one human being deceives another human being). For this reason, activities such as hunting and fishing must be seen as morally abhorrent by anyone who shares an attitude of respect for nature, on condition that there is no overriding reason for indulging in such activities, for example because a human being cannot live without killing an animal. (I shall have more to say about such situations later.)

Taylor summarizes the three obligations which express an attitude of respect for nature, in the following way and also shows thereby how the fourth biocentric rule, the 'rule of restitutive justice', enters the picture:

> The three rules of duty so far discussed in this section can be understood as defining a moral relationship of justice between humans and wild living things in the Earth's natural ecosystems. This relationship is maintained as long as humans do not interfere with an animal's or plant's freedom or with the overall workings of ecological interedependence; and as long as humans do not betray a wild animal's trust to take advantage of it. (Ibid., pp. 186–7)

If, however, human beings offend against these duties, their actions disturb the balance of justice between human beings and nature. When human beings cause damage to nature, justice requires that human beings compensate the injury. This duty is set out in the fourth ethical rule:

(4)   *The rule of restitutive justice*: we have a duty to compensate other living beings when we have treated them in a morally unacceptable way: that is, we have treated them in a way contrary to any of the rules (1), (2) or (3).

Taylor distinguishes between three different ways in which a living being can be morally violated (ibid., pp. 187f). The first possibility occurs when an *individual* organism has been unjustly treated. In a situation where the organism has been injured but not killed by human beings, the rule of restitutive justice requires that it be sufficiently restored for it to achieve what is beneficial for it as an individual, in the same way that it was able to do prior to the injury. On the other hand, where the organism has been killed, the rule of restitutive justice requires that some form of compensation is paid out to the 'relatives' of the organism, that is to the species to which the dead organism belonged.

The other possibility is that the members of a whole species have been treated in a morally reprehensible way. A typical example is when a group of animals has been drastically reduced within a certain definite area as a result of hunting or fishing. In this kind of situation, it is appropriate that compensation be given to the remaining members of the species.

A final way in which living beings can be morally violated is when human beings destroy a biotic community, for example, when a meadow or wood is completely wiped out so that a new housing development can go ahead or when a whole mountainside is destroyed for the sake of a mining project. Taylor holds that there are at least two different ways in which, in these circumstances, compensation can be arranged in accordance with the principle of restitutive justice. One possibility is that compensation should go to another biotic community which has an ecosystem of the same type as that which has been destroyed. Another possibility is to compensate an arbitrarily selected, untouched part of nature which is threatened by human exploitation.

Ethical Priority Principles

Taylor is aware that the four rules of environmental ethics which he puts forward can occasionally come into conflict with one another. He therefore sets up certain priority principles which are to apply in this kind of conflict situation. Two of the rules – the rule of non-maleficence and the rule of non-interference – cannot, however, conflict with one another. The duty not to injure cannot come into conflict with the duty not to violate the freedom of other beings. Refraining from violations of nature can never of itself entail injury for wild animals and plants (Taylor, 1986, pp. 192–8).

The most important principle of priority, according to Taylor, is that the rule of non-maleficence overrides the rule of fidelity and the rule of justice. The rule of non-maleficence conflicts with the rule of fidelity if, for example, park managers have encouraged animals to live in a national park by forbidding hunting within its confines but it turns out that the number of animals of a certain species have increased to such a degree that the whole ecosystem of the park is threatened. In such a situation, the rule of non-maleficence carries more weight than the rule of fidelity because the lesser evil would seem to be to break our promise to certain of the animals of the species in question in order not to injure others, by tempting them or in some other way removing them from the national park (to kill them would not be morally acceptable).

Another kind of conflict situation arises when one is faced with choosing between the 'rule of non-maleficence' and the 'rule of restitutive justice'. Taylor holds, however, that in the majority of cases there is no need for such conflicts to arise. If wildlife managers are very careful to plan their interventions in nature, for example when they set out to save an endangered species, it is entirely possible that no other living creatures need to be harmed in the process. In spite of this, conflicts can naturally arise. In such a situation, the rule of non-maleficence is overriding because certain actions otherwise entail that in addition to the evil we have already done (and which must be compensated), we commit further transgressions.

The rule of non-interference and the rule of restitutive justice can also conflict with one another. In such a situation, the latter rule is accorded greater weight. This implies, for example, that it is morally permissible to set up a fence around an area where there is a leakage from radioactive waste in order to protect animals from potential injury, even though such a measure implies a limitation on the freedom of other living beings. In a similar way, Taylor holds that in a conflict situation the 'principle of restitutive justice' overrides the 'rule of fidelity'. An example of such a situation is when people help seabirds, whales or other creatures to be free of the oil which covers their bodies as the result of an oil spill. In order to catch the animals so that the oil can be removed, it is necessary to deceive them in one way or another. Such deception, according to Taylor, is justified since it results in creatures recovering from the injury which our previous actions had caused them.

Taylor is also aware that these ethical rules can in certain situations come into conflict not only with each other but also with the ethical rules which form part of human ethics. He writes:

> In these cases if we carry out our duties to animals and plants in natural ecosystems we fail in our duties towards our fellow humans, but if we fulfill the latter we do not do what is required of us regarding the good of nonhumans. So even when we have worked out an acceptable ordering among the rules of the ethics of respect for nature we still must decide on what priorities hold between that system and the rules that bind us in the domain of human ethics. (Ibid., pp. 170–71)

These situations where, on the one hand, human interests and, on the other hand, the interests of animals and plants come into conflict with one another are perhaps the most difficult situations with which a biocentrist such as Taylor has to deal. Examples of such situations are when a freshwater ecosystem is destroyed to allow a hotel to be built on a lakeside or when a mountainside is laid waste so that a mine can be operated. These inevitable confrontations between nature and culture must, however, be solved. How should a biocentric ethic relate to human ethics? Taylor makes the following admission:

> Not only must humans make use of the natural environment and thereby compete with animals and plants that might also need that environment as their habitat and food source, but humans must also directly consume some non-humans in order to survive ... Furthermore, from the human standpoint those species of animal and plant life that are harmful to our survival and health must be controlled or gotten rid off. (Ibid., p. 257)

This situation, however, creates difficult ethical problems for biocentrists such as Taylor since, as we have seen, they reject the idea of human superiority and instead advocate the principle of species impartiality. Thus it is not possible for them – as it would be for anthropocentrists – in a competitive situation consistently to assign to human interests greater moral importance than to the interests of other living creatures. According to an anthropocentric ethic, human actions of the kind presented above concerning the building of a hotel and mining operations need not in general come into conflict with the rules of human ethics, since these actions do not need to infringe any human rights.

Nor can the acute problems of these biocentric thinkers be solved by embracing vegetarianism, since Taylor takes the view that the eating of plants requires just as much justification as the eating of meat. Irrespective of whether it is a matter of plants or animals, to 'kill or otherwise harm such creatures is always something morally bad in itself and can only be justified if we have no feasible alternative' (ibid., p. 269). It is therefore necessary to work out, on the basis of a biocentric position, a number of *priority principles* to govern how much weight is to be assigned to human and non-human interets in cases of conflict. These principles may not assign a higher value to human beings than to other living things since this would contravene the requirement of species impartiality.

For his own part, Taylor suggests five such principles of priority. The first of these, the 'principle of self-defence', allows greater importance to be attached to human interests than to those interests of other living things in situations where human life is in danger (ibid., p. 264). According to the principle of self-defence, human beings would be entitled to kill a bear or some other predator if attacked by the latter or to exterminate insects which directly threaten human existence. However, Taylor qualifies this principle in the following way. First of all, the principle of self-defence is valid only when human beings cannot be expected to avoid being exposed to organisms threatening their lives. In other words, we ought to do what we reasonably can to avoid situations where organisms constitute a threat to us. Secondly, we are not allowed to employ whatever methods we like in self-defence but only those which cause the least injury to the organisms in question and at the same time achieve the object of protecting human life. The principle could therefore be formulated as follows:

(P1) *The principle of self-defence*: we have a moral duty to protect ourselves against other living beings if they threaten our existence, assuming that we have done all that can be expected of us to avoid such situations and provided that we do not employ more force than is necessary.

Common to the following four priority principles which Taylor identifies as being compatible both with respect for human beings and with respect for nature is that they are applicable in situations which are not covered by the principle of self-defence. In other words, they are applicable to situations where other living creatures do not constitute a threat to human existence.

A further common feature shared by these priority principles is that they all presuppose a distinction between 'basic interests' and 'non-basic interests'. In general, interests are things which preserve or promote an organism's well-being. There are, however, certain interests which it is more important for an organism to satisfy than others. For example, it is more important for human beings to have food and shelter than it is to have an opportunity to drive a car or to indulge in holiday travel. Acquiring food and shelter are two examples of human basic interests. We can say that an interest is *basic* if its non-satisfaction injures the organism in question. (According to Taylor, they are interests which an organism has a moral right to satisfy.) They are universal interests because they are common to all beings of a species. On the other hand, driving a car or holiday travel are examples of 'non-basic interests'. We could say that non-basic interests are those which individuals can strive to satisfy but are such that their non-satisfaction does not endanger their well-being. (According to Taylor's definition, they are interests which a being does not have a moral right to satisfy.) These interests are not universal but relative to the individual: in other words, they vary from individual to individual.

The distinction between basic and non-basic interests is more or less generally accepted. What is new and interesting is that Taylor wishes to introduce a further distinction. He wants to subdivide the set of non-basic interests into two groups. Taylor asserts that in environmental ethics we ought to distinguish between (a) human non-basic interests such as building a museum of art (with the result that certain natural habitats must be destroyed) or building an airport, railway, harbour or motorway (which entail serious disturbances to natural ecosystems) and (b) human non-basic interests such as capturing and killing reptiles such as snakes and crocodiles in order to make fashionable shoes from their skins, or hunting and fishing when these activities are not needed for human survival. In Taylor's view, the promotion of the interests belonging to the first group is – at least in certain cases – compatible with an attitude of respect for nature. The interests belonging to the second group, on the other hand, are always incompatible with such an attitude.

Taylor's second principle, 'the principle of proportionality', is intended to regulate conflicts between human (non-basic) interests of type (b) above and the basic interests of other living creatures. Let us call such human interests *peripheral* non-basic interests, since Taylor looks upon them as not being of central importance for the maintenance of a high level of culture, while at the same time they are quite incompatible with non-human interests. The principle of proportionality is thus applicable to situations where human peripheral non-basic interests are not compatible with the basic interests of other living beings. In such situations, it forbids us to satisfy human interests at the cost of the basic interests of other living beings. This principle, as we have seen, is violated when human beings for example kill reptiles to make fashionable shoes and handbags of their skin. The principle also forbids hunting and fishing where these activities are not necessary for human survival. We can define the principle in the following way:

(P2) *The principle of proportionality*: in situations where our peripheral, non-basic interests are incompatible with the basic interests of other living beings, we have a duty to assign to the latter interests a greater moral weight or importance.

Taylor's third principle of priority, the 'principle of minimum wrong', on the other hand, applies in situations where some of our non-peripheral, non-basic interests come into conflict with the basic interests of other living beings. He writes:

> The principle of minimum wrong ... applies to conflicts between the basic interests of wild animals and plants and those non-basic human interests that are so highly valued that even a person who has respect for nature would not be willing to abstain from pursuing them, knowing that the pursuit of such interests will bring about conditions detrimental to the natural world. (Ibid., p. 278)

It is thus morally permissible for us to seek to satisfy such human, non-basic interests which rational and informed persons consider of central importance for our civilization as a whole, although we know that other living beings will suffer (ibid., p. 288). These interests may be called *central* non-basic interests. The examples which Taylor gives of such interests include building libraries, museums of art, airports, railways, motorways, harbours, dams for hydroelectric schemes or public parks, despite the fact that they entail natural ecosystems and habitats being destroyed or severely damaged and animals and plants being killed or injured. In carrying out such interventions in nature, it is always required that we try to minimize the violations of the rule of non-maleficence. We must always try to choose to act so that it entails the least possible suffering for non-human life. Thereby the principle of minimum wrong demands that we must show concern for what is beneficial for non-human life in the positioning and construction of buildings, motorways, airports and harbours.

The principle can be formulated as follows:

(P3) *The principle of minimum wrong*: in situations where our central non-basic interests come into conflict with the basic interests of other living beings, we have a duty to try to satisfy these human interests in such a way that the least possible suffering or injury is caused to other living beings.

Taylor poses the question whether the principle of minimum wrong is compatible with the idea that wild animals and plants have an intrinsic value. For my own part, I cannot see any objection to this. The difficult question for Taylor – which he refrains from discussing – is rather whether the principle is compatible with the idea that all life has *equal* value. Is the principle of minimum wrong really *species impartial*? In other words, does it treat all living creatures (including human beings) as if they have the same value in the sense that irrespective of the species to which a being belongs, it is assigned equal weight and consideration? In my view, this is very doubtful.

Compare this with the way we judge similar situations in human ethics. If, in building a library, harbour or public park, certain people were likely to be killed or seriously injured, or to lose the capacity to secure certain basic living necessities, would we then not maintain that it was immoral to go through with the project on these terms? It would hardly constitute an adequate explanation if those responsible told us that there was no better alternative if we wished to achieve the ends which the project made possible. It would scarcely be the case even if we learned that those responsible envisaged compensating other people (near relatives) for the losses brought about by the project and sustained by the people directly involved. In striving to satisfy one or more of my central non-basic interests (for example, to have paid work) I have no right to kill or injure other people, even if I am prepared to pay damages to the relatives of the injured or to some other people. For this reason, it would seem that, as far as this point is concerned, Taylor nevertheless assigns to human beings a higher value or embraces the principle of the moral superiority of human beings.

If my argument is correct, in order to be consistent Taylor must surrender the principle of minimum wrong and instead modify the principle of proportionality so that it is also applicable in cases of conflict between environmental ethics and human ethics.[8] The principle would then be formulated as follows:

(P2*) *The principle of proportionality*: in situations where our (peripheral or central) non-basic interests are incompatible with the basic interests of other living beings, we have a duty to assign to the latter interests a greater moral weight or importance.

Taylor calls the fourth priority principle 'the principle of distributive justice'. It applies in situations where human beings are not threatened by other living beings but where *basic* human interests inevitably come into conflict with the *basic* interests of other living things. In such cases, the principle is designed to ensure that there is a just distribution. Taylor writes: 'The idea of justice in all this is to distribute benefits and burdens equally among the parties. Fair shares are equal shares' (ibid., p. 304). In other words, the principle of distributive justice becomes applicable in situations where the principles of self-defence, proportionality and minimum wrong do not apply. Let us formulate the principle in the following way:

(P4) *The principle of distributive justice*: in situations where our basic interests inevitably clash with the basic interests of other living beings, we have a duty to assign an equal weight to the interests of both parties.

The principle implies that, even if it is morally permissible in certain situations to give priority to human interests, in other situations non-human basic interests must be given precedence. Secondly, the principle of distributive justice entails that, in general, both parties ought to be given priority to the same extent.

Taylor chooses to discuss only one concrete example of this type of conflict between environmental and human ethics, namely the human use of animals and plants as food. From the perspective of a biocentric ethical theory like Taylor's, a moral justification of the human consumption of *both* animals and plants is required

---

[8] He can also naturally discard the principle of species impartiality and maintain that human beings have a higher value than other living beings. This alternative formulation of biocentrism is discussed in the last part of this section.

since all life has an equal value. Taylor, however, is of the opinion that conscious suffering is greater than other suffering simply because it is conscious. For this reason, even if there are situations where hunting and fishing are morally permitted (for example, in the Arctic), people who embrace an attitude of respect for nature must be *vegetarians*. A vegetarian lifestyle also implies that we 'can drastically reduce the amount of cultivated land needed for human food production by changing from a meat-eating culture to a vegetarian culture' (ibid., p. 296). The land areas which in this way can be saved (or transformed) can then be left free to be used by living beings other than humans.

What is lacking in Taylor's discussion is an example of conflict situations where it would be appropriate to give priority, not to our own interests, but to those of *other* living beings. If we generalize from the sole example Taylor gives, where human interests are given priority (although a transformation from a meat-eating lifestyle to a vegetarian one is required), the principle of distributive justice cannot be given the above formulation. Instead, the principle would say that, in situations where human interests inevitably clash with the basic interests of other living beings, we have a duty to attach greater weight to human interests. (The principle of minimum wrong could in such a situation be used as an argument in favour of vegetarianism.)

Compare this with the way we deal with a similar situation in human ethics. Suppose that the basic interests of two groups of people (say, those of immigrants and those of native-born Swedes) were to clash and we consistently gave priority to the interests of the latter. We would then violate the principle of distributive justice as it is formulated above. As we have seen, Taylor writes, 'The idea of justice in all this is to distribute benefits and burdens equally among the parties. Fair shares are equal shares' (ibid., p. 304). If therefore, in situations where it is a matter of food, we give priority to our own basic interests, we must in other situations, such as protection against the elements (housing and clothing), correspondingly give priority to the interests of other living beings. (A question which can be raised is naturally whether such priorities can be carried out in practice. Note, however, that such doubts presumably entail a rejection of a value-undifferentiated biocentric theory of environmental ethics like that of Taylor. We shall have reason to return to this issue when we discuss value-differentiated biocentrism.)

Some doubts arise in relation to this point regarding whether Taylor has fully taken account of the principle of species impartiality in his arguments. The principle of distibutive justice, at least as I have formulated it, is certainly species-impartial, but the question is whether Taylor in his one-sided interpretation does not tend in practice, from a biocentric viewpoint, to give human interests an unjustified priority.

Taylor is naturally aware that a wholly just distribution between human interests and those of other living beings cannot be guaranteed. As a result, a fifth principle of priority, the 'principle of restitutive justice', is necessary. Because we cannot achieve an ideal distribution, we must be prepared to compensate other living beings for their losses. He writes,

> the principle of restitutive justice is applicable whenever the principles of minimum wrong and distributive justice have been followed. In both cases harm is done to animals and plants that are harmless, so some form of reparation or

compensation is called for if our actions are to be fully consistent with the attitude of respect for nature. (In applying the minimum wrong and distributive justice principles, no harm is done to harmless humans, so there occurs an inequality of treatment between humans and nonhumans in these situations.) (Ibid., pp. 304–5)

The basic idea with compensation is that the principle of restitutive justice requires that non-human lives are compensated in a way which corresponds to the wrong which they have suffered. The general proposal which Taylor makes with respect to adequate measures for compensation is that special areas are set aside as protected areas so that the plants and animals affected can strive to attain what is beneficial for them as individual organisms.

The principle can be formulated as follows:

(P5) *The principle of restitutive justice*: in situations where we give priority to our central non-basic and basic interests before the basic interests of other living beings, we have a duty to recompense these beings for their losses.

Taylor emphasizes that these five principles of priority do not cover all possible situations of conflict which can arise between human ethics and environmental ethics. However, the principles can give us important guidance and, in situations which lie outside their sphere of application, Taylor writes that we must instead allow ourselves to be guided by the basic vision which is expressed by an attitude of respect for nature, namely the ideal of a world order where human civilization exists in harmony with nature. By 'harmony' Taylor means 'a condition on Earth in which people are able to pursue their individual interests and the cultural ways of life they have adopted while at the same time allowing many biotic communities in a great variety of natural ecosystems to carry on their existence without interference' (p. 309).

Taylor believes not only that this type of non-anthropocentric ethic is theoretically defensible, but also that it can be put into practice. In their day-to-day lives, people can follow the ethical rules which biocentric ethic puts forward as norms for our individual and social behaviour. Although Taylor does not directly recommend political, legal or economic changes which an attitude of respect for nature would demand, he holds that a first necessary step is an inner change in our moral convictions. At the same time, he has no illusions about how difficult it would be for many people to change their values and lifestyle if they really did adopt an attitude of respect for nature.

Three Versions of Biocentrism

We have seen that Taylor, despite the fact that he advocates the demand for species impartiality, tends in his more practically oriented arguments *de facto* to assign to human beings a special status in relation to all other living beings. In this connection, I have chosen to reformulate the ethical principles which he puts forward, so that they do not come into conflict with his basic normative position, namely that all life has equal value. This shows, nevertheless, that biocentrism can be given different interpretations. As we have see, a view that is common to all biocentrists is that they maintain that living organisms and only they have an intrinsic value and are therefore beings to which we have certain moral obligations. They can be treated in a morally right or wrong way. In other words, they are moral subjects.

At the same time, it is not necessary for biocentrists to share Taylor's view that all life has equal value. It is entirely possible simultaneously to maintain that all life has moral standing and to deny that all living things have the same value. Robin Attfield, for example, holds that plants and bacteria

> could have a moral standing and yet have almost infinitessimal moral significance, so that even large aggregations of them did not outweigh the significance of sentient beings in cases of conflict. It could be that their moral significance only makes a difference when all other claims and considerations are equal (or nonexistent). Yet, as Goodpaster says, as long as plants have moral standing, it is worth bearing this standing in mind (Attfield, 1983, p. 154)

If biocentrists permit such value differentiation, usually human beings and certain other animals who can experience suffering are assigned a higher value than all other animals and plants. For example, Carl-Henric Grenholm maintaintains that 'Human beings have an intrinsic value which is higher than that assigned to other living beings. In a conflict between the well-being of animals and human well-being, the latter has in general a higher value than that of animals' (Grenholm, 1997, p. 94).

Another possible position is that adopted by proponents of animal rights such as Tom Regan. He holds that only certain animals in addition to human being can be assigned an intrinsic value. Other animals and all living plants lack an intrinsic value. According to Regan, all living beings which are 'subjects-of-a-life', that is to say, animals which possess self-consciousness and a capacity both to suffer and to experience well-being, have equal worth (Regan, 1983, p. 243). In short, all mammals have an intrinsic value. Representatives for the movement for animal rights such as Regan, however, can only be classified as biocentrists if we modify the definition of biocentrism which was given earlier. According to such a modified definition, a sufficient condition for a viewpoint to be classed as biocentrism would be that *it attributes an intrinsic value to at least one animal species in addition to human beings*. This is quite possible, but since Regan's view is not usually reckoned by biocentrists to be a biocentric one,[9] let us instead interpret the ethic which proponents of animal rights put forward as if it also attributed an intrinsic value to plants and lower animals in accordance with Attfield above.[10] This latter intrinsic value is thus considerably less than that ascribed to human beings and sentient animals (or somewhat more narrowly to subjects-of-a-life).

---

[9] See Callicott (1995a, p. 678) and Des Jardins (1997, pp. 130, 147).

[10] Regan at least leaves the issue open as to whether animals which are not subjects-of-a-life and plants might have an intrinsic value. His position is instead agnostic.

We would thus be able to distinguish at least three different formulations of biocentrism:

(1) *Strong biocentrism* is the view that individual behaviour as well as proposed environmental policies should be judged on the basis of how they affect the well-being of all living beings, irrespective of what these living beings are.

(2) *Weak biocentrism* is the view that individual behaviour as well as proposed environmental policies should be judged on the basis of how they affect the well-being of all living beings, but primarily the well-being of human beings.

(3) *Animal rights biocentrism* is the view that individual behaviour as well as proposed environmental policies should be judged on the basis of how they affect the well-being of all living beings, but primarily the well-being of human beings and of sentient animals.

A number of advocates of biocentrism are prepared to assign to animals or at least sentient animals, certain rights, so-called biotic rights.[11] This is particularly true of the animal rights biocentrists. The extent of these biotic rights and the weight attached to them in a conflict with human interests, however, vary depending on which of these three formulations is accepted. Since those who advocate weak biocentrism assign a higher value to humans than they do to animals, it follows that it is not always wrong, for example, to expose animals to suffering in medical experiments. However, as Grenholm writes, if 'it is possible to free humanity from illness and suffering without exposing animals to suffering, these alternative methods of achieving knowledge should be preferred' (Grenholm, 1997, p. 97). In addition, according to Grenholm, it is our moral duty to carry out animal experiments in such a way that animal suffering is kept to a minimum. Also as far as weak biocentrism is concerned, it does not necessarily imply vegetarianism. Animals can be used for food. What is demanded, however, is that we respect their right to well-being to the extent that we do not permit animal factories where creatures are held in confined and stressful conditions or that animals during transport or at the slaughterhouse itself are exposed to unnecessary suffering. All hunting for pleasure, and all sports where animals are injured or suffer, are judged to be morally wrong. The same is true of all cosmetic tests carried out on animals. All such activities are morally wrong since the human interests which thereby are satisfied are not of sufficient importance to outweigh the rights of animals to be spared unnecessary injury and suffering.

Both strong biocentrism and animal rights biocentrism, however, entail a total ban on the use of animals in science, commercial agriculture and in hunting, whether for commercial purposes or for pleasure. Hunting is certainly permitted when it is a question of protecting ourselves against the dangers to our health and well-being which animals can sometimes occasion. It is also permitted when we have no other possibilities for obtaining food (Regan, 1983, p. 323). But, in general, hunting is not compatible with a respect for the equal value of animals, and

---

[11] Taylor is an important exception. See Taylor (1986, ch. 5).

vegetarianism is therefore morally obligatory. It is also our duty to refrain completely from scientific experiments involving animals. Regan writes that we should 'not be satisfied with anything less than the total abolition of the harmful use of animals in science – in education, in toxicity testing, in basic research' (Regan, 1983, p. 393).

According to animal rights biocentrists, the basic fault of commercial agriculture is not that sentient animals are exposed to unnecessary suffering, as weak biocentrism maintains, although it certainly makes matters worse. The basic fault is that we look upon sentient animals as our resource and as something which exists for our sake. Just as it is wrong to use other people as our slaves (because all human beings have equal worth), it is also wrong to make use of sentient animals purely as a resource since they too have a value equal to our own. This is the reason why we, according to Regan, 'should not be satisfied with anything less than the total dissolution of commercial animal agriculture as we know it, whether modern factory farms or otherwise' (Regan, 1983, p. 351).

Taylor's priority principles – the ethical principles intended to guide us in situations where our interests come into conflict with those of other living beings – must therefore be given a partly different formulation if weak biocentrism or animal rights biocentrism are to be accepted instead of strong biocentrism. In this chapter, I have previously argued that if the demand for species impariality is to be taken seriously, Taylor's *principle of proportionality* must be interpreted to mean that in situations where our (peripheral or central) non-basic interests are incompatible with the basic interests of other living beings, we have a duty to assign to the latter interests a greater moral weight or importance. Animal rights biocentrists, unlike Taylor, hold that the range of application of this principle must be limited to sentient animals. Such a restriction is necessary because they maintain that only such animals have a value equal to that of our own. Thus, according to animal rights biocentrists, we have the right to give priority to our own needs, even if these are not directly necessary for our well-being (on the ground of their non-basic character) where they come into conflict with the well-being of non-sentient animals and plants. At the same time, respect for nature entails that these living beings must not be exposed to unnecessary damage.

Advocates of weak biocentrism, on the other hand, believe that human beings have a higher value than all other living beings in nature. As a result, they do not merely limit the principle of proportionality but totally reject it as it has been formulated. They accept the principle only in its original, weaker form: in situations where our peripheral non-basic interests are incompatible with the basic interests of other living beings, we have a duty to assign to the latter interests a greater moral weight or importance. Thus it is morally wrong to capture and kill animals in order to make fashionable shoes, clothes and handbags from their skins, to keep animals because they are beautiful to look at, to injure animals or plants in producing cosmetics, to hunt animals purely for pleasure, and so on. In all these situations, the interests of the animals should be given priority. In other cases, where we try to satisfy interests which can be deemed to be of central importance for a sophisticated human culture, we have the right to kill other beings and to expose them to injury and suffering. In this latter connection, however, Taylor's *principle of minimum wrong* applies: we must act in relation to other living beings in such a way that the least possible wrong or injury is done to them.

As far as both weak biocentrism and animal rights biocentrism are concerned, the *principle of restitutive justice* is applicable in situations where the principle of proportionality and the principle of minimum wrong are used. This principle of justice says that in situations where we give priority to our interests before the basic interests of other living beings, we have a duty to recompense these beings (or their 'relatives') for their losses.

Taylor's principle of of distributive justice holds in situations where other living creatures do not constitute a threat to us, but where their basic interests conflict with our basic interests. The principle says that, in such situations, we must attach equal importance to the interests of both parties. In operational terms, this means that, if in certain situations we give priority to basic human interests, then in other situations we must give priority to the basic interests of non-human beings. In general, priority should be equally distributed among the parties. Analogously, as in the case of the principle of proportionality, animal rights biocentrists accept this principle only if it is limited to sentient animals. Advocates of weak biocentrism, on the other hand, completely reject this principle of justice and hold that, in such situations, human interests have priority because human beings can justly be assigned a higher value than other living beings in nature.

Ecocentric Ethics

The chief characteristic of the second form of non-anthropocentric ethics, namely ecocentrism, is that its advocates maintain that ecological wholes such as species, ecosystems and the biosphere as a totality have an intrinsic value or have moral standing. According to the ecocentrist, the land forms an interconnected whole to which we have certain responsibilities. Baird Callicott asserts that the two key ideas in this type of non-anthropocentric ethic are 'the shift in emphasis from part to whole – from individual to community – and second, the shift in emphasis from human beings to nature, from anthropocentrism to ecocentrism' (Callicott, 1989, p. 8).

Ecocentrism is thus characterized by an 'ethical holism', the view that ecological entities as wholes and not simply parts (or individuals) have moral standing. While biocentrists (in contrast to anthropocentrists) maintain that life, whether human or not, has an intrinsic value, ecocentrists believe that non-living natural objects also have an intrinsic value. Mountains, rivers, glaciers and forests are moral subjects towards which we can act rightly or wrongly. A key point is thus that ecosystems are not simply to be given instrumental values, that is to say to be valued as means towards the survival and well-being of individuals: they ought to be assigned a value in themselves.

This suggests the following formulation of ecocentrism:

An *ecocentric ethic* is a view which holds that species, ecosystems, the land or the biotic community in addition to living beings have an intrinsic value or have moral standing (in the sense that they can be treated in a way which is right or wrong and that human beings have certain duties towards them).

The ecocentrists look upon this extension of things to which we must show moral consideration in our way of living and behaving, to embrace species and ecosystems, as a further step naturally brought about by increased ethical awareness. From at first covering only free men, the circle during the course of history has been successively enlarged to embrace women, slaves, children and certain (mainly domestic) animals. Now the time is ripe for the circle to be extended so that not only all animals but all plants, species, ecosystems and indeed the very biosphere in its entirety are included (see Leopold, 1949, p. 202). However, as we shall see, this extension of moral standing entails, paradoxically, in certain formulations of ecocentrism that the moral legitimacy of the individual parts becomes depreciated.

Leopold's Land Ethics

The thinker who has perhaps played the greatest role in the emergence of an ecocentric ethic in the Western world is Aldo Leopold (1887–1948). Leopold writes that 'the land ethic' is a natural extension of the human community to embrace a community of the land. 'The land ethic simply enlarges the boundaries of the community to include soils, waters, plants, and animals, or collectively: the land' (Leopold, 1949, p. 204). We can no longer look upon the earth as 'dead' matter or as a property we can use and fashion however we like. Instead, the earth should be seen as a living organism which can be injured and can be healthy or sick. 'Land, then, is not merely soil; it is a fountain of energy flowing through a circuit of soils, plants, and animals' (ibid., p. 216).

Leopold's land ethic entails a radical removal of human beings from their central position. It is not – as Brundtland says in her address to the United Nations report, *Our Common Future* (World Commission, 1987, p. xiv) – human well-being but rather the well-being of ecosystems or the land which is the ultimate goal of an acceptable environmental policy. '[A] land ethic changes the role of *Homo sapiens* from conqueror of the land-community to plain member and citizen of it' (Leopold, 1949, p. 204). It shows that Leopold's land ethic is, in a fundamental and radical way, non-anthropocentric. Human beings occupy no special position but are merely one of several members of the biotic community, no more and no less.

It is important to observe that this extension of the domain of ethics is not simply a matter of including more individuals. In actual fact, Leopold shifts the emphasis from individuals to the biotic community and to the land. What determines whether an environmental policy is morally acceptable or not is the extent to which it benefits the biotic community as a whole rather than the extent to which it benefits the good of its separate individual members. Leopold's assertion that a 'thing is right when it tends to preserve the integrity, stability and beauty of the biotic community. It is wrong when it tends otherwise' (ibid., pp. 224–5) forms the starting point and principal criterion for an ecocentric ethic. Let us call this basic principle *Leopold's principle of integrity and stability*.

A crucial difference between ecocentrism and biocentrism thereby becomes apparent. Contrary to what apparently is implied by biocentrism, we do not need to be especially concerned about killing mosquitoes or elks, felling trees or relaying our lawn, since it is the health and status of the ecosystems and land which must primarily be our concern and which we should seek to promote. It is morally justifiable to kill elks and eat their flesh as long as the integrity, stability and beauty of the elk population is not threatened. It is to the species as such that we have a responsibility and not to its individual members. It can even be the case from an ecocentric position that it is not merely morally acceptable but indeed morally obligatory to reduce the number of elks in a given area by hunting. Such measures are justified if the stability of the elk population or the balance of the ecosystems of which the elk forms a part is in danger. On the other hand, certain animals or plants which are endangered, and simultaneously are of great importance for the continued survival of the ecosystems, require special care and consideration. An ecocentrist like Callicott emphasizes therefore that, 'In every case the effect upon ecological systems is the decisive factor in the determination of the ethical quality of actions' (Callicott, 1989b, p. 21). Thus entities as wholes can have greater moral significance than their individual parts: 'oceans and lakes, mountains, forests, and wetlands are assigned a greater value than individual animals' (ibid., p. 37).

This implies, however, that the intrinsic value of the individual parts tends to become depreciated because their value is determined primarily in relation to ecological wholes such as species and ecosystems. Callicott writes as follows:

> The land ethic manifestly does not accord equal moral worth to each and every member of the biotic community; the moral worth of individuals (including, take note, human individuals) is relative, to be assessed in accordance with the particular relation of each to the collective entity which Leopold called 'land'. (Ibid., p. 28)

An initial formulation of ecocentrism maintains that only ecological wholes such as species and ecosystems have an intrinsic value, while the individuals which form part of these systems merely have an instrumental value. Individuals and the species of which they are part are to be valued and graded according to the extent to which they contribute to the survival and flourishing of ecosystems, not to their own survival and flourishing. Some individuals and species contribute more than others to ensure that the earth's ecosystems are preserved as well-functioning entities and are thereby more valuable. Moreover they only possess a value inasmuch as they have this function. What makes this formulation of ecocentrism really radical is that certain ecocentrists are not prepared to make any distinction between nature and culture and between human beings and other natural objects. It is not only when we speak about animals and plants that we must see their value in relation primarily to the totality of which they are part: the same is true for human beings. It is no longer justifiable to assign to human beings special treatment because according to these ecocentrists, they are to be seen not as conquerors but merely *'plain members'* of the biotic community. For this reason there is no basis for according human beings and their interests a special status when it comes to matters of morality.

We have thus identified two poles of the debate in the discussion of environmental ethics. At one pole is the view (anthropocentrism) that only human beings have moral standing while at the other pole we have the view that only ecosystems or the land have moral standing. Let us call this latter view *radical ecocentrism* or *ecocentric monism*. Radical ecocentrism assigns an intrinsic value only to the biotic community. The only value which an individual being possesses is determined by its function and importance in an ecosystem.

This form of of ecocentrism has startling consequences for the form given to environmental policy making. Given the assumption (a) that human life and customs have on the whole a negative effect on the integrity, stability and beauty of the ecosystems, and (b) that the value of human beings is determined entirely by how much they have contributed to the continued existence of the ecosystems, it follows that an endangered organism which is of vital importance for an ecosystem ought to be considered much more valuable than many human lives. Callicott appears to accept such a conclusion when he refers to and comments upon Edward Abbey's statement, in *Desert Solitaire*, that he would rather shoot a human being than a snake: 'Abbey may not be simply depraved; this is perhaps only his way of dramatically making the point that the human population has become so disproportionate from the biological point of view that if one had to choose between a specimen of Homo sapiens and a specimen of a rare even if unattractive species, the choice would be moot' (Callicott, 1989b, p. 27). Callicott writes also that 'The extent of misanthropy in modern environmentalism thus may be taken as a measure of the degree to which it is [ecocentric]' (ibid.).

Thus we could formulate radical ecocentrism more precisely in the following way:

> *Radical ecocentrism* is the view that only ecological wholes (such as species, ecosystems, the land or the biotic community) have a value in themselves and that the value of the ecological parts (the individual living organisms, including human beings) is determined by how far they contribute to the survival and well-being of the ecological wholes.

The problem with this formulation of ecocentrism is a practical rather than theoretical one. Because radical ecocentrism involves the highly controversial view that human beings only have an instrumental value and thus possess no value in themselves, it is reasonable to suppose that it will never have the broad popular support which is necessary if it is to form the basis for developing an environmental policy or for drawing up ethical guidelines to regulate environmental management at a more concrete level. The values upon which radical ecocentrism is founded deviate too much from accepted norms and are likely to prevent it in the foreseeable future from have any real political significance. Because one of the subsidiary aims of the present book is precisely that of providing a critical analysis of the possible values a politically based environmental policy making could reasonably be based upon, I shall choose certain, less radical, formulations of ecocentrism as a basis for my discussion. These formulations are at the same time very different in character from the intergenerational anthropocentric ethic upon which modern environmental policy making is based.

If, instead, we choose to entertain the idea that other objects in nature besides ecosystems and species have an intrinsic value, and naturally posit in addition that human beings have moral standing, we find ourselves embracing 'ecocentric pluralism' rather than ecocentric monism. Ecocentric pluralism is thus the view that both ecological wholes such as ecosystems and species, on the one hand, and individual human and non-human organisms, on the other, have intrinsic value. Leopold's principle of integrity and stability for deciding whether an action is right or wrong must therefore be reformulated. What is good or bad cannot be decided purely on the basis of whether or not it promotes the well-being of the biotic community. Every action which can influence nature must be judged both on its effects on ecological wholes and on the consequences it has for the lives of individual organisms. Ecocentric pluralism thus allows at least two alternative interpretations of Leopold's principle of integrity and stability. The first says that *the most important* (but not the sole) determinant in judging whether an environmental policy proposal is morally acceptable is whether it promotes the good of the biotic community. The second says that *one important* (though not necessarily the most important) determinant in judging whether an environmental policy proposal is acceptable is its effect on ecological wholes such as the earth's ecosystem. I shall call the first view *strong ecocentrism* (or, more exactly, *strong ecocentric pluralism*) while the second view I shall call *weak ecocentrism* (or, more exactly, *weak ecocentric pluralism*). Let us now try to describe in more detail the basic ideas of strong and weak ecocentrism.

Strong Ecocentrism

According to strong ecocentrism, both ecological wholes such as species and ecosystems and individual organisms whether human, animal or plant, have a value in themselves. Thus strong ecocentrism rejects the thesis of radical ecocentrism that biological individuals (including human beings) merely have instrumental value. It follows that we can no longer claim that the integrity and stability of ecocological wholes is the only criterion for deciding whether individual behaviour or environmental policies are morally defensible since biological individuals also have a value in themselves and what is good for them can be different from what is good from the viewpoint of the biotic community.

But what are to be our priorities when the interests of the biotic community conflict with the interests of its individual members? The answer which strong ecocentrists give is that, as a rule, ecological wholes are more important than their parts, but that this need not always be so. Leopold's principle of integrity and stability can thus be interpreted to mean that the most important – but not the sole – criterion for judging whether or not an action influencing nature is acceptable is the effects on ecological wholes such as the earth's ecosystem. According to this interpretation, the principle implies that, in cases of conflict between the good of the biotic community and the good of its individual members, the good of the former should, *ceteris paribus*, normally be given priority.

If we go back to our earlier formulation of a non-anthropocentric environmental ethic, we might say, in somewhat simplified terms, that

> *Strong ecocentrism* is the view that both ecological wholes (such as species, ecosystems, the land or the biotic community) and the individual members (such as human beings, animals or plants) making up these wholes have a value in themselves but as a rule the ecological wholes have a higher value than that of their individual members (including human beings).

Alternatively, we might say that[12]

> *Strong ecocentrism* is the view that individual behaviour or proposed environmental policies should primarily be judged according to how they affect the well-being of species and ecosystems and secondarily according to how they affect the well-being of human generations, whether present or future, as well as the well-being of other living beings.

Callicott's view can I think most appropriately be seen as an expression of this form of ecocentrism. He writes that 'the good of the community as a whole, serves as a standard for the assessment of the relative value and relative ordering of its constitutive parts and therefore provides a means of adjudicating the often mutually contradictory demands of the parts considered separately for *equal* consideration' (Callicott, 1989b, p. 25). The parts thus have a value in themselves. But situations where the interests of the various individual parts come into conflict with each other are to be decided by how much they respectively contribute to the survival and well-being of the biotic community: 'Animals of those species, which, like the honey bee, function in ways critically important to the economy of nature ... would be granted a greater claim to moral attention than psychologically more complex and sensitive ones, say, rabbits and voles, which seem to be plentiful, globally distributed, reproductively efficient, and only routinely integrated into the natural economy' (ibid.).

The problem, however, is that because Callicott – exactly like Leopold – holds that human beings do not have a privileged position in nature, even this form of ecocentric ethic is open to the objection to radical ecocentrism which we discussed above. As we have already seen, Callicott holds that the value of human beings, just like that of animals and plants, should be judged on the basis of their relation to the biotic community or biosphere as a whole (Callicott, 1989b, p. 28). Despite the fact that a strong ecocentrist such as Callicott assigns an intrinsic value to the individual members of the biotic community, it is still possible to sacrifice not only animals

---

[12] In choosing between these definitions, our choice is determined at least partly by whether we accept a deontological or consequentialist ethic.

and plants but also human beings for the sake of the whole. A culling of individual animals is often considered biologically desirable provided the species is numerous. Since *Homo sapiens* is quite clearly a very numerous species, we cannot rule out a culling of the human race as something desirable from the viewpoint of the biotic community. Strong ecocentrism thus risks undermining respect for individuals. The animal rights ethicist, Tom Regan, has therefore accused adherents of Leopold's land ethic of embracing a form of 'environmental fascism':

> The difficulties and implications of developing a right-based environmental ethic ... include reconciling the *individualistic* nature of moral rights with the more *holistic* view of nature. ... Aldo Leopold is illustrative of this latter tendency. ... The implications of this view include the clear prospect that the individual may be sacrificed for the greater biotic good, in the name of 'the integrity, stability, and beauty of the biotic community'. It is difficult to see how the notion of the rights of the individual could find a home within a view that ... might be fairly dubbed 'environmental fascism'. (Regan, 1983, p. 361–2)

In a review of Regan's book, *The Case for Animal Rights*, Callicott asks rhetorically: 'Well, who would ever want to be an environmental fascist?!' (Callicott, 1989c, p. 42), with the implication that he naturally would not wished to be classified as one. That is scarcely suprising, but the question remains. Callicott has tried in certain other contexts to show that this accusation is misleading. He does not deny that, if Leopold's principle of integrity and stability is held to constitute the only or most important source about what is right or wrong then ecocentrism *can* be formulated in such a way that the sacrifice of living human beings can be justified by reference to the way it promotes the integrity, stability and beauty of the ecosystems. Callicott writes that because of the drastic increase in the world population of human beings, William Aitken maintains 'from the point of view of the land ethic, therefore [that] "massive human diebacks would be good. It is our duty to cause them. It is our species' duty, relative to the whole, to eliminate 90 per cent of our numbers"'.[13]

Aitken's view must be classified as particularly radical. Exactly how radical it is depends naturally on how this 'elimination' would take place. Are we simply to exterminate 90 per cent of the current human population or is the idea that ecocentrism cannot justify such a direct slaughter of human beings and that the reduction of the human species must be brought about by some other means, for example, by massively reducing the birthrate in future generations? If it is the latter which is envisaged, it could imply that every family in future generations would be allowed (that is to say, would be morally justified) to consist of a man, a woman and *one child only* until the population goal had been achieved. There is hardly any doubt among environmentalists in general that a reduction of the human population is desirable and, as we shall see, both strong and weak ecocentrism lead to the view that we have a moral duty here and now to try to reduce population growth. The extent to which we should carry out this reduction, remains an open question.

---

[13] Aitken, cited in Callicott (1989e, p. 92).

How then does Callicott try to show that strong ecocentrism does not need to imply a form of environmental fascism? He writes that nature's law is eat or be eaten and that life and death are what makes the biotic community work well. For that reason, it is something which is considered good in the land ethic. In other words 'a "right to life" for individual members is not consistent with the structure of the biotic community and hence is not mandated by the land ethic' (Callicott, 1989c, p. 92). This may seem unjust and inhuman, and deviates from the Christian or humanist social ethic we are already familiar with. However, in Callicott's view, our insight that we are part of the biotic community does not prevent us from simultaneously remaining members of the *human* community. The land ethic does not replace the moral obligations which membership of human society involves: we must continue, for example, to respect basic human rights. This is so because obligations to our family in general takes precedence over obligations to the nation, and human ethical obligations take precedence over the obligations of environmental ethics. For this reason, strong ecocentrism need not be fascist. It does not release us from the claims of human ethics. Callicott writes that, if we accept this form of ecocentrism, we are

> still subject to all the other more particular and individually oriented duties to the members of our various more circumscribed and intimate communities. And since they are closer to home, they come first. In general, obligations to family come before obligations to more remotely related fellow humans. For example, pace [Peter] Singer one should not impoverish one's own children just short of starvation in order to aid actually starving people on another continent. But neither should one promote or even acquiesce in human starvation, no matter how distant, to achieve environmental goals – as some overzealous environmental activists have actually urged. Similarly, one should not allow a wild predator to help herself to one's free-range chickens, members of one's immediate mixed community. But neither should one interfere, other things being equal, in the interaction of the wild members of the biotic community. (Callicott, 1989d, p. 58)

In other words, Callicott means that what we may call a *principle of kinship* is morally and ecologically defensible. This principle says that every being on earth which can be reckoned as a moral agent is morally justified, when there is a conflict with equally weighty obligations to other beings with moral standing or to processes such as ecosystems, in giving priority to the obligations which apply to the parties which are genetically closest and most socially concerned. More concretely, the principle of kinship implies in the context of environmental ethics that human beings have a moral right to consider primarily themselves in the sense of the human community and only thereafter to be concerned with the biotic community in general.

On the other hand, Callicott asserts, ecocentric ethics does not leave human ethics unaffected, in the same way that obligations to the nation, such as to pay tax and, in certain countries, to do military service, do not leave family ethics unaffected. The land ethic can, for example, demand that one 'make certain sacrifices oneself or impose certain restrictions on the animal members of one's mixed community for the sake of ecological integrity. Dairy cattle, for example, can be very destructive of certain plant communities and should be fenced out of them when other pasture or fodder is available – despite their own preferences and the economic interests of dairy farmers' (ibid., pp. 58–9) .

A problem with this qualification of the Leopold principle of environmental ethics is how it can be combined with what Callicott says in his discussion of Abbey's statement that he would rather shoot a human being than a snake. But perhaps we should not take Callicott's pronouncements in this context too literally. He has later admitted that the article was primarily 'intended to provoke controversy' (Callicott, 1989a, p. 6). Is he, after all, an advocate of weak ecocentrism? There is a way of interpreting the kinship principle so that it is compatible with what seems nonetheless to be one of Callicott's key assertions: 'In every case the effect upon ecological systems is the *decisive* factor in the determination of the ethical quality of actions' (Callicott, 1989b, p. 21, emphasis added). In my judgment, this assertion constitutes the kernel of strong ecocentrism.

If Callicott or ecocentrists in general wish to maintain that the decisive factor (albeit not the sole factor) in deciding in environmental ethics whether an action or an environmental policy is morally acceptable is its effect on the earth's ecosystems, the kinship principle must be interpreted so that it only gives human beings the right, in situations where the ensuing effects of their actions constitute a marginal, or are at least not a real, threat to the continued existence of the ecosystems, to give priority to their own good before the good of the biotic community. Let us formulate the principle more precisely, as follows:

> *The principle of kinship*: human beings have a moral right to place their family and species, that is the human community, first when their interests do not constitute a threat to the continued existence and well-being of the biotic community.

In every situation where the effects of human actions on species and ecosystems do not constitute a major threat to their continued existence or functional capacity, human beings, according to this principle, have a right (but not a duty) to have regard primarily to their own needs and interests. If we formulate the kinship principle in this way, it is compatible with strong ecocentrism.

Weak Ecocentrism

The proponents of strong and weak ecocentrism agree that what promotes the good of the biotic community constitutes a criterion for judging whether human actions involving nature or politically sanctioned environmental measures are morally defensible. However, while the advocates of strong ecocentrism in addition maintain that the integrity, stability and beauty of the ecological wholes constitute the *decisive* factor, the proponents of weak ecocentrism limit themselves to saying that the integrity, stability and beauty of the ecological wholes form an important – but not necessarily the most important – factor in deciding what form environmental policy making should take. Holmes Rolston, III can be classified as a supporter of weak ecocentrism when he maintains that '*an* important ethical constraint in environmental decisions is concern for the integrity, stability and beauty of biotic communities' (Rolston, 1994a, p. 82, emphasis added). I shall take Rolston as my chief example of the way proponents of weak ecocentrism argue.[14]

What other factors besides the effect on species and ecosystems should we bear in mind in making an ethical assessment of an environmental policy? One possibility for proponents of weak ecocentrism is to maintain (1) that all individual members are equally important or even more important than the ecological wholes of which they form part and that it is these individuals which we must consider. This is an interpretation which brings them close to biocentrism. However, the problem with such a formulation of weak ecocentrism is that ecocentrists in general do not seem to see any real problems with killing individual animals: a culling of certain animal populations may not simply be morally permissible – it may be morally obligatory. Callicott argues, as we have seen, in such a way. Rolston writes: 'The well-being of a species, even though it is a so-called insignificant one, can be more important than the well-being of animals that we think are significant, even charismatic, if only individuals are at stake' (ibid., p. 64). He therefore has no qualms about the fact, for example, that the US Fish and Wildlife Service shot thousands of wild goats to save three endangered plant species on San Clemente Island off the Californian coast (ibid., p. 65). Neverthless, Rolston is not prepared in general to maintain that the well-being of plants and animals at the species level has greater moral importance than human beings (at least not in the case of people alive at present) at an individual level. To some extent he assigns to human beings a privileged position in comparison with animal and plant species. In another connection, he writes:

> The [ecological] system does not center indiscriminately on life, with one life being equal to another, and the system does not center functionally on humans, who in the ecological sense have little role in the system. Microbes are more important than humans instrumentally. All value does not 'center' on humans though some of it does ... Nevertheless, humans are of the utmost value in the sense that they are the ecosystem's most sophisticated product. They have the highest per capita intrinsic value of any life form supported by the system. (Rolston, 1988, p. 73)

An important difference between strong and weak ecocentrism is thus that, in the weak version, human beings are assigned a higher intrinsic value than other natural beings, objects or processes. (Note that the privileged treatment of human interests which is justified according to Callicott's kinship principle is not based on the fact that human beings have a higher value than other living beings and processes.

---

[14] I shall not maintain, however, that it is impossible to interpret Rolston as embracing a strong form of ecocentrism. In this context, I would nevertheless stress the differences to be found when Rolston and Callicott are compared. These differences allow Rolston to be interpreted as an advocate of weak ecocentrism. Callicott suggests that he looks upon Rolston's ecocentrism as being too weak (see Callicott, 1995a, pp. 681–2).

Rather, it is based on behaviour which can be assumed to be common for the majority of living creatures, namely that they seek primarily to protect their own or their nearest.)

Thus a more reasonable proposal than (1) above, is that weak ecocentrism implies (2) that the well-being of present and future generations of human beings – in addition to the integrity, stability and beauty of ecological wholes – is seen as a decisive factor in making decisions about the form environmental management is to take. Note, however, that this emphasis in weak ecocentrism on the 'unique' position of human beings in the biotic community does not mean that non-human organisms lack moral standing. It merely implies that their intrinsic value relative to the intrinsic value of species, ecosystems and human beings is rated relatively low. Callicott's statement that ecocentrism or Leopold's land ethic 'provide only "respect" for individual members of the biotic community, but "biotic rights" for species' expresses rather well the viewpoint of both weak and strong ecocentrism (Callicott, 1989d, p. 58). However, the value of plants and animals is not so low that it lacks relevance in deciding on the form environmental management is to take.

Observe too that, even if the value of human beings *per capita* is the highest, weak ecocentrism allows that the combined value of other living beings or processes can in certain situations surpass that of human beings and thus weigh more in a possible case of conflict. It can, for example, be more important to preserve a million existing species than that a further million human beings are born (see Rolston, 1988, p. 138).

According to advocates of weak ecocentrism, the continued existence of both present and future generations of human beings, as well as of species and ecosystems, should be at the core of environmental policy making. However, what is still unclear is to decide which of these two values is the more important when they conflict with one another. What has the greater priority – the human community or the biotic community? Those who espouse weak ecocentrism can provide different answers to this question, but the greater the emphasis on human interests as opposed to those of species and ecosystems, the nearer their view approaches anthropocentrism or the ethic of sustainable development. But what is required for a view to be classified as weak ecocentrism, according to my formulation above, is that moral standing is assigned to the ecological wholes and their non-human members. It is therefore reasonable to assume that, in all forms of weak ecocentrism, some form of moral concern is shown about this group of objects, beings or processes in setting out an environmental policy.

If we try to formulate weak ecocentrism analogously to the way we earlier formulated strong ecocentrism, our formulation, somewhat simplified, might look like the following:

> *Weak ecocentrism* is the view that ecological wholes (such as species, ecosystems or the land) as well as the individual members making up these wholes (such as human beings, animals or plants) have a value in themselves, although human beings have the highest individual value.

Alternatively,

> *Weak ecocentrism* is the view that individual behaviour and proposed environmental policies are to be judged primarily on the basis of how they affect the well-being of present generations of human beings and thereafter by how they affect the well-being of species and ecosystems.

Ecocentric Ethical Principles

The question we must try to answer is this: what are the ethical principles which ecocentrists believe ought to form the basis of human attitudes and behaviour towards nature and in devising environmental programmes? It turns out, however, that ecocentrists are very often far from clear about exactly which ecocentric policies their ethical principles imply. An explanation of this lack of clarity – which is much commoner in the case of ecocentrism than in the parallel cases of anthropocentrism and biocentrism – is that ecocentrism (if we except radical ecocentrism) is the environmental ethic which assigns moral standing to the most objects. In no other environmental ethic are there as many beings or processes which must be taken into account in our actions as there are in ecocentrism. Ethics has been expanded from a sphere containing only human beings (anthropocentrism) to one which apart from individual animals and plants (biocentrism) also includes ecological wholes such as species and ecosystems. Ecocentrists would thus find it more difficult to specify exactly which ethical principles governing our actions and relevant priority principles, partly because it it is reasonable to suppose that the larger number of objects possessing moral standing makes it correspondingly difficult to decide how conflicts between these objects are to be resolved.

In what follows, I shall nevertheless try to identify, systematize and make precise ecocentrism's ethical principles which very often have only been implicitly expressed by the ecocentrists themselves. As a result, it has often been necessary to provide not so much a recapitulation of the meaning of ecocentrism as a reconstruction.

Ecocentrists share not only the view that the earth's ecosystem forms a key factor in deciding what is right or wrong: they also maintain that we have moral obligations with respect to these ecosystems. Rolston asserts: 'Humans are not free to make whatever uses of nature suit their fancy, amusement, need, or profit ... [They] have some duties to the ecosystems of which they are part' (Rolston, 1988, p. 226). In his view, the ecosystem is the fundamental entity in biological evolution and for this reason it has not only an intrinsic value but a high intrinsic value. It is the high intrinsic value of ecosystems which makes wrong 'such seemingly trivial behavior as putting soap into geysers, carving names on trees and boulders, carving mountains into monuments to human pride, tossing toilet paper off the Mount of the Holy Cross, or bulldozing a giant fire off the lip of Glacier Point. Mere sport hunting is wrong on this count alone, even if those killed feel no pain' (ibid., p. 225).

But even if we allow that ecosystems are fundamental entities of this kind, how can we meaningfully speak of our moral obligations to ecosystems? What is needed? The basic idea is that, just as it is meaningful to speak about what is good for cultural wholes such as states, bureaucracies or business corporations, so too we can speak meaningfully about what is good for, or what promotes the well-being of, ecological wholes such as ecosystems, species and animal populations. We can, for example, discuss the circumstances in which a business corporation or a bureaucracy can flourish. In an analogous way, we can speak about the conditions which promote the good of ecosystems. What is good for an ecological whole, however, is not necessarily what is good for its constituent parts. What is good for a business corporation as a whole need not be good for the various subdivisions which make it up. What is good for an animal species is not necessarily good for its individual members. In order to be able meaningfully to speak about moral obligations to some entity or other, we require at the very least that this entity have some good of its own which we can either promote or oppose with our actions. Ecological wholes such as ecosystems and species fulfil this requirement. The good of these entities can be promoted or injured and the moral duties which we have with respect to them cannot automatically be reduced to the obligations which we have to their constituent parts.

Even if it is clear that ecocentrists consider that we *have* moral duties to ecosystems, they are not for this reason unanimous about *how* these duties should be expressed or formulated. Very often, all that is said is that we have a duty to ecosystems. However, in order to decide how relevant ecocentrism is for the form environmental management takes or for our intercourse with nature, we must nevertheless be able to explain relatively clearly the meaning and content of these 'ecosystemic' principles.

Rolston provides us with some guidance. He writes: 'The duty [to ecosystems] remains a prima facie one: humans ought to preserve so far as they can the richness of the biological community' (ibid., p. 230). But this ecosystemic duty is not as informative as one would wish, for what still remains unclear is at what point Rolston considers that we have done *what we can* to preserve the diversity and integrity of the ecosystems. What are to be our priorities? One measure which we could carry out, if we want to preserve the global ecosystem, is consciously to reduce human population over a number of generations to 10 per cent of its present size. Another, less radical, measure is to content ourselves with trying to keep intact those regions of wilderness which still remain on earth. Rolston's ecosystemic duty, however, gives us no guidance on this point.

A further obstacle to a more precise formulation of our duties to ecosystems is that they naturally must be related to other duties we have to species, individual animals and plants and in particular to other human beings. Rolston holds that our duty to preserve as far as possible the ecosystem intact is not 'In a capstone sense ... the ultimate one, since the cultural values supervening on nature are more eminent. But in a foundational sense it is ultimate, since it is out of projective nature that everything is created and maintained. Such [a] duty must be heeded or reasons given why not' (ibid., p. 230).

Here it is apparent that Rolston adopts a weak ecocentric viewpoint. The integrity and stability of ecological wholes form an important, but not always the most important factor in deciding whether a human action involving nature or an environmental policy is morally acceptable.

A more substantial moral duty towards the ecosystems which is endorsed by Rolston, appears instead in the following quotation: 'I do not say that there is no further cultural development needed, only that we do not need further cultural development that sacrifices nature for culture, that enlarges the sphere of culture at the price of diminishing the sphere of nature' (Rolston, 1994b, p. 231). Human beings have thus no right to devastate, modify or exploit more regions of wilderness than they have already done. Human beings have a duty to preserve what remains of wild nature. What are Rolston's arguments in reaching this conclusion? He writes as follows:

> About 2 percent of the contiguous United States is wilderness (1.2 percent designated; 1 percent under study). The remaining 98 percent is developed, farmed, grazed, timbered, or designated for multiple use. Another 2 percent might be suitable for wilderness or semiwild staus. So the 'balance' is 98–2 or perhaps 96–4. In dispute, we might be tempted to compromise, but then that would make it 99–1, or 97–3. (Rolston, 1994a, p. 27)

Rolston estimates that, all in all, wild nature amounts to about 5 per cent of the world's land surface (ibid., p. 68). According to him, this figure should only be taken as an illustration. It indicates that a compromise between cultural and natural values only further accentuates an imbalance that already exists. What this imbalance shows (on the assumption that, as an advocate of weak ecocentrism, one assumes that the two basic values are to promote the well-being of the present and future human generations and to respect the integrity, stability and beauty of the biotic community) is that every action or environmental policy which leads to the exploitation of existing areas of wilderness, on the supposed basis that they promote the good of humankind, is morally repugnant. Let us call this ecosystemic duty the 'principle of wildlife preservation' and formulate it as follows:

> *The principle of wildlife preservation*: we have a duty to leave the remaining areas of wilderness untouched.

Note that this principle expresses an obligation towards the ecosystem and not to future generations. Irrespective of the value which future people will derive from the preserved areas of wilderness, we ought to preserve them for their own sake. Areas of wilderness are to be protected because they have a high intrinsic value.

How, then, shall we relate to the ecosystems which are part of a cultivated landscape? According to Rolston, human beings have the right to transform areas of wilderness into rural and urban settlements. However, the ecocentric ethic

> requires that rural places be kept as full of nature as is consistent with their being agricultural places as well ... It limits road-building to minimize the impact on wildlife. It likes brushy fencerows and dislikes clean (and barren) ones ... It leaves the hardwoods along the stream courses when converting the uplands to pinewoods for paper pulp ... It says that humans ought to let sand dune ecosystems be – sometimes, at least. (Rolston, 1988, p. 226)

Moreover Rolston holds that it was presumably necessary for the new settlers in the United States to reduce the herds of buffalo so that they had room to pasture their cattle. But the settlers had no right to exterminate them: 'respect for those bison in their plains ecosystems should have preserved ample grasslands wilderness and national parks in every plains state' (ibid., p. 227). Once common ecosystems such as the prairie *ought* to be preserved. Thus it is not merely the earth's remaining areas of wilderness which must be left untouched: the original ecosystems which form part of cultural landscapes must also be preserved. A second ecocentric principle relating to our duties to ecosystems could thus be formulated roughly as follows:

> *The preservation principle with respect to natural ecosystems*: we have a duty in transforming areas of wilderness to cultural landscape to leave a place for the original ecosystems and their inhabitants.

According to Rolston, we have transformed approximately 95 per cent of the earth's areas of wilderness to either rural or urban settlements. Is this division between nature and culture morally defensible? Does ecocentrism require us to try to make recompense for the damage we have caused the earth's ecosystems? In other words, is there an ecocentric rule corresponding to biocentrism's rule of restitutive justice? The answer to these questions depends partly on how we weigh the interests of nature against the interests of culture, in short on whether we embrace a strong or weak version of ecocentrism. Rolston comments as follows: 'It has been necessary in the course of human history to sacrifice most of the wildlands, converting them to rural and urban settlements, and this is both good and ecological' (ibid., p. 226). Thus Rolston at any rate considers that it is morally acceptable for human beings to have transformed the majority of areas of wilderness to cultural landscapes of various kinds. The rule of restitutive justice with respect to ecosystems (namely that we have a duty to recompense ecosystems when we have treated them in a morally unacceptable way) would thereby come into play in situations where the remaining wilderness is damaged or threatened by human beings.

However, in other contexts, Rolston suggests that human beings have acted wrongly with respect to ecosystems. We have not respected their integrity (or dignity) sufficiently. As we have seen, he holds that the new settlers in the United States had a right to reduce the herds of buffalo. But they had no right to destroy them altogether. Instead they or the authorities in the country should have 'preserved ample grasslands wilderness and national parks in every plains state' so that some of these animals could have continued their existence in their natural habitat ... (ibid., p. 227). 'Alas, the United States has not a single grasslands national park or grasslands wilderness with free-ranging buffalo' (ibid., p. 227). To a limited extent, Rolston appears to consider that weak ecocentrism can imply also that some of the wilderness which has already been transformed into cultural landscape should be restored to as original a state as possible (see also Rolston, 1994a, p. 93). In general, however, the ecocentric moral directive is intended to apply to the future relation between culture and nature:

How to trade gains in culture against losses in ecosystemic communities is often puzzling. As a general rule, humans count enough to have the right to flourish within ecosystems, but they do not count so much that they can degrade or shut down ecosystems – not at least without a considerable burden of proof that they are obtaining greater value in culture in exchange ... If this cannot be a rule with which to judge the past in our now greatly modified rebuilt environments, at least it can help envision the future. (Ibid., p. 83)

Can we expect advocates of strong ecocentrism to content themselves with these two ecosystemic principles which we have found are accepted by proponents of weak ecocentrism? Hardly. A decisive factor in judging the moral qualities of an action or an environmental policy is their effect on the ecosystems (see, once more, Callicott, 1989b, p. 21). This implies that, in weighing the interests of human beings against the integrity of ecosystems, the latter carries more weight in the eyes of proponents of strong, as opposed to weak, ecocentrism. In other words, strong ecocentrism would appear to imply a more comprehensive duty to ecosystems than that which is expressed in the preservation principle, even if the kinship principle is taken into account. Although we human beings have a right to consider primarily the interests of our nearest relations (that is, other human beings), it is nonetheless reasonable to suppose that human beings could (and thus ought to) live in such a way that a much smaller part of the earth's surface is transformed into cultural landscape.

According to the deep ecologists, Bill Devall and George Sessions, the strong ecocentric viewpoint leads to the practical consequence that 'we should live with minimum rather than maximum impact on other species and on the Earth in general' (Devall and Sessions, 1994, p. 217).[15] Even if the principle of wildlife preservation does not entail that we live in such a way that our actions have a maximum effect on ecosystems, it scarcely implies minimum influence either. Devall and Sessions believe that we ought to accept a way of life which leaves as much as possible of the wild nature undisturbed. But according to them, an altered way of life does not suffice: 'The flourishing of human life and cultures is compatible with a substantial decrease of the human population. The flourishing of non-human life requires such a decrease' (ibid., p. 218). We must also ensure that we reduce the number of people who are straining the carrying capacities of the global ecosystems. It is therefore reasonable to suppose that strong ecocentrism demands more of us with respect to our relation to ecosystems than what is expressed by the principle of wildlife preservation and the preservation principle with respect to ecosystems. Callicott also writes: 'The land ethic, on the other hand, requires a shrinkage, if at all possible, of the domestic sphere' (Callicott, 1989b, p. 34).

How then are we to formulate more precisely a strong ecocentric duty to ecosystems? The problem is that strong ecocentrism allows a number of different formulations of such an ecosystemic principle, depending on the exact value assigned to the integrity and stability of ecosystems, in contrast to the value assigned to the well-being of the present and future generations of human beings. It

---

[15] Deep ecology can be classified as a variant of strong ecocentrism.

is clear, however, that this 'weighting' has the result that more than 5 per cent of the earth's surface ought to be made up of wilderness. But does 'more' here mean 10 per cent, 20 per cent, 30 per cent or even possibly 50 per cent of the earth's total surface? The question is partially decided by how far we *can* restore regions which once were wilderness but now are cultural landscapes, to their original state. As Rolston points out: 'We cannot go back in history and undo the undoing [sic] we humans once did. We cannot go back to yesterday as though we could restore pre-Columbian America' (Rolston, 1994a, p. 93).

However, Rolston estimates that around 5 per cent of the surface of the earth consists of semi-wilderness. Thus it seems reasonable to assume that we could successfully restore these natural areas to pure wilderness. But it seems possible to rehabilitate more than just these areas, although in certain cases there are problems:

> Revegetating after strip mining cannot properly be called rehabilitation ... because there is in fact nothing left to rehabilitate. But one can rehabilitate a prairie that has been not too badly overgrazed. Overgrazing allows many introduced weeds to outcompete the natives; perhaps all one has to do is pull the weeds and let nature do the rest ... Overgrazing allows some native plants to outcompete other natives, those that once reproduced in the shade of the taller grasses. So perhaps, after the taller grasses return, one will have to dig some holes, put in some seeds that have been gathered from elsewhere, cover them up, go home, and let nature do the rest ... The naturalness returns. (Ibid., p. 91)

A restoration, however, seldom achieves the perfection of the original and, for example, the multiplicity of species may be lacking. It is therefore reasonable to imagine advocates of strong ecocentrism holding that we have a duty to restore natural areas only if we can achieve something which approximates the original and stands in historical continuity to it. If this is correct, we would not have the duty to restore natural values which we have destroyed in, for example, a complete deforestation, since a new forest would be something completely new. (On the other hand, we can naturally have an obligation to future generations to plant a new forest.) If all we can achieve is a copy and not a genuine restoration, our duty no longer applies in spite of our liability: the damage is irreversible.

Thus we might formulate the ecosystemic duty which advocates of strong ecocentrism believe should guide environmental management, as follows:

> *The principle of wildlife restoration*: we have a duty to try to rehabilitate the areas of nature which from an ecological standpoint can still be restored to a state of wilderness.

According to this principle, we have a moral duty to try to restore as much of the original wilderness as possible. Only natural science can determine how extensively we can successfully transform areas which we have already settled. However, it is reasonable to suppose that, in addition to the 5 per cent of the earth's surface classified by Rolston as wilderness, a further 5 or 10 per cent of the global surface could meet the requirements of the principle of restoration.

To sum up, ecocentrists emphasize that we have moral obligations to ecosystems and on this point they adopt a quite different view from that of anthropocentrists. But ecocentrists also differ from biocentrists in particular when our obligations to ecosystems conflict with our duties to individual organisms. For example, Rolston writes: 'No duty to sentient life overrides the carrying capacity of an ecosystem, whether wild or modified by agricultural changes' (Rolston, 1988, p. 87). The difference bewteen strong and weak ecocentrism is that, in the weak formulation, the words 'sentient life' refer only or at least primarily to non-human life: those who embrace strong ecocentrism refuse, or at least put off as far as they can, any such qualification of the phrase.

The principles of wildlife preservation and restoration are examples of duties which are based on the ecocentric view that such entities as ecosystems and species have an intrinsic value and have moral standing. Can we identify any ethical principles which determine how we ought to behave towards species? The ecocentric (as opposed to the anthropocentric) perspective is quite apparent in what Rolston writes when he rhetorically asks: 'Do we simply want to protect these endangered forms of life *for* exploitation, or do we sometimes want to protect them *from* exploitation?' (ibid., pp. 129–30). According to Rolston, endangered species are worth preserving for their own sake because of their intrinsic value. This does not imply that these species have a right to exist, but only that human beings have no right to destroy species. Moreover, he writes:

> humans have no duty of benevolence to preserve rare species from natural extinction, although they may have a duty to other humans to save such species as resources or museum pieces. No species has a 'right to life' apart from the continued existence of the ecosystem with which it cofits. But humans have a duty of nonmaleficence to avoid artificial extinction, which superkills the species in the formative process in which it stands. This prima facie duty can on occasion be overridden: for example with the extinction (which we have almost achieved) of *Orthopoxvirus variola*, the smallpox virus or (could we ever achieve it) of *Plasmodium vivvax*, a malaria parasite. (Ibid., p. 155)

Two duties – one positive and one negative – seem to follow from Rolston's argument. The negative duty is that we do not have any environmental (or possibly human) duty to protect animal and plant species from natural extinction. This duty, in other words, corresponds to the negative duty we previously identified as applying with respect to the ecosystem: now it applies at the species level. The second moral duty is about whether it is permissible for us to exterminate living animal and plant species. Let us call this principle 'the principle of non-maleficence towards to other species' and formulate it as follows:

> *The principle of non-maleficence towards other species*: we have a duty to treat animal and plant species in such a way that they are not threatened with extinction as a result of our actions but can be preserved in properly functioning ecosystems.

Rolston says in addition that this principle is a *prima facie* principle: in other words, in special circumstances, it may be overridden. Rolston does not stripulate what these circumstances are, but given that weak ecocentrism assumes that the two basic values are to promote the well-being of present and future generations and to respect the integrity, stability and beauty of the biotic community, it is reasonable to assume that it is human interests which in certain circumstances can weigh so heavily that the foregoing principle no longer holds. The examples which Rolston gives, however, suggest that it is not just any human interests which play a role here. In both cases, it is a matter of organisms which directly threaten human beings. Thus it would seem that only basic human interests such as food, water, and shelter are relevant. What Rolston does not discuss is whether human basic interests can always set aside the above principle of non-maleficence with respect to species or whether there are situations in which this principle nevertheless carries the most weight. This is a question we shall have reason to return to in the next chapter.

According to ecocentrists, there is a crucial ethical dividing line between the ecosystem and the species level, on the one hand, and the organism level, on the other. This contrast is evident in the following passage from Rolston: 'The consumption of individual animals and plants is one thing; it can be routinely justified. But the consumption of species is something else; it cannot be routinely justified' (ibid., p. 158). We have already touched somewhat on the difference between ecocentrism and biocentrism in this respect, but the ecocentric standpoint ought to be made a little more precise. As a result, the dividing line at organism level which is drawn between human beings on the one hand and plants and animals on the other in weak ecocentrism will be clarified and illustrated.

Like Callicott, Rolston holds that human beings belong to two different communities, the cultural and the biological.[16] We are dealing with two different formulations of moral duties. The ecological principles for biological health and well-being cannot be applied to human culture. We must not romanticize nature: 'Realistically, suffering is an integral feature of sentient life in ecosystems. Nature is harsh; herbivores starve; carnivores kill. When humans encounter wild nature, animals have neither a right nor a welfare claim to be spared the pains imposed by natural selection' (ibid., p. 56). So even if we human beings feel sympathy for a vulnerable deer, for example, we have to accept and thus not hinder a hungry wolf from devouring it. While, in the sphere of human culture, we have a moral duty to avoid suffering, we have no such duty when we are faced with suffering in nature. If a child, however, is threatened by being devoured by a wolf, the situation is different. We should then try to save the child. The explanation which Rolston gives for this difference in response is that the deer lives solely within an ecosystem in nature, whereas the child is also part of a culture. It is thus human ethics and not environmental ethics which justifies the saving of the child.

A central ecocentric standpoint is thus the following: 'There is no human duty to eradicate the sufferings of creation' (ibid., p. 56); 'Environmental ethics ... [does

---

[16] In contrast to Callicott (and to a number of biocentrists), Rolston places much more emphasis on the distinction between culture and nature and between human ethics and environmental ethics.

not] give us any duty to revise nature' (ibid., p. 57). According to ecocentrists, there is no principle of benevolence in environmental ethics and no moral duty actively to hinder or to minimize suffering in nature. Thus Rolston writes, 'Wild creatures may have, asymmetrically, some negative claim not (without cause) to be harmed but no positive claim to be helped' (ibid., p. 56). The basic idea is that environmental ethics should follow rather than deny ecology. Suffering is a necessary part of a properly functioning ecological process. Trying to eliminate such suffering is not biologically sensitive but rather biologically insensitive. What *is*, *ought*, in this respect, to be the case. Let us formulate this principle of non-interference as follows:

> *The principle of non-interference with respect to natural suffering*: we have no duty to reduce or diminish the suffering which exists as a natural part of the natural process.

Thus we have no duty to try actively to reduce the amount of suffering in nature. But do we, according to ecocentrists, have a right ourselves to cause nature (animals and plants) suffering? Rolston writes that 'one species must capture the values of others to live. Making a resource of something else is pervasive in the system, even when it inflicts suffering; when humans do this too, they simply follow nature. There is nothing immoral about participating in the logic and biology of one's ecosystem' (Rolston, 1988, p. 60). It is therefore morally permissible for us to use not only plants but also animals for food: 'human consumption of animals is to be judged by the principles of environmental ethics, not those of interhuman ethics ... Humans eat meat, and meat-eating is a natural component of ecosystems' (ibid., p. 79). 'Humans in their eating habits follow nature; they can and ought to do so. But humans do not eat humans because such events interrupt culture.' (ibid., p. 81). Ecocentrism, in contrast to strong biocentrism and animal rights biocentrism, thus does not imply vegetarianism.

Rolston calls the first principle of environmental ethics with respect to animals and plants which is justified by his arguments, 'a homologous principle': 'Do not cause inordinate suffering, beyond those orders of nature from which the animals were taken. One ought to fit culture into the natural givens, where pain is inseparable from the transfer of values between sentient lives. Culturally imposed suffering must be comparable to ecologically functional suffering' (ibid., p. 61). Culture has no right to increase the amount of suffering in nature in excess of that which already exists as a natural part of the global ecosystem. Let us formulate this principle as follows:

> *The homologous principle*: we have a duty not to cause animals more suffering than that which they are exposed to (on average) in the state of wilderness.

The relevant ethical question is therefore not that of Bentham and the biocentrists, namely 'Can animals suffer?', but 'Is the human-inflicted suffering excessive to natural suffering?' (Rolston, 1988, p. 61). The role of the homologous principle is thus primarily to demonstrate a crucial difference between biocentrism and ecocentrism.

Despite the fact that ecocentrists maintain that the eating of animals is a natural biological phenomenon, and therefore should be accepted, Rolston holds that human beings have a moral duty to avoid subjecting animals to unnecessary or meaningless suffering (ibid., pp. 83, 85). He gives no direct reasons for this being the case, but it is reasonable to suppose that this duty is a consequence of the fact that ecocentrists look upon animals as beings with moral standing, in other words beings towards which we can behave rightly or wrongly. The intrinsic value which they assign to individual organisms justifies such treatment. This principle can be called the 'principle prohibiting needless suffering':

> *The principle prohibiting needless suffering*: we have a duty to try to avoid personally causing animals unnecessary or meaningless suffering.

However, this principle is compatible not only with making use of animals for food but also with using animals (and also plants) for producing clothes and medicine. Rolston sees no reason for forbidding the use of animals in the production of products which secure the health and basic well-being of human beings. The products he has in mind include leather for shoes, wool for jackets and coats and insulin for diabetics. Nonetheless, he also notes, 'As these uses of animals pass from the essential through the serious into the merely desirable and finally to the trivial, the ecological pattern rapidly fades, and the justification collapses' (Rolston, 1988, p. 85). The values which animals possess, independent of the value they have for human beings, impose constraints on the way humans may use them for these purposes. Rolston gives the following examples of morally acceptable and morally unacceptable use of animals: 'The use of fur for survival – a jacket on a frontiersman – is much closer to the natural, and the suffering is justified thereby. The use of fur for status – a jaguar coat on an actress – is highly artificial ... The suffering traded for it is not justified by any naturalistic [or ecocentric] principle' (ibid.). Rolston appears to be aware that there is no simple criterion allowing one to distinguish once and for all between what is permissible and impermissible in these matters. But it is at any rate clear that the more the purpose of using the animal is distanced from satisfying basic human needs, the lower its degree of moral justification. Hunting would be justifiable if its purpose was to acquire food: 'Nothing is more natural than hunting for food' (ibid., p. 88). But all forms of hunting where the aim of satisfying human basic desires is not uppermost are morally repugnant from an ecocentric perspective.

Up to now, we have spoken about ecocentric duties towards sentient animals: what about the case of plants and insects? Rolston holds that the ethical principles which apply to plants and insects must be formulated somewhat differently from those applying to higher animals, since plants and insects do not feel. Rolston calls the principle which is compatible with the ecocentric view of this matter *the principle of the non-loss of goods*. It applies in the following way:

The goods preserved by the human destruction of plants ... outweigh the goods of the organisms destroyed; thus, to be justified in picking flowers for a bouquet one would have to judge correctly that the aesthetic appreciation of the bouquet outweighed the goods of the flowers destroyed. One might pluck flowers for a bouquet but refuse to uproot the whole plant, or pick common flowers (daisies) and refuse to pick rare ones (trailing arbutus) or those that reproduce slowly (wild orchids). (Rolston, 1988, p. 20)

The principle of the non-loss of goods thus says that *the value which is obtained by the human use of a plant must exceed the value that the plant possesses in itself or in a virgin state.* Judging from the examples, however, the principle says something more. It says that plants are not to be subjected to unnecessary damage: when we pick a flower, we should avoid pulling up all its roots unless it is absolutely necessary. However, the fact that the principle seems to say this, undermines Rolston's assertion that the two principles which specify our duties towards sentient animals cannot be applied to plants. All that is required is that the word 'suffering' be replaced by the word 'damage' in the two principles. The analogue to the principle prohibiting needless suffering would be:

The principle prohibiting needless damage: we have a duty to try to avoid personally causing plants and insects unnecessary damage.

The homologous principle says that we have a duty not to cause plants and insects damage which exceeds that which they would (on average) sustain in the wilderness. If this is correct, it would imply that the principle of the non-loss of goods would not replace but rather complement the other principles of environmental ethics. The principle of the non-loss of goods helps us in situations where human non-basic interests (such as the interest in picking flowers because we think them beautiful as an adornment for our homes) conflict with the good of the plants, by allowing us to judge which interests shall be given moral priority. The principle is important because Rolston believes that the interests of plants and insects can sometimes carry more weight than the interests of human beings. This is particularly the case in situations where the human interests are trivial in character, but it can also apply in situations where human interests are certainly not trivial but where the combined value of the plants is high (Rolston, 1988, p. 121).

Rolston is aware that it is difficult to give precise ecocentric directives for human beings' moral relation to plants and insects. But he denies that the answers are subjective: 'Answers in environmental ethics ... [are] rough because the questions are novel. They involve immeasurable and seemingly incommensurable values. An answer must be approximate, but approximation ought not to be confused with mere opinion. Damage to wildflowers, trees, butterflies is real; it actually takes place in the world' (ibid., p. 124).

In order to make the ecocentrists' view of the way human beings ought to treat invidual animals and plants less complex and more graspable, we might sum it up in the following two ethical principles:

The utility principle with respect to animals: it is morally acceptable for human beings to make use of (sentient or higher) animals to satisfy their own basic needs as long as they do not cause unnecessary suffering or threaten the continued existence of the species.

The utility principle with respect to plants: it is morally acceptable for human beings to make use of plants (and insects) to satisfy their own needs as long as (1) the value of the plants does not exceed the value which human beings attain by making use of the plants, and (2) they do not cause unnecessary damage or threaten the continued existence of the species.

In contrast to the case of our duties towards ecosystems, there would seem to be no difference between strong and weak ecocentrism as regards our moral duties towards plants and animals.

In the present chapter, we have seen that there are alternatives to the anthropocentric approach to environmental ethics upon which the idea of sustainable development is based. This non-anthropocentric ethic can, however, be formulated in different ways, since *inter alia* non-anthropocentrists give different answers to the questions 'What in nature has an intrinsic value?' and 'Are the objects which are assigned an intrinsic value, equally valuable?' The most important division is that between biocentrism and ecocentrism. Biocentrists maintain that non-human lives have an intrinsic value, but they do not assign any such value to species and ecosystems since these are not living beings. Ecocentrists, on the other hand, maintain that the land, rivers and mountains and not merely living beings, have an intrinsic value. They hold that biological wholes such as ecosystems and the biotic community, as well as biological individuals, have moral standing and that we must be concerned with their good when we are faced with choosing between different courses of action or are engaged in environmental policy making.

CHAPTER FIVE

Environmental Management: Aims and Policies

We have seen that the values which consciously or unconsciously guide people's attitudes and responses to the natural environment derive from at least three distinct ethical approaches: anthropocentrism, biocentrism and ecocentrism. We now need to ask whether these theoretical differences have practical consequences. Does environmental policy making take on a special character depending on whether it is based upon an anthropocentric, biocentric or ecocentric approach? If decision making were to be based on some form of biocentrism or ecocentrism instead of the intergenerational anthropocentrism indirectly recommended in *Our Common Future* or *Agenda 21*, would environmental management and policy making develop along different lines?

What is clear is that both biocentrists and ecocentrists in general believe that their basic ethical standpoints involve an attitude to nature which in practice differs radically from that of anthropocentrism. Paul Taylor writes, 'It makes a practical difference in the way we treat the natural environment whether we accept an anthropocentric or a biocentric system of ethics' (Taylor, 1986, p. 12). According to many biocentrists and ecocentrists, our entire planetary future stands or falls with our choice of environmental ethic and many are also strongly critical of the policy programme drawn up by advocates of sustainable development. In his verdict on the report of the World Commission, Holmes Rolston writes that

> there is here no concern for the integrity of ecosystems, nor for biodiversity. The concern is for justice in sharing the produce of the Earth now and in future generations. Nor is there concern about the escalating human populations; the only goal is meeting essential human needs by sustainable growth. The earth is regarded as a natural resource and a sink for wastes; what really counts is meeting people's needs. Most people do not have enough yet for two reasons: not enough is produced; and what is produced is not equitably shared. It is clear here that sustainable development is for people; the commission anticipates much more growth, people increasingly making a resourceful use of the Earth, as fast as technology can arrange it. (Rolston, 1994a, p. 84)

Writing in a different context, Rolston states his conviction that a model 'in which nature has no value apart from human preferences will imply different conduct from one where nature projects all values' (Rolston, 1988, p. 230).

Bryan Norton is an anthropocentric ethicist with a diametrically opposite point of view. He has tried to defend the hypothesis that 'environmentalists are evolving toward a consensus in policy, even though they remain divided regarding basic values' (Norton, 1991, p.86). According to Norton, the preferred environmental ethic does not make much practical difference since in questions of policy all such ethics give rise to the same kind of environmental management. Norton asserts that his conclusion, if generalized, suggests that 'introducing the idea that other species have intrinsic value, that humans should be "fair" to all other species, provides no operationally recognizable constraints on human behavior that are not already implicit in the generalized, cross-temporal obligations to protect a healthy, complex and autonomously functioning system for the benefit of future generations of humans' (ibid., pp. 226–7). His conclusion is of especial interest here, where we start off by considering the ethic of sustainable development.

The ecocentrist Baird Callicott holds quite simply that 'Norton's "convergence hypothesis", however, is dead wrong' (Callicott, 1995b, p. 22). He even thinks as follows:

> The eventual institutionalization of a new holistic, nonanthropocentric environmental ethic will make as much practical difference in the environmental arena as the institutionalization of the intrinsic value of all human beings has made in the social arena. As recently as a century and a half ago, it was permissible to own human beings. With the eventual institutionalization of Enlightenment ethics – persuasively articulated by Hobbes, Locke, Bentham, and Kant, among others – slavery was abolished in Western civilization. Of course, a case could have been made to slaveowners and an indifferent public that slavery was economically backward and more trouble than it was worth. But that would not have gotten at the powerful moral truth that for one human being to own another is wrong. With the eventual institutionalization of a holistic, nonanthropocentric environmental ethic – today persuasively articulated by Aldo Leopold, Arne Naess, Holmes Rolston, and Val Plumwood, among others – the wanton destruction of the nonhuman world will, hopefully, come to be regarded as equally unconscionable. (Ibid., p. 24)

We will need to return to this discussion among environmental philosophers. As we shall see, Norton's view that non-anthropocentrists often exaggerate the significance of basic values for policy making is right but his 'convergence hypothesis' must still be judged erroneous.[1] Certainly, the various environmental ethical theories are in agreement about a number of practical issues but we should also notice many significant differences, particularly in a situation where many policy decision makers, as we have seen, are scarcely aware of the underlying ethical differences.

We should note, however, that the adoption of a moral stance in regard to the

[1] Such an assertion is particularly apposite in a philosophical and also, to some extent, a theological context. Here the word 'anthropocentrism' has often been used as more or less a term of abuse. Thus Don E. Marietta, in agreement with Norton, points out in his critique of deep ecologists that they have used 'some poor examples, taking the worst offenders against the natural environment as examples of anthropocentric thinking. Were the despoilers of nature really champions of humanity? Were they *anthropo*centric? Regardless of what they might have claimed, were they not petroleum industry centrists, lumber industry centrists, developer centrists, or even egocentrists? Had we thought a little bit about the meaning of *anthropocentrist*, I do not think we could have graced with the name anthropocentrism behaviors and attitudes that do nothing to help the human race' (Marietta, 1995, p.76).

environment would be just as important even if anthropocentrism, biocentrism and ecocentrism had largely the same practical consequences. This is because it is important to distinguish between *what* people do and *why* they do it. Suppose two siblings both try to take care of their grandmother who has been injured in a fall. One helps her out of love. The other's help is motivated by the hope of inheriting her fortune. The chain of practical reasoning has in both cases the same consequences, yet we consider the difference between the two motives as highly significant. Morality and ethics cannot simply be reduced to correct behaviour. This is also true in the case of environmental ethics.

Since anthropocentrism, biocentrism and ecocentrism can take many different forms, I shall restrict myself to comparing the ethic of sustainable development (that is, intergenerational anthropocentrism), weak and strong biocentrism, animal rights biocentrism and weak and strong ecocentrism. How do each of these ethical viewpoints in practice help to influence environmental policy making? One difficulty already noted is that biocentric and ecocentric thinkers in general supply only a few examples of the practical consequences of their basic ethical positions. They do not try to construct biocentric or ecocentric policy programmes. As Rollin observes: 'Writings in this area by and large have tended to focus more on making the case for the attribution of moral status to these entities [other living beings, species and ecosystems] than in working out detailed answers to practical issues' (Rollin, 1995, p. 114). Our task , therefore, will often be to try to reconstruct these alternative policy programmes for environmental management, making use of previously identified ethical rules and ethical priority principles.

We begin, however, by briefly recalling the alternative basic value priorities which these various theories of environmental ethics express. Put simply, when devising an environmental policy programme we must

- consider the needs of human beings living at present and only to these (*traditional anthropocentrism*),
- consider the needs of present and future generations of human beings and only to these (*intergenerational anthropocentrism*),
- consider the needs of all living beings and only to these, with priority given to human needs (*weak biocentrism*),
- consider the needs of all living beings and only to these, with priority given to the needs of sentient beings (including humans) (*animal rights biocentrism*),
- give equal consideration to the needs of all living beings and only to these (*strong biocentrism*),
- consider the needs of all living beings as well as the integrity of species and ecosystems, but as a rule giving priority to human needs (*weak ecocentrism*),
- consider the needs of all living beings as well as the integrity of species and ecosystems, but as a rule giving priority to the integrity of species and ecosystems (*strong ecocentrism*).

The consideration in question here is *moral* consideration, that is, the consideration a moral agent must show towards any person or thing capable of being treated rightly or wrongly. An example of non-moral consideration, by contrast, would be the care taken when I put on my raincoat to go out for a walk. Thus I consider the weather when deciding how to dress. Similarly, when planning to build a road, I consider (in the non-moral sense) the shape of the terrain. Anthropocentrists of course concede that we have to consider, in this second sense, the plants, animals and ecosystems which are involved, but only to the extent that these affect human well-being. Thus, according to the anthropocentrists, we should consider the soundness of ecosystems when devising an environmental policy programme, but only on account of their high instrumental value.

It is clear, all the same, that the different environmental ethical theories depend upon different views regarding the *aims* of environmental management and policy making. For advocates of sustainable development, human well-being is 'the ultimate goal of all environment and development policy' (World Commission, 1987, p. xiv). The Swedish National Environment Protection Board affirms that 'the proposed environmental goals build upon assessments as to what will benefit society as a whole' (Naturvårdsverket, 1997, p. 13). More exactly, the aim of (intergenerational) anthropocentric policy making is *to use natural resources in such an effective and far-sighted way that the needs of future as well as present generations of human beings will be satisfied.* This implies that the ecosystem's long-term productive potential must come before all else. If this is neglected, then, although people who are alive at present may be able to satisfy their needs, it is unlikely that future generations will be able to do so.

Biocentric policy making, by contrast, aims *to ensure that the way people use nature does not violate the right of other living beings to exist and flourish.* Thus Tom Regan considers that 'the overarching goal of wildlife management should not be to ensure maximum sustainable yield; it should be to protect wild animals from those who would violate their rights' (Regan, 1983, p. 357). The ultimate goal of any environmental policy should be the well-being of plants and animals and not simply the well-being of human beings. Environmental programmes must be fair to all living beings. It is a tacit biocentric assumption that, by attaining this goal, we can be sure that the vital needs of future human generations can also be met. Environmental management should thus concentrate on other living beings rather than on present or future human generations.

Ecocentric environmental policy making, finally, aims *to ensure that the way people use nature neither violates the integrity of the biotic community (including in varying degrees that of its individual members) nor threaten its stability.* As we have seen, Leopold holds that a thing 'is right when it tends to preserve the integrity, stability, and beauty of the biotic community. It is wrong when it tends otherwise' (Leopold, 1949, pp. 224–5). Thus one important, indeed decisive factor in the formulation of an environmental programme, apart from the way it may influence the prospects of individual people and animals of satisfying present or future needs, will be the effect the programme has upon the survival and well-being of species and ecosystems. The preservation of species and of ecological units such as rivers, marshes or mountain forests should be central to environmental policy making, irrespective of whether this also serves human welfare.

Thus the question we must try to answer is whether these environmental ethical theories, given their different goals, will also give rise to different *environmental policies*. We shall examine certain key areas such as population size, wilderness management, endangered species and agricultural planning where practical differences can arise, and thus ignore many other important environmental questions. Nonetheless, I trust that the discussion will be sufficiently comprehensive to demonstrate the relevance of environmental ethics for practical work in environmental management.

Human Population Policies

In many parts of the world the population is growing at a rate which cannot be supported by available natural resources. This threatens the productivity of the ecosystems affected, in both the short term and the long term. According to the World Commission, urgent measures are therefore required in order to halt the more extreme population increases. The problem, of course, is not simply the size of the population, but how it is related to available resources and the rate at which these resources are being consumed. As a result, a reduction in the rate of population increase even in the industrialized countries cannot be excluded: 'population growth rates [are not] the challenge solely of those nations with high rates of increase. An additional person in an industrial country consumes far more and places far greater pressure on natural resources than an additional person in the Third World' (World Commission, 1987, p. 95). So if we are to achieve the overriding aim of environmental management, namely that of using natural resources with sufficient efficiency and far-sightedness so that the needs of present and future human generations can be met, an important subsidiary goal will be that of securing an ecologically sustainable level of population.

One interesting difference between the World Commission's report and *Agenda 21* is that in the latter document no direct goal with respect to population density and increase is specified. Instead there is talk of incorporating 'demographic trends and factors in the global analysis of environment and development issues' (*Agenda 21*, 5.5). The emphasis in *Agenda 21* is placed instead on the fight against poverty and on bringing about satisfactory living conditions for rapidly growing populations. I shall, however, refrain from dwelling on this difference and shall simply assume that *Agenda 21*'s silence on this point is not to be interpreted as evidence for a different standpoint on the part of its authors from that expressed in *Our Common Future*. It should instead be seen as evidence that the question is politically very sensitive.[2] *The Rio Declaration*, finally, simply states that countries must promote 'appropriate demographic policies' if sustainable development is to be attained (*The Rio Declaration*, 1992, Principle 8). What 'suitable' means in this context, however, remains vague.

---

[2] Consider the following comment on the Rio conference: 'When, in the final negotiating session, the United States moved to delete all references to consumption in the North, the G-77 retaliated by deleting reference to the urgency of slowing population growth' (Jessica Matthews, cited in Van De Veer and Pierce (eds) (1994), p. 372).

Let us consider the World Commission's report, *Our Common Future*. According to the Commission 'sustainable development can only be pursued if population size and growth are in harmony with the changing productive potential of the ecosystem' (World Commission, 1987, p. 9). Thus the essential content of anthropocentric population policy is that *a population's size must be stabilized at a level compatible with the ecosystem's productive potential*. It is only then that we are able to attain the goal of securing a sustainable level of population. More concretely, as we saw in Chapter 3, it has been recommended that the global population should stabilize at 7.7 billion by 2060, such a stabilization being possible if the number of births reach replacement level by 2010 (ibid., p. 102).

What measures are recommended for achieving such a population policy? First of all we have to realize that population growth today is concentrated in the developing regions of Asia, Africa and Latin America. The total world population is expected to increase from 4.8 billion in 1985, to 8.2 billion by 2025. More than 90 per cent of this increase is expected to occur in these developing regions. The view of the World Commission, therefore, is that 'the challenge now is to quickly lower population growth rates, especially in regions such as Africa, where these rates are increasing' (ibid., p. 56). This can be brought about by industrialized and developing countries both helping to create the preconditions for economic growth in these regions, since 'almost any activity that increases well-being and security lessens people's desires to have more children than they and national ecosystems can support' (ibid., p. 98). It is stipulated, however, that this growth should be of benefit to the majority (ibid., p. 106). Other more concrete measures suggested are that 'the development of smaller urban centres needs to be encouraged to reduce pressures in large cities' (ibid., p. 57) which are now growing at a much faster rate than the authorities can cope with. Another proposal is that concerned governments should develop 'long-term, multifaceted population policies and a campaign to pursue broad demographic goals: to strengthen social, cultural, and economic motivations for family planning, and to provide to all who want them the education, contraceptives, and services required' (ibid., p. 11). Another measure is to improve the health and education of women in particular so that 'fertility rates fall as women's employment opportunities outside the home and farm, their access to education, and their age at marriage all rise' (ibid., p. 106).

What is the goal and what are the policy measures of the non-anthropocentric theories we have identified? Even allowing for the fact that biocentrists and ecocentrists might argue somewhat differently, it is hard to imagine that advocates of these theories would be satisfied with a population policy of seeking merely to limit population growth to a level compatible with the productive potential of ecosystems. As we have seen, William Aiken, for example, champions the very radical view that, from an ecocentric viewpoint, 'massive human diebacks would be good. It is our duty to cause them. It is our species' duty, relative to the whole, to eliminate 90 per cent of our numbers'.[3] Rolston writes that 'conserving the Earth is more important than having *more* people'. It is even 'more important than the

---

[3]   Aiken, cited in Callicott (1989e, p. 92).

needs, or even the welfare, of existing people' (Rolston, 1994a, p. 233). Arne Næss is critical of the lack of 'adequate policies regarding human population increase' (Næss, 1989, p. 23). As noted in our previous chapter, one of deep ecology's basic principles is that 'The flourishing of human life and cultures is compatible with a substantial decrease of the human population. The flourishing of non-human life requires such a decrease' (ibid., p. 29). Thus Naess's view is that promoting a decrease in population is not incompatible with human ethics and that our moral responsibilities towards other living beings demand such a reduction. How comprehensive should such a reduction in population be? Næss notes that a UN study posed the following question:

> 'Given the present world-wide industrial and agricultural capacity, technological development, and resource exploitation, how many people could be supported on earth today with the standard of living of the average American? The answer is just 500 million.' The authors think that 500 million would not result in a uniform, stagnant world and refer to the seventeenth century. Agreed, but the question raised refers only to humans. How about other living beings? If their life quality is not to be lowered through human dominance, for instance agriculture, are not 500 million too many? Or: are cultural diversity, development of the sciences and arts, and of course basic needs of humans not served by, let us say, 100 million? (Næss, 1989, pp. 140–41)

Thus Næss considers that a non-anthropocentric ethics entails a policy implying a drastic reduction in the number of people on earth during the next few generations. Edward Goldsmith puts the limit higher, insisting that an acceptable population would be about 3.5 billion human beings (Goldsmith, 1972, p. 57). Another suggestion is more regionally based. According to Andrew Dobson, S. Irvine and A. Ponton maintain that a suitable population for the United Kingdom would be half of what it is today, that is, about 30 million, while P. Bunyard and F. Morgan-Grenvill opt instead for a figure of 55 million on condition that vegetarianism is accepted (cf. Dobson, 1997, p. 93).

Thus non-anthropocentrists have no agreed answer to the question of optimal human population. This is partly because the answer depends more directly on considerations in human ethics than on anything specific to environmental ethics: should we seek to maximize the number of people at the cost of a minimal standard of living or strive to reduce the number of people for the sake of a high living standard? It is also crucial whether animals and plants are accorded the same value as human beings or whether such a principle of species impartiality is rejected, that is, whether the strong or weak versions of either biocentrism or ecocentrism are accepted. What I have tried to show is that biocentrism and ecocentrism of whatever type assign to animals, plants or ecological wholes (such as species and ecosystems) such a high value that a limitation upon the number of people becomes obligatory. In their view, we have unjustly encroached upon other living beings' living space by allowing unrestrained human population increase and therefore have a responsibility both to limit the spread of our own species and – as we shall see – to restore areas of land which we have commandeered.

Hence a non-anthropocentric ethic does not lead, like the ethic of sustainable development, to a policy implying *stabilization* of the human population, but to one requiring *reduction* (even perhaps a significant reduction) in the number of people. Intergenerational anthropocentrism issues in a policy of stabilization, whereas ecocentrism and biocentrism give rise to a reductionist one by requiring that *the population size should decrease to a level compatible with the well-being of other living beings or with the integrity (or dignity) of species and ecosystems.*

Advocates of biocentrism or ecocentrism do not directly suggest any concrete strategies for carrying out such a policy. Naess, for example, merely stresses that the measures should not be limited to developing countries and that the term 'reduce' must not lead us to think of the genocidal programmes of the Hitler kind. It is to be expected that the programme will take several generations to carry out (Næss, 1989, pp. 30, 140–41; 1997, p. 67).

As we have seen, the population policy of the World Commission neither suggests directly compulsory measures nor does it seek to introduce economic controls to promote more sustainable population increases and gradual stabilization. The question, however, is whether biocentrism and ecocentrism – in at least their stronger forms – do not imply such measures. Consider a country with just two population groups, *P* and *S*, where the individuals of each group are assigned the same moral standing and hence the same basic human rights. Assume also that the increase in population of *P* reaches such proportions as to result directly or indirectly in individuals in *S* being killed, exposed to suffering or forced into exile. In such a situation an ethic affirming the equal rights of all human beings entails not only the introduction of economic controls but also that legal prohibitions and ordinances should be introduced to regulate *P*'s population and thus prevent these adverse consequences for *S*. The example is taken from human ethics but a biocentrist who thinks that animals have the same moral worth as humans could not reasonably argue otherwise. Thus respect for the integrity and right of self-determination of other living beings could result in legislation making it punishable for parents to produce more than a certain number of children: one child if one lives in an industrial country and no more than two or three if one lives in a developing country. Since it is an offence, except in special circumstances, to harm other people and still more to kill them, the same must reasonably be held to apply in regard to other living beings, *if* we think they have the same value as ourselves.

The weaker forms of biocentrism and ecocentrism tend to be more common and are certainly more politically viable. Even these forms of non-anthropocentric ethics are obliged to support measures, certainly less radical than those described above, but still going beyond the World Commission proposals. One example is provided by measures which directly seek to limit population by means of various economic controls. One possibility, in countries where there is a system of child allowances, would be to restrict such allowances to one or two children per family. If one agrees with Rolston that it can be more important to 'protect one million existing species than to bring into existence an additional one million persons', such a view must lead to more direct and comprehensive measures than those proposed by the World Commission (cf. Rolston, 1988, p. 138). Irvine and Ponton give more concrete examples of the type of measures which could be taken:

> There could be payments for periods of non-pregnancy and non-birth (a kind of no claims bonus); tax benefits for families with fewer than two children; sterilization bonuses; withdrawal of maternity and similar benefits after a second child; larger pensions for people with fewer than two children; free, easily available family planning; more funds for research into means of contraception, especially for men; an end to fertility research and treatment; a more realistic approach to abortion; the banning of surrogate motherhood and similar practices; and the promotion of equal opportunities for women in all areas of life. (Irvine and Ponton, 1988, p. 23)

All the same, it is up to biocentrists and ecocentrists in general to try to show more clearly what measures their environmental ethic entails with regard to population growth. It is at any rate clear that a non-anthropocentric ethic in general results in *reductionist policies* as opposed to the *stabilization policies* associated with an ethic of sustainable development. According to non-anthropocentrists, the World Commission is certainly right in claiming that our responsibility to future generations entails that we have a moral duty to take measures now for stabilizing population size at a level compatible with the productive capacity of ecosystems. However the Commission should also see that we have a further responsibility, namely a genuine moral responsibility to other living beings. This responsibility entails a moral duty to reduce the number of future men and women to a level compatible with respect for the well-being of these other living beings and the integrity of species and ecosystems. Biocentrists and ecocentrists are thus agreed that there are too many human beings, even if they have different views as to what a morally acceptable population size would be. According to them, we have illicitly trespassed upon the living space of other living beings by allowing an unrestrained increase in the human population.

The fact that the World Commission does not suggest any reduction in the size of the world's population, but only more limited and controlled growth, implies that *the solution to environmental problems* lies in an exploitation of renewable and non-renewable natural resources which is more efficient, more far-sighted and more equitable. This is further borne out by noting that the population question is touched on only very superficially in *Agenda 21*. For biocentrists, on the other hand, the fundamental aim of environmental management (that of devising a policy which is fair to all living beings) cannot reasonably be pursued without placing the population question at the very centre. Ecocentrists agree. The integrity, stability and beauty of the biotic community cannot be secured with less than people's conscious limitation on the number of children they have.[4]

---

4 Such a conclusion is fully consistent with the assertion in 'The Green Party Manifesto' (1994) that 'growth in human numbers is probably the greatest long-term threat to achieving ecological stability either locally or throughout the world' (quoted in Dobson, 1997, p. 92).

Wilderness Preservation Policies

Closely related to the population problem is the question of how much of nature should be left undisturbed. If we allow a continued increase in human population, natural areas which remain unexploited will need to be turned into agricultural and forestry land in order to meet the increased population's need for food, shelter and other necessities. Thus, even though an anthropocentric population policy requires that population size and growth does not go beyond the productive potentials of ecosystems, we are left with the question of how many such ecosystems we may transform from wilderness into areas of productive agriculture and forestry. Analogously, even if biocentrists and ecocentrists propose a general population policy requiring a successive reduction in population, they still must answer the question of how much land human beings may reasonably use, without setting aside their moral responsibility towards other living beings, species and ecosystems.

The protection of the wilderness is not treated separately by the World Commission or the authors of *Agenda 21*, but the question often arises indirectly through a discussion of the need to safeguard the earth's natural resources as well as its biological diversity. In other words, the question of how much of nature should be left undisturbed is seen in the light of the anthropocentric goal of preserving and exploiting natural resources efficiently and far-sightedly so as to satisfy the needs of present and future generations of human beings. How much wilderness is to be preserved in order to satisfy mankind's present and future needs? The World Commission reports that protected areas comprise at present around 4 per cent of the earth's total land surface (World Commission, 1987, p. 147). It notes further that, since 1970, the total area protected has increased by 80 per cent. But, according to the Commission, experts agree that the area of such protected regions would need to increase threefold if a representative selection from the earth's ecosystems is to be preserved for future human beings. The Commission concludes that there is 'still time to save species and their ecosystems. ... Our failure to do so will not be forgiven by future generations' (ibid., p. 166).

Nonetheless, it is not completely clear whether the World Commission means that it is our moral duty to future generations to try to ensure that around 12 per cent of the land surface is left untouched, or if they merely consider that this is desirable rather than obligatory. It is clear that 'the network of protected areas that the world will need in the future must include much larger areas brought under some degree of protection' than is currently the case (ibid., p. 13). More concretely the Commission wishes to increase substantially the present almost non-existent protection of the tropical rain forests: 'Many experts suggest that at least 20 per cent of tropical forests should be protected, but to date well under 5 per cent has been afforded protection of any sort – and many of the tropical forest parks exist only on paper' (ibid., p. 152). The Commission thinks, however, that perhaps even this 20 per cent is not enough since it depends upon what happens to the remaining 80 per cent. They note: 'In Amazonia, if as much as half the forest were to be safeguarded in some way or another but the other half were to be eliminated or severely disrupted, there might well not be enough moisture in the Amazonian ecosystem to keep the remaining forest moist' (ibid.).

The rain forests are in particular need of preservation since they form the habitat of at least a quarter – perhaps even a third – of all the earth's animal and plant species. Loss of these species deprives present and future generations of important genetic material, since scientists have investigated in detail only 1 per cent of the earth's plant species and even less of its animal species. The view of the World Commission is that, 'if nations can ensure the survival of species, the world can look forward to new and improved foods, new drugs and medicines, and new raw materials for industry' (ibid., p. 147). The preservation of protected areas and hence of biological diversity is a basic requirement for long-term sustainable development. Thus according to *Agenda 21*, 'the current decline in biodiversity ... represents a serious threat to human development' (*Agenda 21*, 15.2). But both *Our Common Future* and *Agenda 21* emphasize that, besides these commercial and scientific arguments, there are cultural, aesthetic and spiritual reasons for keeping some natural areas and their inhabitants undisturbed, even if these reasons are not spelled out.

A question we now have to ask is whether biocentrists and ecocentrists can agree with supporters of sustainable development as to how large a part of nature should be left untouched. Do the various environmental ethical theories all support a similar wilderness policy? Another important question, to be discussed in the following section, is whether an anthropocentric system of values can really give full protection to the pristine ecosystems and species concerned. If, for example, we wish to preserve between 5 per cent and 12 per cent of the earth's natural ecosystems, does the argument put forward in *Our Common Future* and in *Agenda 21* that these land areas have a high instrumental value, suffice?

Let us turn, however, to the question of the proportion of land to be left unexploited. It is clear that advocates of sustainable development think it is our moral duty to future generations not to exploit all of the earth's land. What is unclear is how large these unexploited natural areas should be. Should they make up 4 per cent or perhaps even as much as 12 per cent of the earth's total land surface? The answer is closely connected to the principle of intergenerational justice which we consider is entailed by the notion of sustainable development.[5]

If we accept the *weak principle of intergenerational justice* which entails that we are morally obliged to use natural resources in such a way that future generations will also be able to satisfy their basic needs, 4 per cent seems sufficient. Presumably, an even lower level would be acceptable, since this principle states only that we are morally obliged not to endanger the capacity of future generations to attain at least a minimal standard in regard to food, water, shelter, energy, health care and education.

The *strong principle of intergenerational justice*, on the other hand, specifies that future generations have the same right in principle to the earth's resources as we have. It is therefore our moral duty to use the earth's resources in such a way that

---

[5] Cf. Chapter 3, pp. 45–8.

future generations can be expected to attain a standard of living equal to our own. If they have the same right in principle to the earth's resources then we are surely obliged to make sure that they have access to at least a representative selection of the earth's ecosystems. According to this strong principle, moral consideration towards future generations would require us to treat maybe as much as 12 per cent of the earth's land surface as strictly protected areas.[6]

Does acceptance of a biocentric or ecocentric environmental value system lead to different conclusions regarding the desirable extent of unexploited land? We can begin with weak ecocentrism, since it appears rather close to intergenerational anthropocentrism on this issue. As we have seen, Rolston holds that we have a duty to leave at least those remaining uncultivated lands and ecosystems untouched (the *principle of wildlife preservation*).[7] He estimates that these areas amount to about 5 per cent of the land surface. He thus reckons on a much lower figure than the World Commission's.[8] However, since he believes that we have no right to exploit more land areas than we do already, we can accept the Commission's 12 per cent without any essential modification to Rolston's conclusions. *If* anthropocentrists accept the strong principle of intergenerational justice, intergenerational anthropocentrism and weak ecocentrism will result in the same policy for uncultivated land, namely that *we should try to ensure that about 12 per cent of the land surface is left untouched.* Thus, in the short run, these environmental ethical theories are indistinguishable in practice as far as this issue is concerned.

Note, however, that this is not the case in the long run. The principal argument advanced by proponents of sustainable development, in claiming that we have a duty to protect these land areas, is that their exploitation deprives future generations of important genetic material. These ecosystems make up a resource base which *we* must preserve intact for coming generations. But such areas of wilderness can only supply important genetic material for future human beings if one assumes that *the latter,* unlike us, have a right to use them. Thus nothing prevents human beings in the future from using much more than 88 per cent of land, especially if we accept a continued increase in population.

The ecocentric standpoint, in contrast, is that even if such areas of wilderness contain important genetic material, people do not have the right to exploit them, either now or in the future. While anthropocentrists want to protect nature *for* human beings, ecocentrists (and even other non-anthropocentrists) intend to

---

[6] The question is actually more complicated than this. Ecosystems and species are certainly examples of renewable resources, but if certain natural ecosystems or species are wiped out, the same reasoning we employed earlier in connection with the use of non-renewable resources for fossil fuel will apply (Cf. Chapter 3). When we consume non-renewable natural resources, succeeding generations are denied the option of using these resources themselves. Although we cannot directly compensate them for this loss, according to the strong principle of intergenerational justice we must compensate them in some way or other. We can do this through developing substitute products ensuring that succeeding generations can be expected to retain a quality of life like our own. Wiping out a renewable natural resource is therefore permissible where we can develop an acceptable replacement.

[7] Cf. Chapter 4, p. 93.

[8] A possible explanation is that Rolston's concept of wilderness is more restrictive than that of the World Commission.

protect nature *against* humans beings. For an ecocentrist, as we saw, it is important to distinguish between natural resources for future consumption and *preserving* nature from both present and future consumption. We should leave these protected land areas untouched, irrespective of the profit present or future generations might gain from them.

Thus the anthropocentrist's and the weak ecocentrist's policy for preserving wilderness are not in fact the same. The anthropocentric policy is that we should try to ensure that about 12 per cent of the land be left untouched *for future human generations*, while the weak ecocentrist says we should try to ensure that about 12 per cent of the land be left untouched *for plants and animals*. This policy, according to ecocentrists, entails application of the *principle of restitutive justice towards ecosystems* (namely, that we have a duty to recompense ecosystems whenever we have treated them in a morally unacceptable way). This principle of restitutive justice would come into play in situations where land which is still unexploited were to be damaged or threatened by present or future generations. In short, there seems to be agreement over policy between anthropocentrists and weak ecocentrists regarding protected areas in the short term, but disagreement about the long term.

A strong ecocentric viewpoint, on the other hand, is saliently different from anthropocentrism even in the short term. According to strong ecocentrism, it is the well-being of the biotic community and not of the human community which should be the main concern of environmental management. This form of environmental ethics radically downgrades the human species to being merely one among many members of the biotic community. This implies that, when human interests conflict with the integrity of ecosystems, the latter carries much more weight in the eyes of an advocate of strong ecocentrism than of someone embracing weak ecocentrism. Strong ecocentrism is therefore assumed to contain not only a principle of wildlife preservation but also a *principle of wildlife restoration*, namely that we have a duty to try to rehabilitate natural areas which, viewed ecologically, can still be restored to their original state.[9] It is unclear how far we are obliged to carry out such a transformation of natural areas which we have already settled or how successfully this can be done. However, it may be reasonably assumed that, in addition to the earth's 12 per cent of genuine wilderness, a further 5–15 per cent could be restored in accordance with this principle of wildlife restoration.

Thus strong ecocentrism, like anthropocentrism and weak ecocentrism, supports a *policy of preservation*, but in addition it also supports a *comprehensive policy of restoration*. Nor need one expect this policy to demand wide-ranging active human intervention in natural processes. Given a proposed policy which implies a substantial reduction in future human population, nature herself can be expected to take care of much of this restorative work.

Biocentrists tend as a rule to focus less on unexploited areas or natural ecosystems than on the individual organisms to be found in such areas. Environmental management, at least for advocates of strong and animal rights biocentrism, is primarily about the need to 'protect wild animals from those who

---

[9] Cf. Chapter 4, p. 96.

would violate their rights – namely, sport hunters and trappers, commercial developers who destroy or despoil their natural habitat in the name of economical interest, and the like. *It is, in short, human wrongs that need managing, not the "crop" of animals'* (Regan, 1983, p. 357). Regan thinks that caring for the wilderness should in the first place be a matter of leaving the animals in peace, allowing these 'other nations' to live their own lives (Regan 1983, p. 357). Neither Regan nor any of the other biocentrists studied here, however, have explicitly dealt with the question of which areas members of these other nations should rightfully possess.

Let us see, however, if we can devise a reasonable biocentric policy for determining the extent of such wilderness. We can begin with the most radical form of biocentrism, namely strong biocentrism, the advocates of which, as we have seen, start from a *principle of species impartiality*. The idea of the superiority of human life *vis à vis* non-human life, in other words, of a hierarchical view of nature, is rejected. The principle states that, since all life is of equal worth, human beings may not rightfully promote their own good at the cost of the good of any other organisms, providing that no considerations (such as a direct threat to human life) which outweigh this intervene. When weighing human interests against the interests of other living beings, we must try to be impartial if we want to act rightly. In other words, it seems quite obvious that a division of the earth giving human beings a right to use and decide over 88 per cent of it, while other animals or plants have only the right to use and decide over 12 per cent is *species-partial* and therefore unjust. This is so even though other living beings may also live, on our terms of course, on large parts of 'our' land area. Perhaps the land area which 500 million people would need for a life of good quality should suffice for us.

Weak biocentrism, on the other hand, ascribes a higher intrinsic value to human than to other living beings. But, as it is unclear how much higher this value is thought to be, it is impossible to formulate unambiguously a weak biocentric policy for determining the total extent of the wilderness. In fact, we risk at least a partial misunderstanding of biocentrism by asking its advocates this type of question. We can see why this is so if we try to conduct a parallel discussion within human ethics. Thus, if one wishes to emphasize that all human beings are of equal worth, the important question is not necessarily that of how much land area to allot to the different human nationalities. Rather, it is that of how people should treat one another wherever they live or meet. A biocentrist, therefore, who proclaims the rights or intrinsic value of animals is not especially interested in drawing boundaries between the human and 'other nations'. Biocentrists have no objections in principle to human beings and animals living together over the whole surface of the earth. The important question, instead, is how one *treats* animals (and possibly plants). What form should intercourse between these various species take? Hence a policy concerning the *human treatment of domestic and wild animals* will lie at the centre of biocentric environmental management.

Ecocentric talk about moral consideration for ecological wholes such as species and ecosystems is rejected by biocentrists, or else reduced to the consideration which is to be shown to individual organisms forming part of these species and ecosystems. Whereas the treatment of ecosystems and species is an important question for ecocentrists, the important thing for biocentrists is how individual animals (and plants) are treated, whether they are to be found in wild or settled areas. So advocates of weak and animal rights biocentrism, at least, should in principle be able to approve an anthropocentric policy for unexploited areas implying that 12 per cent of land should be preserved in its natural state. Of more concrete significance for environmental management, however, are the different programmes, relating to the treatment and use of animals within both wild and productive agricultural and forestry areas, which are supported by biocentrism.

Wilderness Management Policies

Having considered policy differences concerning how much wilderness should be preserved, we move on to the question whether advocates of different environmental ethical theories draw correspondingly different conclusions as to how these wilderness areas should be administered. Anthropocentrists, biocentrists and ecocentrists all value 'unspoiled' natural areas, but for different reasons. Yet these natural areas are threatened, due to the prevalence of human beings and their way of life. Wilderness adminstrators have tried to restore some of these natural areas through intervention of various kinds, so that the autonomous functions of ecosystems can be sustained. This has taken place through such measures as reintroducing wolves or bears in areas from which they had previously been rooted out through hunting. Our question now is whether our choice of environmental ethics has any effect on the type of environmental policies adopted.

A difference arises directly, of course, when questions regarding hunting and fishing in the wilderness are mooted. None of the biocentric theories presented support a categorical rejection of hunting or fishing as such. Hunting and fishing are morally permissible in situations where people, such as Eskimos, cannot obtain food or other vital necessities in any other way. But this does not prevent a biocentrist such as Regan from maintaining that recognition of animal rights implies the total abolition of recreational or commercial hunting and trapping. He points out that hunters act wrongly

> because they are parties to a practice that treats animals as if they were a naturally recurring renewable resource, the value of which is to be measured by, and managed by reference to, human recreational, gustatory, aesthetic, social and other interests ... but wild animals are not natural resources *here for us*. They have value apart from human interests, and their value is not reducible to their utility relative to our interests. (Regan, 1983, p. 356)

Taylor writes that, 'besides breaking the Rule of Fidelity, hunting, trapping, and fishing also, of course, involve gross violations of the Rules of Nonmaleficence and Noninterference' (Taylor, 1986, p. 183). People's intercourse with animals both wild and domestic should be guided in principle by the same basic ethical rules that ought to guide people's behaviour towards one another. Thus we have a *prima facie* duty not to cause damage or suffering to other living beings (the *rule of non-maleficence*), not to limit or violate the freedom of other living beings (the *rule of non-interference*) as well as not to mislead other living beings or abuse their confidence in us (the *rule of fidelity*). Under normal circumstances, hunting or fishing entail breaking all these ethical rules. Hence both strong and animal rights biocentrism lead to a policy for hunting and fishing whereby *no recreational or commercial hunting or fishing is allowed.*

In reality these biocentrists stand for a general 'hands off' policy regarding the management of the unexploited wilderness. Regan writes that we should 'let wildlife be. Wildlife management ought to be designed to protect wild animals against hunters, trappers and other moral agents' (Regan, 1983, p. 395). Taylor declares that the rule of non-interference implies that 'we must not try to manipulate, control, modify, or "manage" natural ecosystems or otherwise intervene in their normal functioning' (Taylor, 1986, p. 175).

If this environmental ethic were accepted in policy making, the existing management of wild areas would need to be basically rethought. Many common current measures aim at influencing in various ways, by active intervention, the distribution of animal species within a given area of wilderness. Measures are taken, for example, to root out animals that have gone wild simply because they do not belong to any of the species indigenous to a given area of wilderness. In the United States, this policy has been applied to prairie horses and pack-mules. Another example, which we discussed when presenting ecocentrism, concerned the handling of feral goats on San Clemente Island, off the Californian coast (Rolston, 1994a, p. 116). The US Fish and Wildlife Service put down almost 30 000 goats on that island in order to protect three plant species threatened with extinction and to hinder continued degradation of the island's ecosystem. Another type of measure often taken is to order local authorities to regulate a given breed of animal, for example moose or elk, by allowing hunters to shoot a given number each year, so that they will not threaten the spread of other species or the ecosystem in which they are found. But if the task of wildlife management is to 'defend wild animals in the possession of their rights, providing them with the opportunity to live their own life, by their own lights' then all measures like these must be condemned and given up (Regan, 1983, p. 357). They must be condemned and given up because we have a duty not to harm other living beings and not to limit or violate their freedom.

Even policy measures involving only the sterilization of animals (rather than harming or killing them) or their transfer from one area to another are generally incompatible with strong or animal rights biocentrism, since the rights of these animals are thereby violated. Thus a not uncommon measure is to capture and move wolves, bears or tigers from one area of wilderness to another so as to increase the area of distribution of the species, secure its survival or promote biological diversity in the area concerned. This is questionable from the biocentric viewpoint since we cannot move other humans around in this way merely as fancy takes us. In the context of human ethics, we would not approve if, for example in Sweden, in a situation where the indigenous Lapps were threatened with extinction, the authorities forcibly moved some of the remaining families to another part of the country. Such a measure would imply a violation of the Laplanders' integrity, exhibiting lack of respect for their intrinsic value and right of self-determination. The same must consequently apply to all creatures having the same moral standing as ourselves, irrespective of the species they belong to. Similarly, solving the problem of prairie horses in the United States by sterilization or removal to certain clearly designated areas cannot be accepted by those biocentrists who assert that the horses have as much right to exist and be left in peace as human beings.

Capturing wild animals able to survive by themselves in a state of freedom and removing them to zoos is of course equally unacceptable. For these biocentrists, it is analogous to accepting that white people should exhibit Indians or Lapps in enclosures. Taylor writes that, 'with regard to individual organisms, ... [the rule of non-interference] requires us to refrain from capturing them and removing them from their natural habitats, *no matter how well we might then treat them*' (Taylor, 1986, p. 174).

Does biocentrism forbid all types of 'hands on' policies for the management of natural areas of wilderness? This seems at first sight to be the case. Taylor emphasizes:

> [the] general policy of nonintervention is a matter of disinterested principle. We may want to help certain species-populations because we like them or because they are beneficial to us. But the Rule of Noninterference requires that we put aside our personal likes and our human interests with reference to how we treat them. Our [the biocentrists'] respect for nature means that we acknowledge the sufficiency of the natural world to sustain its own proper order throughout the whole domain of life.This is diametrically opposed to the human-centered view of nature as a vast piece of property which we can use as we see fit. (Ibid., p. 177)

But Taylor himself indicates an exception. It is morally permissible (but not obligatory) to violate the rule of non-interference when we choose to help an injured animal, provided that we intend to set it free again as soon as possible (ibid., p. 174). Although he gives no explanation why, the situation can be seen as analogous to situations in human ethics where we have a right to help, say, an injured baby or a senile person despite the fact that this violates the rule of non-interference. Thus this rule is absolute neither in human ethics nor in environmental ethics. Another type of acceptable 'hands on' policy might be the following. In Sweden attempts have been made to prevent lakes and watercourses acidifying through the use of lime. The aim, according to the National Environment Protection Board, has been to 'bring about an environment where naturally occurring species can survive as a vigorous stock' (Naturvårdsverket, 1993, p. 244). It is calculated that through the use of lime, the total area of acidified lakes has shrunk to about 2 000 square kilometres, or somewhat less than half of what it was. A measure of this kind seems fully compatible with biocentrism, since it does not involve injury to other living beings (the rule of non-maleficence) or violation of their freedom (the rule of non-interference). Note, however, that this or similar measures are, according to Regan and Taylor, not morally obligatory. On their view we have no duty to do good to other living beings. There is no equivalence within environmental ethics to the rule of benevolence (in its weak or strong form) which is found within human ethics.

Many ecocentrists have severely criticized biocentrism for its general tendency to issue in a radical 'hands off' policy as regards management of natural wild areas. It has been important to me for this reason (among others), not simply to distinguish between two types of environmental ethics, namely anthropocentric and non-anthropocentric, as is more usually done. Callicott writes,

> Neither Singer's nor Regan's prototype of animal welfare ethics will also serve as environmental ethics. For one thing, neither provides moral standing for plants and all the many animals that may be neither sentient nor, more restrictively still, subjects of a life – let alone for the atmosphere and oceans, species and ecosystems. Moreover, concern for animal welfare, on the one hand, and concern for the larger environment, on the other, often lead to contradictory indications in practice and policy. Examples follow: Advocates of animal liberation and rights frequently oppose the extermination of feral animals competing with native wildlife and degrading plant communities on the public ranges; they characteristically demand an end to hunting and trapping, whether environmentally benign or necessary; and they may prefer to let endangered plant species become extinct, rather than save them by killing sentient or subject-of-a-life animal pets. (Callicott, 1995a, p. 678)

Biocentrists' basic mistake, according to Callicott, is their exclusive focus upon biological individuals and not upon ecological wholes such as species and ecosystems. Ecocentrism, in contrast, 'provides only "respect" for individual members of the biotic community, but "biotic rights" for species and, in the last analysis, "the integrity, beauty, and stability of the biotic community" is the measure of right and wrong actions affecting the environment' (Callicott, 1989d, p. 58). Thus our obligations towards species and ecosystems outweigh our respect for individual animals. It follows that it is morally permissible, perhaps even obligatory, to shoot wild horses, although sterilization or adoption is preferable. The elimination of feral goats on San Clemente Island can be similarly justified.

Rolston even sets up as a general ethical principle: '*Protect species over individuals.* Individuals can be replaced, but species cannot ... The well-being of plants at the species level outweighs the welfare of the goats at the individual level' (Rolston, 1994a, pp. 64–5). Since the species is accorded a higher moral value than its individual members, the ecocentrists can even approve a policy adjusting, for example, the elk population, if this promotes the survival of the species. Rolston writes, 'When we move to the level of species, we may kill individuals for the good of their kind', since what may be harmful for individual members can benefit the species as a whole (Rolston, 1994, p. 114). He concludes, 'The ecological ethic [ecocentrism], which kills in place, is really more advanced, harmonious with nature, than the animal-rights ethic [biocentrism], which kills no animal at all, in utter disharmony with the way the world is made' (ibid., p. 125). Since, ultimately, it is the good of the biotic community and not the good of individuals which environmental management should primarily seek to promote, a policy involving the removal of certain animals from one natural area to another so as to ensure biological diversity is compatible with an ecocentric ethic.

Two central value components of the ethic of sustainable development, identified in Chapter 3, are the principle of nature as a resource (nature should be exclusively viewed as a resource which we human beings have the right to use for our own ends) and the principle of intergenerational justice (we have moral obligations to future human generations). These, together with the thesis on limited natural resources and the thesis on nature's vulnerability, have generated a general anthropocentric policy regarding our use of nature: it should be efficient and far-sighted.[10] This principle of efficiency and far-sightedness should result in the following management directive: *animals and plants should be treated so that they can be used in as efficient and far-sighted a way as possible.* This implies that an anthropocentric ethic allows (a) that hunting and fishing may be pursued in open natural areas, on condition that there is no threat to the ecosystem's carrying capacity and the distribution and diversity of species, (b) that wild animals may be killed to protect endangered plants, if these plants are considered as having a higher instrumental value (for example, recreational or genetic value) than the animals, and (c) that wolves, bears or other animals may be moved from one area of wilderness to another when attempting to ensure the species' survival or to protect the autonomy of a particular ecosystem, given that the species or ecosystem can be accorded higher instrumental value than these individual animals.

Simplying somewhat, we could say that the more general choice between 'hands on' policies and 'hands off' policies is not for anthropocentrists, as it is for biocentrists, primarily an *ethical* choice (are we treating animals and plants fairly?), but an *ecological* choice (do we know enough about the effects of the measures we are taking to be able to decide with sufficient certainty whether they are useful and not harmful to the ecosystems and species concerned?). Finally, anthropocentrism and ecocentrism can often result in similar measures for managing areas of wilderness. This is because ecocentrists, unlike biocentrists, ascribe higher *intrinsic* value to species and ecosystems than to individual organisms, while anthropocentrists ascribe a higher *instrumental* value to species and ecosystems than to individual plants and animals. Thus, despite the failure of anthropocentrists and ecocentrists to agree about what has moral standing, there is a structurally similar assignation of value priority of biological wholes over biological individuals in these two forms of environmental ethics.

Policies Regarding Endangered Species

The preservation of endangered species is of course an important part of wilderness management, but, since such preservation extends also to species found in productive forest and agricultural areas or other types of settled land, I have chosen to discuss this question separately.

A decisive difference between environmental policy making based on biocentric values and policy making based on ecocentric values centres on *which* species' survival and well-being we primarily aim at ensuring. Regan makes clear

---

[10] Cf. Chapter 3 for discussion of these principles and theses.

the biocentric point of view in the following way: 'Species are not individuals, and ... [the biocentrists do] not recognize the moral rights of species to anything, including survival' (Regan, 1983, p. 359). So the reason why 'we ought to save the members of endangered species of animals is not because the species is endangered but because the individual animals have valid claims and thus rights against those who would destroy their natural habitat' (ibid., p. 360). Thus biocentrists support protection for the animals of endangered species, not because they are few in number but because 'they are equal in value to all who have inherent value, ourselves included, sharing with us the fundamental right to be treated with respect' (ibid., p. 360). Regan emphasizes this because he, *inter alia*, considers that the attempts made to save endangered species can create a wrong mentality which entertains the view that it is only morally wrong to harm or kill animals when these belong to an endangered species: otherwise it is acceptable. Moreover he thinks that both anthropocentrists and ecocentrists are often mistaken in their priorities. They place too little weight on animals which are 'subjects-of-a-life' (such as mammals) but too much weight on other forms of life. Regan thinks that it is rather the organisms which have a value equal to that of ourselves which should be given priority.

A biocentric policy of preserving species could thus be formulated as follows: *Preserve in the first instance the members of those endangered species which have intrinsic value or have the highest intrinsic value*, that is, sentient animals or, somewhat more restrictively, animals which are 'subjects-of-a-life'. If we are forced to choose between an endangered plant species and an endangered animal species we ought, therefore, to save the animal species. Regan also thinks that, if a situation arises in which we are forced to choose between either saving some individual animals having moral standing or some endangered species of plant, it is our moral duty to save these individual animals:

> If, in a prevention situation, we had to choose between saving the last two members of an endangered species or saving another individual who belonged to a species that was plentiful but whose death would be a greater prima facie harm to that individual than the harm that death would be to the two, then the rights view [Regan's biocentrism] requires that we save that individual. (Ibid., p. 359)

Regan is consistent on this point. We can compare it with the way anthropocentrists would have to choose in a similar situation. Assume a situation in which one has to choose between saving either an endangered plant or animal species or some individual human lives. Since anthropocentrists accord intrinsic value to other people, but only instrumental value to plants and animals, it follows that they should save the people.

We can now contrast the biocentric policy for preserving species (which is that we should in the first place preserve endangered species containing individual members having intrinsic value) with anthropocentric and ecocentric policies. We shall begin with the latter. Ecocentrists deny that all living beings (strong biocentrism) or all human beings and sentient animals (animal rights biocentrism) have equal value. Callicott asserts, as we have seen, that an ecocentric ethic will not accord to all members of the biotic community the same moral standing, claiming rather that these members' value depends on their significance for the community as a whole. He writes,

> the good of the community as a whole, serves as a standard for the assessment of the relative value and relative ordering of its constitutive parts and therefore provides a means of adjudicating the often mutually contradictory demands of the parts considered separately for *equal* consideration ... Animals of those species, which, like the honey bee, function in ways critically important to the economy of nature ... would be granted a greater claim to moral attention than psychologically more complex and sensitive ones, say, rabbits and voles, which seem to be plentiful, globally distributed, reproductively efficient, and only routinely integrated into the natural economy. (Callicott, 1989b, p. 25)

An ecocentrist such as Callicott, therefore, *contra* Regan, would give priority to endangered plants over non-endangered sentient animals. Even if these sentient animals were endangered, ecocentrists would not necessarily invest limited resources in saving them. Priority among endangered organisms would depend on their significance for the survival and well-being of the ecosystem concerned. Thus an ecocentric policy for preserving species would be that *we first of all should preserve endangered species which contribute to the survival and well-being of the ecosystems.*

Representatives of both strong and weak ecocentrism agree on this point. Rolston writes that the guidelines for preserving species ought to be '*Protect keystone species.* Species that play vital roles in the ecosystem ought to receive greater protection ... These can be big animals, such as predators ... like pumas and jaguars ... Or they can be invertebrates that are at the base of the food chain pyramids, like the plankton in the sea' (Rolston, 1994a, p. 62). Since whatever promotes the integrity, stability and beauty of the *biotic* community is morally right (Leopold's principle of integrity and stability) we should preserve in the first place the endangered species which contribute to the survival and well-being of ecosystems.

On the other hand, anthropocentrists maintain – if we retain the ecocentric terminology – that something is morally right if it now and in the future preserves the integrity, stability and beauty of the *human* community. Joel Feinberg clarifies the basic anthropocentric viewpoint, as follows: 'We have duties to protect threatened species, not duties to the species themselves as such, but rather duties to future human beings, duties derived from our house-keeping role as temporary inhabitants of this planet' (Feinberg, 1974, p. 56). Their more general principle of practical management, as we saw, is that animals and plants should be treated so that they can be used as efficiently and far-sightedly as possible, that is, so that the needs of future human generations can also be satisfied. Thus the Swedish National Environment Protection Board affirms, 'The maintenance of biological diversity presupposes that methods of cultivation, production and consumption be so developed that the biological resources such as genes, species and ecosystems represent can be used prudently so as to be permanently available without continued losses' (Naturvårdsverket,

1993, p. 31). The authors both of the World Commission's report and of *Agenda 21* are agreed that the preservation of endangered species and of biological diversity is important. These documents led also to the drawing up of a convention on biological diversity at the 1992 Rio Conference, which was signed by 157 countries. It contains the following statement:

> The objectives of this Convention, to be pursued in accordance with its relevant provisions, are the conservation of biological diversity, the sustainable use of its components and the fair and equitable sharing of the benefits arising out of the utilization of genetic resources, including by appropriate access to genetic resources and by appropriate transfer of relevant technologies, taking into account all rights over those resources and technologies, and by appropriate funding. (*Convention on Biological Diversity*, 1992, article 1)

Even though it is accepted in the Convention that countries have a sovereign right to exploit their own natural resources (article 3) there is agreement about the need to preserve endangered species and to restore ecosystems by setting up a system of protected areas where special measures can be taken to preserve biological diversity (article 8). This biological diversity is to be preserved in both areas of wilderness and areas of human settlement, that is, in all areas, irrespective of the degree of human dominance. Thus the Convention deals with both wild and domesticated species. The greatest attention is to be accorded to those genes, species and ecosystems needing 'urgent conservation measures and to those which offer the greatest potential for sustainable use' (*Convention on Biological Diversity*, 1992, article 7). Regarding species, this implies conserving those species which are 'threatened; wild relatives of domesticated or cultivated species; of medicinal, agricultural or other economic value; or social, scientific or cultural importance; or importance for research into the conservation and sustainable use of biological diversity, such as indicator species' (ibid., Appendix 1).

A clearer picture of the priorities assigned to these different values is lacking. This is no great problem when the species concerned both need 'urgent conservation measures' and 'offer the greatest potential for sustainable use'. But which is to have priority if these two criteria conflict with each other? Should we bother or, rather, feel morally obliged, to set aside means for conserving species for which urgent measures are needed but which have little or no potential use (in other words which possess at most a very low value in economic, cultural or scientific terms)? To the extent that the UN Convention on Biological Diversity rests on anthropocentric values, the answer seems obvious:[11] An anthropocentric policy for

---

[11] The convention begins, however, with the following words: 'Conscious of the intrinsic value of biological diversity and of the ecological, genetic, social, economic, scientific, educational, cultural, recreational and aesthetic values of biological diversity and its components' (*Convention on Biological Diversity*, 1992, Foreword). Thus the signatory countries would in addition seem to consider that biological diversity, besides its resource or instrumental value, has also an intrinsic value. But this declaration has no relevance at all to the succeeding argument since it implies no specific restrictions upon human behaviour. Hence a reasonable interpretation of it might be that those parties to the document either fail to understand what it means to ascribe intrinsic value to something or that, despite the declaration, they remain committed to an anthropocentric value system.

preserving species means that *we ought first to preserve those endangered species which constitute a resource for present and future human generations; that is, those species which are of high instrumental value.*

We should give highest priority to those endangered species which are judged as of greatest use for human beings now and in the future. Thus the endangered species which should primarily be preserved are those with the highest recreational, cultural, scientific and economic value. Anthropocentrists can, however, have different notions among themselves as to which of these instrumental values are the most important in possible situations of conflict. The emphasis upon ecosystems' productive potential among advocates of sustainable development suggests that it is probable, though not certain, that they would often accept the same priorities as ecocentrists, for example primarily conserving keystone species or other species of central importance for the survival and well-being of ecosystems.

The disquiet of ecocentrists regarding a policy of species preservation having an anthropocentric formulation does not primarily centre upon whether anthropocentrists have the right priorities in a situation when they have to choose which of a group of endangered plant or animal species is to be preserved: for example, keystone species or sentient animals. The source of their disquiet is rather (a) that such a policy does not protect sufficiently many of the endangered plants and animals, and (b) that the priorities of the anthropocentrists are misguided when they are forced to choose between protecting endangered species and promoting other human interests such as building museums, sports facilities and motorways or providing for people in poverty.

Robyn Eckersley thinks that 'if we restrict our perspective to a human welfare ecology perspective [anthropocentrism] we can provide no protection to those species that are of no present or potential use or interest to humankind' (Eckersley, 1992, p. 38). Rolston shares Eckersley's view. He writes that 'if all ninety-three plants now on the endangered species list [in 1988 in the United States] disappeared, it is doubtful that the ecosystems involved would measurably shift their stability. Few cases can be cited where the removal of a rare species damaged an ecosystem' (Rolston, 1988, p. 130). Thus, in the case of many endangered species, their existence or non-existence lacks any directly decisive significance for the survival of an ecosystem as a whole.

Nor is it the case, in Rolston's view, that every endangered species has significant scientific, cultural or economic value:

> Let's be frank. A substantial number of endangered species have no resource value. Beggar's ticks (*Bidens* spp.), with their stick-tight seeds, are a common nuisance through much of the United States. One species, tidal shore beggar's tick (*Bidens bidentoides*), which differs little from the others in appearance, is increasingly endangered. It seems unlikely that it is either a rivet or potential resource. (Ibid., p. 130)

If Rolston is right – and this is a scientific rather than an ethical question – it looks as if ecocentrism offers more comprehensive protection to endangered animal and plant species than does anthropocentrism. It can cost too much, quite simply, to give priority to endangered species judged to have at most very low instrumental value. This is particularly so when they are weighed against other things which also have instrumental value for human beings. In reality, there is no moral obligation, from an anthropocentric perspective, to try to preserve species which cannot be seen as being of use to human beings.

Although ecocentrists think that the consumption of individual animals and plants can be routinely justified, this does not apply to the extinction of species. It does not apply because species, unlike their individual members, are accorded a very high moral significance. It is true that, for a weak ecocentrist such as Rolston, 'the obligation to protect humans trumps the obligation to protect *individual* animals and plants, short of extenuating circumstances and even if critical animal and plant goods sometimes outweigh nonbasic human goods. But it does not follow that the obligation to protect one or even a group of humans trumps the obligation to protect whole *species*' (ibid., p. 138). Any extinction of species, for Rolston, is not merely a matter of killing, but 'a kind of superkilling' and a 'shutdown of the life stream is the most destructive event possible' (ibid., pp. 144–5).

This brings us to the second reservation ecocentrists have concerning an anthropocentrically based policy towards endangered species. It is an objection which ecocentrists believe applies to anthropocentric management in general. In his reply to Norton's thesis that an environmental policy based on ecocentrism is no different from one based on anthropocentrism, Callicott writes,

> If all environmental values are anthropocentric and instrumental, then they have to compete head-to-head with the economic values derived from converting rain forest to lumber and pulp, savannahs to cattle pasture, and so on. Environmentalists, in other words, must show that preserving biological diversity is of greater instrumental value to present and future generations than lucrative timber extraction, agricultural conversion, hydroelectric empoundment, mining, and so on. For this simple reason, a persuasive philosophical case for the intrinsic value of nonhuman natural entities and nature as a whole would make a huge practical difference. (Callicott, 1995b, p. 22)

The problem is thus not simply that anthropocentrism cannot offer any protection to species which have no potential use (that is, resource value); it is also that anthropocentrists who want to preserve biological diversity must show that the instrumental value thereby attained is *higher* than the value which a transformation of the natural habitats of these species into, for example, productive forest and agricultural land would accomplish. The need to preserve endangered species can end up being dismissed when the instrumental value of these species is unfavourably compared to the instrumental value for present and future human generations of other, competing resources. As Joseph R. Des Jardins points out, this means that

> an environmental ethics that is based solely on the instrumental value of the environment may prove unstable. As human interests and needs change, so too would human uses of the environment. The instrumental value of the Colorado River as a water and hydroelectric power source for southern California will

quickly override its instrumental value as a scenic wilderness or recreation area. Emphasizing only the instrumental value of nature effectively means that the environment is held hostage by the interests and needs of humans, and it immediately evokes the necessity to make tradeoffs among competing human interests. (Des Jardins, 1997, p. 129)

Even endangered species having a high instrumental value are forced to compete with other things to which we human beings assign a resource value. *Ceteris paribus*, the damming of a river in order to supply energy to a hydroelectric power station which can provide present and future generations with energy will outweigh in the judgment of anthropocentrists the potential genetic or recreational value which some animal or plant species are judged to have, particularly if these species can be preserved artificially in scientific laboratories, animal parks or zoos. The destruction of the more or less unique ecosystems containing these species is an unhappy but acceptable loss. Whatever has the highest instrumental value should naturally have priority. Accordingly, the Swedish National Environment Protection Board declares that the environmental goals which they promote 'build upon judgements as to what will be of use for the whole of society' (Naturvårdsverket, 1997, p. 13). That is to say, whatever has the highest instrumental value for our society should have priority.

However, if we grant that these species have an intrinsic value, the order of priorities becomes quite different. As we saw at the beginning of this chapter, Callicott asserts that such a fundamental change in our values makes as much practical difference in the environmental arena as the general acceptance of each person's intrinsic value has had in the social arena (Callicott, 1995b, p. 24). This analogy is worth developing in order to be able to assess ecocentrism's practical relevance.

Consider a slaveowner with a number of slaves whom he uses as labourers on his plantation. Suppose in addition that he does not treat these slaves especially well. An acquaintance of the slaveowner sees this and tells him that he also has moral responsibilities towards his heirs. Consequently, he should use his slaves more far-sightedly and not use them so intensively, so that their 'carrying capacity' is not threatened. The slaveowner sees that his friend is right and begins to use his slaves with more of a view to the longer term. Among other things, he provides better dwellings for them and gives them more nourishing food. Quite simply, he takes better care of this part of his property. But he has, of course, other things which also take up his concern, such as good crops, well maintained buildings, a modern and well functioning assortment of machines. He also wants to treat himself and his family to a couple of holidays abroad each year. All this has high instrumental value for him.

His daughter, however, considers that the slaves have the highest instrumental value. So, as soon as any slave is seriously hurt or sick, she tries to set aside resources for 'rehabilitating' such a slave. Her father agrees that the slaves have a high instrumental value, but his resources are limited and there are other things which are also of value for him. It is his opinion that, instead of saving all the slaves, it is better to set aside resources only for the care of younger slaves and to use the rest of the capital for buying a new tractor. He tells his daughter that sometimes one has to choose, and even if the older slaves are also of value to him, a new tractor is even more valuable. If the daughter still wants to 'preserve' the older slaves, she must prove – if she can – that these slaves, though they do not perhaps have higher instrumental value than a tractor, could nonetheless, if they were healthy, generate a higher value through their work than, for example, the recreational value generated by the families' annual holidays.

The ecocentrists' point here is that if the daughter could insist instead upon these slaves having an intrinsic value apart from their use to her father then the negotiating situation would change drastically. She would no longer need to be able to prove the slaves' usefulness in order to motivate setting aside resources for their maintenance and well-being. It would suffice to make her father aware of their intrinsic value (which would presumably also lead him to emancipate them). This applies particularly to a situation in which it is the slaveowner's own behaviour and directives which caused these people to suffer.

The causal connection is important, since, to return to environmental ethics, an acceptance of ecocentrism does not entail any moral responsibility to benefit species. We have no duty within environmental ethics (though we may still have a duty within human ethics) to seek to protect animal or plant species from natural extinction. As we have seen, Rolston writes,

> humans have no duty of benevolence to preserve rare species from natural extinction, although they may have a duty to other humans to save such species as resources or museum pieces. No species has a 'right to life' apart from the continued existence of the ecosystem with which it cofits. But humans do have a duty of nonmaleficence to avoid artificial extinction, which superkills the species in the formative process in which it stands. This prima facie duty can on occasion be overridden: for example with the extinction of ... the smallpox virus... But a prima facie duty stands nevertheless. (Rolston, 1988, p. 155)

If we advocate an ecocentric policy programme then what I earlier called the *principle of non-maleficence towards other species* ought to guide our actions. The principle means that we have a duty to treat animal and plant species in such a way that they are not threatened with extinction but can be preserved in properly functioning ecosystems. Thus ecocentrism offers no protection to those plant or animal species threatened with natural extinction; it only offers protection to species threatened as a consequence of human activities.

According to the biologist Edward O. Wilson, somewhere between 4 000 and 6 000 species a year become extinct and the speed of this extinction is about ten thousand times greater than it would be if humanity did not exist. He writes that, if we continue to live as we do today, only a tenth of the plant and animal species now in existence will survive until the end of the present millennium (Wilson, 1992). Our lifestyle, therefore, brings us into conflict with the principle of non-maleficence to other species and so we arrive at a situation where the *principle of restitutive justice to species* becomes applicable. This principle means we have a duty to compensate species (since they have intrinsic value or moral standing) when we have treated them in a morally unacceptable way.

It is because we cause harm to other species that we have a moral duty to devise an environmental policy which is able to preserve endangered species and, if need be, rehabilitate them. Thus there is normally no need for discussion as to whether these species have any instrumental value or, if they have, how their value compares with other material assets having an instrumental value for us. Similarly, I cannot say, if I harm another person, that I would rather invest my money in building a larger house for myself (since this has higher instrumental value for me) than pay the hospital costs of the person I have injured. When I have caused harm to another person, what is of instrumental value to me is of little weight compared to the person's intrinsic value.

Thus accepting the intrinsic value of species entails a shift in the burden of proof, as Warwick Fox points out. He writes that 'anyone who wants to interfere with any entity that is intrinsically valuable is morally obliged to be able to offer a sufficient justification for their actions. Thus recognizing the intrinsic value of the nonhuman world shifts the onus of justification from the person who wants to protect the nonhuman world to the person who wants to interfere with it – and that, in itself, represents a fundamental shift in the terms of environmental debate and decision making.'[12]

According to the ecocentrists it is therefore reasonable to believe either (a) that the anthropocentric values, upon which the sustainable development policy for preserving species is based, do not in reality protect all or even the majority of endangered species, or (b) that it is unable to supply convincing arguments for giving priority to setting aside resources for preserving all or even the majority of endangered species, in a situation where there is competition from other things which we human beings value instrumentally.

Ecocentrists, we have seen, accord to species and ecosystems such a high value that in certain contexts it counts for more than the value of human beings. This applies particularly to strong ecocentrists, but even a weak ecocentrist like Rolston can insist on such a view.[13] In certain situations they are prepared to grant a higher moral worth to the integrity of species and ecosystems than to the satisfaction of even the basic needs of certain individual human beings. This type of value conflict is unusual in countries such as Sweden, though it is common in many developing countries. The greatest number of animal and plant species are found in the rain forest areas and it is there that the problem of endangered species is most acute. At the same time, many human beings in these areas are very poor and there is a high rate of population increase. Dealing with this situation is thus a major challenge for decision makers. What comes first? Should we give people food or save endangered species? How are we to judge the priorities when the resources are limited?

---

[12] Fox, cited in Callicott (1995b, p. 23).

[13] 'the obligation to protect humans trumps the obligation to protect *individual* animals and plants, short of extenuating circumstances and even if critical animal and plant goods sometimes outweigh nonbasic human goods. But it does not follow that the obligation to protect one or even a group of humans trumps the obligation to protect whole *species*' (Rolston, 1988, p. 138).

There seems to be a conflict on this point between ecocentrism and anthropocentrism. Rolston asks, 'Ought we to save nature if this results in people going hungry? In people dying? Regrettably, sometimes, the answer is yes' (Rolston, 1997, p. 220). He emphasizes, however, that our being compelled today to this type of choice results from social injustices. But the fact remains that 'human rights to development, even by those who are poor, though they are to be taken quite seriously, are not always and everywhere absolute, but have to be weighed against all the other values at stake' (Rolston, 1994a, p. 154). In some areas, for example, where many endangered species are to be found or, more generally, where 'the natural values at stake are quite high ... there will be no development ... even if people there remain in the relative poverty of many centuries, or even if, with escalating populations, they become more poor' (Rolston, 1997, p. 222). The integrity of endangered species, viewed from a moral point of view, counts for more than the integrity of these individual human beings.[14]

In the *Rio Declaration*, on the other hand, we can read that 'Human beings are at the centre of concerns for sustainable development' (Principle 1) and the World Commission insists that people's 'well-being is the ultimate goal of all environment and development policies' (World Commission, 1987, p. xiv). It is consistent with the ethic of sustainable development, therefore, that as long as the productive potential of ecosystems is not seriously threatened we ought to give higher priority to people's basic needs than to the survival of endangered species. The basic needs of people now living in terms of food, clothing and shelter, are more important than any use which future generations might have for these endangered species. Embracing anthropocentric values leads, therefore, to different priorities from those of ecocentric values in these situations.

Agricultural Policies

It is a basic principle for advocates of sustainable development that there are limits to the way in which we may use land and water. If these limits are overstepped, the long-term productive potential of ecosystems is threatened and thereby biological diversity as well. Ultimately, the well-being of human beings suffers. The agricultural exploitation of land (including forestry, of course) affects ecosystems and biological diversity more than other human activities do since it concerns such large areas of land. When creating a sustainable society, the devising of an agricultural policy is, therefore, of great importance.

The World Commission, consequently, cites the conserving and strengthening of 'the resource base' as one of the seven overarching aims which in their view are subsumed in the concept of sustainable development (World Commission, 1987, p. 49):

---

[14] Rolston is careful, however, to emphasize the question's complexity. He asks, *inter alia*, 'Ought we to feed people first and save nature last? We never face so simple a question. The practical question is more complex' (Rolston, 1997, p. 223). He also points out the other factors which have to be taken into account (cf. ibid., pp. 223f.).

> If [human] needs are to be met on a sustainable basis the Earth's natural resource base must be conserved and enhanced. Major changes in policies will be needed to cope with the industrial world's current high levels of consumption, the increases in consumption needed to meet minimum standards in developing countries, and expected population growth. (Ibid., p. 57)

The problem, according to the Commission, is that traditional policies lead to an impoverishment of the resource base's agricultural potential. In addition to general problems of waste and pollution, these policies lead to soil erosion, acidification of the land, deforestation, the spreading of deserts and a final reduction in fertility. The demand for food will simultaneously increase as a result of population growth and altered patterns of consumption. In general, the Commission reckons that global food production will have to increase annually by 3–4 per cent (ibid., p.128).

The challenge is one of being able to increase food production in line with demand, while so restructuring agriculture that ecosystems' long term productive capacity is no longer threatened. According to *Agenda 21*, therefore, the goal is 'to improve farm productivity in a sustainable manner, as well as to increase diversification, efficiency, food security and rural incomes, while ensuring that risks to the ecosystem are minimized' (*Agenda 21*, 14.26).

Today more food is produced per person than ever before. This increase is due above all to increased productivity but also to the widening of the resource base and the conversion of more territory into cultivated land. The problem, however, is that the wrong areas are converted in this way and that too much food is produced in the industrialized countries and too little in the developing countries (World Commission, 1987, pp. 128f). Many countries which do not grow enough food to feed their own population nevertheless possess the largest remaining unexploited agricultural areas, while in the Western world there are few areas still unexploited and therefore there is a great surplus of food. Much of the surplus is exported, often as aid, to the developing countries. The problem is that such measures tend to undermine efforts to develop these countries' food-producing potential. All this takes place at a time when there is an impoverishment of the resource base in the United States, Canada and the former Soviet Union, among others, through the overcultivation of marginal areas vulnerable to erosion.

Hence a basic conviction of both *Our Common Future* and *Agenda 21* is that ensuring a sustainable agricultural policy and guaranteeing care of the poor are mutually reinforcing aims. One measure suggested for putting agriculture on a permanent basis, therefore, is to reduce the state-supported stimulatory measures which lead to overproduction in the industrialized countries. Instead, one should transfer food production to countries suffering from shortages (World Commission, 1987, p. 132). Such a transfer is also regarded as a question of justice. It is important that one 'requires the systematic promotion of equity in food production and distribution' (ibid., p. 141). According to the authors of *Agenda 21*, the goal should be 'the long-term objective of enabling all people to achieve sustainable livelihoods' (*Agenda 21*, 3.4). The increase in consumption envisaged here depends upon the developing countries attaining a minimally acceptable standard in regard to food, shelter, health and education (ibid., 4.7; World Commission, 1987, p. 57).

In other words, a *weak principle of intragenerational justice* is presupposed on this point. This principle declares, as we saw in Chapter 3, that we have a moral obligation to use natural resources in such a way that the basic needs of at least all people now living can be met. Thus a distribution of food and other necessities will be just if this entails that the basic needs of all persons now living are satisfied as far as this is possible while the acquisition of other natural resources, or their transmission to the population, takes place in an ethically acceptable manner (in accordance with, for instance, the principle of just acquisition and the principle of just transfer).[15]

Another measure suggested is that certain areas now used as agricultural land should be left completely fallow or used agriculturally in a different, less intensive way. The underlying motivation for this measure is the view that 'inappropriate and uncontrolled land uses are a major cause of degradation and depletion of land resources. Present land use often disregards the actual potential, robustness and limitations of land resources, as well as their diversity in space' (*Agenda 21*, 14.34). The World Commission calls the first group of lands 'restoration areas'. They include areas that have quite lost their productive capacity or seen it drastically reduced. Alongside this group one also distinguishes between 'enhancement areas' (those tolerant of intensive agriculture) and 'prevention areas' (those not open to intensive agriculture or those which should be worked in a different way) (see World Commission, 1987, p. 133). The treatment of restoration areas needs to be varied from place to place, but it can require constraints on human activity so as to make a renewal of natural vegetation possible. These areas can also be protected by being designated as national trust territory.

It is further suggested, *inter alia*, that land reforms should be carried out in countries where the land is very unequally distributed or, more generally, that programmes should be devised and implemented to remove the social and economic causes of the spoiling of land; that agriculture's technical resources in the developing countries should be strengthened so that productivity can be improved there; that irrigation and fisheries should be encouraged; and finally that an improvement in the status of women should be brought about in the developing countries.

Thus the general agricultural policy of those advocating sustainable development is that *we should take measures to ensure that all forms of agriculture are pursued in an ecologically sustainable way, that is, in such a way that the productive potential of ecosystems is not threatened.* It is our moral obligation to future human generations to ensure that animals, plants and the ecosystems sustaining them are treated in an effective and far-sighted way and that such treatment benefits everyone.

Do biocentrism and ecocentrism lead to a policy as regards the practical organization of agriculture different from the one suggested by advocates of sustainable development? The answer, we shall see, is yes. However, biocentrism has in general more to say on this point than ecocentrism. This is partly because

---

[15] Cf. Chapter 3, pp. 45.

biocentrism has been mainly concerned with human treatment or exploitation of domestic animals, while ecocentrism concentrates more upon wilderness rather than those already radically transformed areas of countryside which make up most agricultural land.

The biocentric goal for agriculture is not, primarily, that people's use of natural resources should become effective and far-sighted, but that their use of nature *should not violate the right of other living beings to exist and flourish*. Biocentrists believe that the question forgotten by sustainable development advocates, because of their anthropocentrist views, concerns whether plants and, above all, animals are treated within today's farming in a morally acceptable way. Such people fail to note the fact that the final goal of sound environmental policy making should be the well-being not just of human beings but also of other living creatures. The task, according to biocentrists, is therefore to formulate an environmental policy which is also fair and just with respect to other living beings.

For biocentrists the problem is not simply traditional agriculture but the fact that the new types of sustainable agriculture proposed in *Our Common Future* and *Agenda 21* tend to conflict with those ethical principles which should guide our intercourse with other living beings. These forms of agriculture clash even under normal circumstances with such duties as to refrain from causing other living beings harm or suffering (the rule of non-maleficence), to refrain from limiting or violating the freedom of other living beings (the rule of non-interference) and to refrain from deceiving other living beings or abusing the trust they feel for us (the rule of fidelity). Thus Taylor writes,

> when we raise and slaughter animals for food, the wrong we do to them does not consist simply in our causing them pain. Even if it becomes possible for us to devise methods of killing them, as well as ways of treating them while alive, that involved little or no pain, we should still violate a prima facie duty in consuming them. They would still be treated as mere means to our ends and so would be wronged. (Taylor, 1986, pp. 294–5)

Admittedly, Taylor grants that there are exceptions. These ethical rules are of a *prima facie* character. Thus it is morally permissible to deceive animals, to limit their freedom and even cause them suffering and death if this is necessary for our survival. We have no duty, therefore, to sacrifice ourselves and our lives for their sakes. But even if there are undoubtedly people totally dependent upon farming which involves the consumption of animals, it is equally indubitable, according to these biocentrists, that this is not the case with most people on earth. It follows that both traditional and ecologically sustainable agriculture conflict in an unacceptable way with the rule of non-maleficence.

A problem for advocates of strong biocentrism, nonetheless, is that, in principle, our consumption of plants also requires moral justification. This difficulty arises on account of their view that all life (including that of plants) has equal value. Neither human beings nor any other animals occupy a special place in this respect. Taylor thinks that there are at least two reasons why anyone rejecting a hierarchical view of nature should maintain that it is less bad to use plants, in making the choice between using plants or sentient life for food. The first reason is that plants, unlike animals, cannot experience pain, while the second directly concerns environmental policy making. Vegetarians need to use much less of the earth's surface than do meat eaters, and because we already occupy too much space (given that we do not have a higher value than other forms of life), plant consumption is preferable to consumption of animals. Taylor writes that 'one acre of cereal grains to be used as human food can produce five times more protein than one acre used for meat production; one acre of legumes (peas, lentils, and beans) can produce ten times more; and one acre of leafy vegetables fifteen times more' (ibid., p. 296). If this is correct, a biocentric agricultural programme would entail a drastic reduction in the land used for human food production when compared with anthropocentric programmes. According to Taylor, the areas thus freed should, in view of previous human violations, be established as a sanctuary for plants and animals.

Animal rights biocentrists, of course, share much of Taylor's view even if they claim, as a rule, that only sentient animals have a value equal to that of human beings. Vegetarianism is morally obligatory for them, too. Regan draws up guidelines for a biocentric policy, writing that 'we should not be satisfied with anything less than the total dissolution of commercial animal agriculture as we know it, whether modern factory farms or otherwise', the reason being that animals' rights are routinely violated in such agriculture (Regan, 1983, p. 351). Hence it is also clear that a biocentric and an anthropocentric agricultural policy differ essentially. While according to the sustainable development policy we must take measures ensuring that all forms of agriculture be so practised as not to threaten ecosystems' productive capacity in either the short or the long run, according to a biocentric policy *we should take measures ensuring that agricultural production goes over from vegetable and animal production to purely vegetable production.* Agriculture involving commercial exploitation of animals should be abolished. Thus what is fundamentally wrong with modern agriculture is not that animals and plants are used in a non-sustainable way, but that animals are viewed and treated as one of our resources, even as a renewable resource, which we can use as we wish as long as we do not violate any *human being's* rights.

We need, however, to qualify the above somewhat, since weak biocentrism does not lead to such a radical change in the organization of agriculture. Weak biocentrists assert that humans have a higher value than that of other living beings. In any conflict, therefore, between human well-being and that of animals, greater importance is generally assigned to human well-being. An advocate of weak biocentrism such as Carl-Henric Grenholm does not explicitly discuss vegetarianism, but in his discussion of scientific experiments on animals he asserts, *inter alia*, that it is our moral responsibility to carry out experiments on animals in such a way that their suffering is minimized (Grenholm 1997). Thus it is reasonable to assume that, if we have no moral duty to abstain from experiments on animals, we can scarcely have a duty to abstain from using animals as food either.

According to a weak biocentric ethic, it is generally the case, as we have seen, that in situations of conflict between the interests of human beings and those of other living creatures we have a duty, when peripheral or non-basic human interests appear incompatible with the basic interests of other living beings, to assign greater moral importance to the latter group of interests (*the weak principle of proportionality*).[16] Thus it is morally wrong to capture and kill animals to make fashionable shoes, clothes and handbags from their hides, to keep animals captive because they are beautiful to look at, to expose animals or plants to harm when manufacturing cosmetics, to hunt animals simply for pleasure, and so on. Instead, in all these situations, the animals' interests should come first. In some other situations, taking into account humankind's higher worth, priority can be given to human needs. Nonetheless, the *principle of minimum wrong* always holds; namely, that we must so act that the least possible suffering or harm is caused to other living beings.

Thus animals can be used as food. What is required, however, is that we respect their right to well-being inasmuch as we do not permit animal factories, where animals are kept in cramped conditions, or allow animals in transit or at the slaughterhouse to be exposed to needless suffering. It is a weak biocentric agricultural policy that *we should take measures to ensure that the use of animals for farming takes place in such a way that they are caused the least possible suffering and that attention should be paid to their well-being.*

This policy conflicts with the basic management directive issuing from the anthropocentric principle of efficiency and far-sightedness; namely, that animals and plants should be so treated that they can be used in as efficient and far-sighted a way as possible. In order to create sustainable, highly productive industrial farming which meets the food requirements of present and future generations, it is not required that the animals involved be given more space or more natural surroundings or that they be shielded from unnecessary suffering. Such measures, rather, could constitute a hindrance to really efficient and land-economizing meat production. A biocentric agriculture structured to consider the needs and well-being of animals, and not only of human beings, cannot fulfil *Agenda 21*'s directive 'to intensify agriculture by diversifying the production systems for maximum efficiency in the utilization of local resources, while minimizing environmental and economic risks' (*Agenda 21*, 14.25). An intensive agriculture, even when ecologically sustainable, is not a 'humane' or 'animal-friendly' agriculture.

There is reason to believe that an ecocentric ethic and a weak biocentric ethic lead to similar attitudes regarding the use of animals in agriculture. Ecocentrists, as we have seen, consider that the eating of animals should be approved as a natural biological phenomenon. At the same time, however, Rolston, for example, asserts that people have a moral responsibility to avoid exposing animals to needless or meaningless suffering (Rolston, 1988, pp. 81f). The intrinsic value ecocentrists assign to individual organisms justifies such consideration. Ecocentrists advocate, therefore, the *principle of prohibiting needless suffering*, which declares that we have a moral duty to try to avoid ourselves causing animals unnecessary or meaningless suffering.

The question of suffering, nonetheless, is not central to the ecocentrists' criticism

---

[16] Cf. Chapter 4, p. 79.

of the treatment of animals in modern farming. Although ecocentrists like Rolston or Callicott share the animal rights biocentrists' criticism of the way animals are treated, Callicott, for example, nonetheless wants to emphasize that 'the pain and suffering of research and agribusiness animals is not greater than that endured by free-living wildlife as a consequence of predation, disease, starvation, and cold' (Callicott 1989b, p.35). He wants to emphasize this because the important question for an ecocentrist is not really whether an animal suffers, but whether the amount of suffering we cause to animals exceeds the amount they would be exposed to if they were still wild (the *homologous principle*).[17]

Instead, Callicott holds, in agreement with Mary Midgley, that 'a big part of the immorality of the treatment of animals in the current industrial phase of human civilization is that we have broken trust with erstwhile fellow members of our traditionally mixed communities. Animals have been depersonalized and mechanized' (Callicott, 1989d, p. 55). The descendants of the animals once entrusted to us are treated like machines in modern industrial farming. In this way we have broken the silent social contract between humans and animals once entered into, namely that we are permitted to use them if we treat them well, with respect. Callicott's conclusion is that, 'On the ethical question of what to eat, it [ecocentrism] answers, not vegetables instead of animals, but organically as opposed to mechanico-chemically produced food' (Callicott, 1989b, p. 36).

Nonetheless, an ecocentric system of values seems to underwrite the same kind of policy as weak biocentrism, namely that we should ensure that farm animals are so treated that they are not exposed to unnecessary suffering and that their well-being is not neglected. As far as this is concerned, an ecocentric farming policy coincides with a weak biocentric farming policy. Thus ecocentrists, out of consideration for animals' well-being (a consideration which results from conceding moral standing to these animals) are also critical of *Agenda 21*'s insistence that we should seek to attain maximum efficiency regarding the sustainable exploitation of natural resources. They think that such an approach violates animals' moral dignity. People of course have a right to use animals to satisfy their own basic needs, but only on condition that they do not cause them unnecessary suffering but take genuine account of their well-being.

Rolston holds that there is another area where ecocentrism and the ethic of sustainable development lead to different agricultural policies. In a direct polemic against the World Commission's report, he writes:

> the UN commission has played down respect for the integrity of natural systems, and that leaves us wondering if even the health of natural systems is likely to be good, so long as humans are bent on meeting escalating human needs above all else. There is reason to think that agriculture in Iowa has gone too far: there is no national park, no national grassland, no national forest, no wilderness in the state; soil (the 'black gold') is being lost at a rapid rate; wetlands are being destroyed; free-ranging bison are extinct in the state. State parks and other conservation areas contain fragments of prairie, but statewide there is less than

---

[17] Cf. Chapter 4, p. 99.

0.1 per cent of the native prairie left, only one acre in a thousand. There is hardly any mesic prairie at all, once the natural glory of the state. *All this development is a good thing, by the UN criteria, if it meets people's essential needs (growing corn and wheat), provided only that future generations can grow crops there, too.* Now we begin to wonder if the sustainable development approach can appreciate natural values, and if, given its fixation on growth, development really is going to be sustainable. (Rolston, 1994a, p. 86, emphasis added)

Rolston's point is that provided that farming in Iowa does not in the long term threaten the productive capacity of the land used, such farming is compatible with the demand for a sustainable development. The World Commission's purely anthropocentric definition of sustainability, namely that a development is sustainable if it meets the needs of the present without compromising the ability of future generations to meet their own needs, does not imply that a use of land entailing the extinction of virtually the whole of natural animal and plant life there would be wrong, if the land could still be used in a productive way by future generations too. The World Commission writes, for example, 'There is nothing inherently wrong with clearing forests for farming, provided that the land is the best there is for new farming, can support the numbers encouraged to settle upon it, and is not already serving a more useful function, such as watershed protection. But often forests are cleared without forethought or planning' (World Commission, 1987, p. 127). Farming in Iowa will have gone too far only if some of the land used is not suitable for farming or should really to be saved for watershed protection or to preserve some endangered species of high instrumental value for human beings.

An ecocentric ethic, on the other hand, 'requires that rural places be kept as full of nature as is consistent with their being agricultural places as well' (Rolston, 1988, p. 226). Original ecosystems forming part of land areas used for crop cultivation must be preserved too, irrespective of whether these areas are of any use to anyone. They should be preserved because they have an intrinsic value which we have no right to violate. According to ecocentrists, the *preservation principle with respect to natural ecosystems* applies here. This principle states, as we saw, that when converting areas of wilderness into settled areas we have a moral duty to leave some space for the original ecosystem and its inhabitants.[18]

In his criticism of the World Commission's report, however, Rolston does not pay full attention to the farming policy proposed by advocates of sustainable development, including (as it does) suggestions that some arable areas should be taken out of production and that biological diversity should be preserved not only in protected nature reserves but also in productive areas of forestry and agriculture. According to the Convention on Biological Diversity we should 'as far as possible and as appropriate ... [r]egulate or manage biological resources important for the conservation of biological diversity whether within or outside protected areas, with a view to ensuring their conservation and sustainable use' (*Convention on Biological Diversity*, 1992, article 8). The national committee for Agenda 21 summarizes the follow-up of *Agenda 21* in Sweden thus: 'The preservation of

---

[18] Cf. Chapter 4, p. 94.

biological diversity has become an integral part of the use [of agricultural and forest land]. ... The wealth of species has increased through the creation of diffusion corridors on cultivated land. Irrigated border-zones and dikes along with dams and wetlands capture nutrients and act as a refuge for wild animal and plant species' (Statens offentliga utredningar, 1997 p. 57). The Swedish National Environment Protection Board writes, regarding a parliamentary decision of 1990, 'the environmental aim of the new food policy is to take care to maintain a rich and varied agricultural terrain' (Naturvårdsverket, 1997, p. 36). Thus advocates of sustainable development in Sweden (and presumably also in the other countries that have signed the Convention on Biological Diversity) support a programme for structuring agriculture which seems to satisfy the requirements of the ecocentric principle of preservation with respect to ecosystems.

To develop agriculture in such a way that present and future generations can satisfy their vital needs (for example, in the case of Iowa, to grow corn and wheat) is thus not the only UN criterion for a sustainable development of arable land. It is true that according to the World Commission the goal of environmental management and social development is 'the satisfaction of human needs and aspirations' (World Commission, 1987, p. 43) or, as the Swedish National Environment Protection Board puts it, that 'the environmental goals suggested are based upon values as to what is of benefit to society as a whole' (Naturvårdsverket, 1997, p. 13). But, given that a varied agricultural land area rich in animal and plant species can have a scientific, economic, cultural or recreational value for human beings, along with its value in terms of food production, it is possible for anthropocentrists to assert that such an area has a higher instrumental value and should therefore be preferred to agricultural land (according to Rolston, common in Iowa) which is more specialized and possesses less diversity in animal and plant life.

Nonetheless, an anthropocentric policy programme which sets out to protect an agricultural area richer in plants and animals than is necessary for ensuring this area's long term productive capacity will always be to a high degree negotiable. What has greater instrumental value for us: setting aside wealth to improve theatres and museums or preserving hayfields or agriculture in, say, Stockholm's archipelago? How are we to balance the economic profit which an increased investment in advertising tourism in Sweden would bring against the cultural, historical, scientific and aesthetic value embodied in maintaining and improving those arable islet ploughlands created by traditional Swedish agriculture? As the Swedish National Environment Protection Board puts it, one is ultimately asking which is of greater use for society as a whole. But it is just here that an ecocentrist is entitled to feel disquiet. Is the motivation underpinning an anthropocentric policy for a species-rich and diverse agricultural milieu sufficient? According to ecocentrists, as we have seen, environmental goals should be based, not on what is judged of use for the whole *human* community, but on what is judged of use for the whole *biotic* community. Thus they reject the basically anthropocentric values on which the National Environment Protection Board bases its arguments.

Why should not an anthropocentrically inspired programme for maintaining such a varied agricultural environment, rich in plant and animal species, be sufficient? In a country like Sweden, with few mouths to feed and a generally good economy, it is perhaps not so difficult to allocate resources to preserving hayfields and those islet ploughlands. But what should an intergenerational anthropocentrist's priorities be in poor industrial countries or in developing countries where there is considerable population pressure? What is quite obvious is that we should try to ensure that the long term productive capacity of agricultural land is not threatened. But beyond that? Should resources be set aside for preserving fringe areas, islet farmlands and fens, together with endangered species, none of which are necessary, so that – as Rolston expresses it – future generations can grow corn and wheat on these lands too? The emphasis in the World Commission's report in needing to give 'overriding priority' to satisfying the basic needs of human beings, particularly in poor countries (World Commission, 1987, p. 43), clearly indicates that the instrumental value which the maintenance of a species-rich and varied agricultural area beyond the level of sustainability might possess ought to carry little weight for anthropocentrists in poor industrial countries or in developing countries with high population pressure. It is the use of land for maximally efficient food production which should be assigned priority in these countries.

Embracing ecocentric values, on the other hand, results in different priorities in this matter. An agricultural area which satisfies only the requirement that future generations also be able to cultivate corn and wheat or similar crops on the land concerned does not 'respect the nature that is the original source of our being.' It is both possible for us and required of us, according to Rolston, to 'have nature, modified by culture, still flourishing on prairie landscapes' (Rolston, 1994a, p. 87). Agricultural land should be so organized that the plant and animal species naturally at home there can be fitted in. This requirement remains valid even when a pressing human need for food has to be weighed against preserving these remaining unexploited fringe areas or islands. The *integrity* of nature (its dignity) and not only its *sustainability* (its long term productive capacity) has to be respected even when managing an agricultural area. Here, once again, we have a field where the ambitions of ecocentrists to protect nature against human beings (in contrast to anthropocentrists, who want to conserve nature for human beings) is of direct practical relevance, since preserving nature, according to them, is the paramount task of environmental management, even if this does not always serve human well-being.

The question treated in this chapter has been whether anthropocentric, biocentric and ecocentric ethics not merely stand for different basic values but also lead to different conclusions regarding environmental management and policy making. I have tried to answer this question by examining population problems, problems regarding the proportion of land to be kept as wilderness and the appropriate management of these areas, the problem of endangered species and of the principles governing the use of animals and plants in farming. A number of other important topics, such as patterns of consumption, the use of energy, questions of transport and forestry planning, have not been broached, but our discussion is sufficiently comprehensive to show that our choice of environmental ethic is of crucial practical relevance for environmental policy making. Differences in basic values often generate divergent policies.

CHAPTER SIX

The Relevance of Environmental Ethics

According to *Agenda 21*, 'increased ethical awareness' in environmental decision making is desirable (*Agenda 21*, 31.8). Among the measures proposed in order to achieve this is increased cooperation at national and international levels 'to develop codes of practice and guidelines regarding environmentally sound and sustainable development, taking into account the Rio Declaration and existing codes of practice and guidelines' (31.10). The authors of *Agenda 21* propose that this is brought about, *inter alia*, by appointing 'national advisory groups on environmental and developmental ethics' and through 'education and training in developmental and environmental ethical issues [being extended] to integrate such objectives into education curricula and research priorities' (31.10).

The present work can be seen as falling within this area. The aim has been to bring about an increased ethical awareness by defining more precisely and scrutinizing critically the values and moral principles on which the notion of sustainable development is based (as this is expressed in such key policy documents as *Our Common Future*, *Agenda 21*, the *Rio Declaration* and the Swedish National Environment Protection Board's *En miljöanpassat samhälle* (A Sustainable Society). These normative principles have then been presented in a systematic fashion and have been developed into a more explicit environmental ethics, which I have chosen to call 'intergenerational anthropocentrism'. I have, however, also gone beyond *Agenda 21*'s directive in trying to decide how far there are viable alternatives to this ethic or to the complex of values which is involved in the notion of sustainable development. When one system of values is accepted, alternative systems are likely to be indirectly discarded. An important task for research in environmental ethics is therefore to tell us which of the alternative ethical standpoints are indirectly ruled out by the ethic of sustainable development.

It is worth noting that, although in the policy documents which have been studied attention is paid to the fact that environmental problems have a normative dimension, and it is even asserted that a new ethic is needed, there is no discussion of the ethical principles which form the normative basis for current environmental policy making and management. This is problematic from a number of points of view. In order to have a frank and critical discussion of environmental issues in a democracy, an account is needed *both of the facts and of the normative principles* which form the basis of decisions and proposed policies. Without such an account, it is difficult for people to decide whether their possible disagreements are based on a questioning of the reliability of a given piece of information or whether they are based on doubts about the correctness of certain particular moral judgments or ethical principles.

My impression is that this lack of clarity is not intentional. It is in all probability not a question of a conscious attempt to hide the normative premises with the aim of pretending that the matter is one of a purely scientific or empirical character. Rather, it is more likely that it arises from a lack of interest in ethical theory or a lack of acquaintance with research in environmental ethics. At the same time, this tendency reinforces the erroneous impression among decision makers that environmental problems are essentially scientific problems and thus something to be solved by science and technology. What has to be emphasized is that there is no automatic connection between factual assertions and value judgments. We cannot formulate and become engaged in any environmental policy making unless we supplement the scientific information with certain value judgments about what we as human beings value, about the kind of lives we should live, about our proper place in nature and about our responsibility towards other living things and, ultimately, towards the Earth's ecosystems.

It is hoped that a positive effect of the present book is therefore that any illusion that science and technology alone can solve the problems we are faced with will be removed, and decision makers and scientists will become aware that great emphasis must be placed on the normative aspects of environmental issues. It is not enough simply to know how the biogeochemical cycles and the 'social' cycles work: we must also make our minds up about how the relationship between the two cycles *ought* to be. How should nature and culture relate to one another? This naturally also implies that research funds must be set aside for this task.

As Ronald Engel has rightly pointed out, there is a great need for elucidating

> the values that inform public policy statements on environment and development issues. Documents such as the World Conservation Strategy and the World Charter are peppered with moral concepts such as 'democracy', 'equity' and 'respect for nature' which, though crucial to their message, are often used in a vague and even contradictory fashion ... Yet the internal coherence of public policy statements, and consequently their practical effectiveness, depends upon reasoned justification for the values and choices espoused. Ethical clarity cannot be generated casually, but requires the same kind of rigorous intellectual attention as that devoted to scientific, technical and legal considerations. (Engel, 1990, p. 7)

A certain disquiet about this point is justified. To some extent perhaps, the Brundtland Commission and the authors of *Agenda 21* can be pardoned for failing to give a clearer account of the values which form a normative basis for the environmental goals and policies which they propose. These documents, after all, constitute only a starting point for a detailed discussion of the scientific, economic, political and ethical aspects of environmental issues. However, there is reason to consider how much importance is really assigned to the 'new' ethics. In spite of the fact that the UN has appointed countless committees of enquiry and has been involved in the initiation of major environmental research programmes, we still do not have a detailed analysis of the ethic of sustainable development, and of the question why alternative value systems which indirectly conflict with it should be rejected.

This ambivalent attitude to our values and the importance of ethics in the dicussions about environment also reappears in the tutorial material which has been produced for use in courses on environmental studies at universities and colleges. For example, in the introduction to his book *Miljökunskap* (The Study of the Environment), Torsten Persson writes: 'A number of environmental issues can be defined in terms of natural sciences but ultimately it is a question of morality and ethics. What right have human beings to exploit nature in a way which leads to the extinction of other species?' (Persson, 1994, p. 10). But if one really believes that environmental issues ultimately boil down to morality and ethics, how does it come about that one can write a whole book devoted to the ecological, economic and legal aspects of the environment without at the same time providing at least some elementary knowledge of ethical theory and research in environmental ethics?

A valuable subject for investigation would be the extent to which the directives of *Agenda 21* to 'develop codes of practice and guidelines regarding environmentally sound and sustainable development', to appoint 'national advisory groups on environmental and developmental ethics' and to extend 'education and training in developmental and environmental ethical issues' have been implemented at international and national levels (31.8–31.10). To take a concrete example, in the case of Sweden I know of no resources whatsoever having been set aside for research and teaching positions in environmental ethics at any Swedish university. By contrast, a great number of other environment-related posts have been created at the universities.

Here there is a striking difference between the relationship between ethics and environmental research, on the one hand, and the relationship between ethics and biomedical research on the other. In the environmental sphere, there is a gap between decision makers and ethicists which does not seem to exist in the sphere of medicine and genetics. To give an example, 3–7 per cent of the total funding for the HUGO programme (the mapping of the human genome) and the GENOM programme (the mapping of the genome of other organisms) has been set aside for projects which investigate the ethical, social and legal implications of this research. As a result, it has been possible to carry out at a national and an international level a whole series of research projects dealing with ethical implications of this area of biomedical investigation. In this way, a competence in medical ethics has been built up. There has been little or no conscious attempt – at least in Sweden – to build up a comparable competence in the area of environmental ethics. Yet, as Engel points out, ethical clarity and reflection requires as much rigorous intellectual attention as is needed in scientific, technological and legal studies, and this is also true in the case of environmental ethics.

The reason why decision makers and environmental scientists have not taken the ethical dimension seriously, may have to do with the fact that they make the (conscious or unconscious) assumption (a) that ethical principles do not constitute a subject for serious and constructive research or (b) that the type of environmental ethic one adopts is irrelevant in a practical sense: that is, the ethical differences with regard to environmental issues have only a marginal importance for shaping environmental management and for social planning as a whole. I hope that what has been written in earlier chapters shows that serious and constructive research in environmental ethics is possible. Concerning point (b), it is important to provide an answer not only to the question of what ethical alternatives there are to intergenerational anthropocentrism but also to the question of how environmental management would be transformed if one of these alternatives were to be chosen instead as a basis for policy making.

In order to answer these questions, we began initially by distinguishing between two formulations of non-anthropocentric ethics, namely biocentrism and ecocentrism. Biocentrists hold that we, as advocates for sustainable development suppose, do not merely have moral obligations towards present and future generations of human beings but also have them towards other (non-human) living beings. Ecocentrists in this matter go still further maintaining that our obligations extend beyond biological individuals (human beings, animals and plants) to apply to ecological wholes such as rivers, mountains and forests. We can violate not only the integrity of human beings or other living beings but also that of ecosystems and other ecological wholes. Non-anthropocentric ethicists do not usually discuss the practical implications of their ethical principles for environmental policy making and management. As Rollin notes, 'Writings in this area by and large have tended to focus more on making the case for the attribution of moral status to these entities [other living creatures, species and ecosystems] than on working out detailed answers to practical issues' (Rollin, 1995, p. 114). Part of my work has therefore been devoted to trying to create a bridge between ethical theory and practice.

It is clear that these various environmental theories of ethics underpin different aims in environmental policy making. The goal of (intergenerational) *anthropocentric* policy making is to use natural resources in such an efficient and far-sighted way that it will answer to the needs not only of now living human beings but also of future generations. By contrast, the object of *biocentric* policy making is to try to ensure that human beings, in making use of nature, do not violate the right of other living things to exist and flourish. The ultimate goal of all environmental policies is the well-being, not merely of human beings, but of animals and plants as well. The task is therefore to design an environmental programme which is just to all living beings. Finally, the aim of *ecocentric* policy making is to try to ensure that in making use of nature we do not violate the integrity of the biotic community (and in varying degrees its particular individuals) or threaten its stability. The preservation of species and ecological entities such as rivers, marshes and forests must be the central concern of environmental policy making, irrespective of whether or not it also promotes human well-being.

These theories of environmental ethics support different policy programmes, for example with regard to population, the extent of wilderness, the management of the wilderness, endangered species and agricultural management.

An urgent problem is how we are to deal with the global increase in population which in a variety of ways, constitutes a direct threat to nature. Anthropocentrists, on the one hand, and biocentrists and ecocentrists on the other, tend to approach this issue in quite different ways. Intergenerational anthropocentrism supports a *stabilization* policy: the size of the population must be stabilized at a level which is compatible with the productive potential of the ecosystems. Ecocentrism and biocentrism, on the other hand, advocate a *reduction* policy: the size of the population must be reduced to a level which is compatible with a respect for the welfare of other living beings and for the integrity of species and ecosystems. This difference of approach arises from the fact that biocentrists and ecocentrists assign, respectively, to animals and plants or to species and ecosystems such a high moral value that a limitation in the number of human beings is morally obligatory.

The central argument which proponents of sustainable development give for our obligation not to exploit all the land areas of the earth is that such exploitation deprives future generations of important genetic material. But these areas of wilderness can only constitute important genetic material for future generations of human beings if it is assumed that *the latter* (as opposed to us) have a right to use them. The ecocentric view, however, is that, even if such areas of wilderness constitute important genetic material, human beings have the right to exploit them neither now nor in the future. Irrespective of the utility which present or future generations might derive from the areas of wilderness which have been preserved, it is our duty to leave them undisturbed.

A crucial difference of view about the direction of environmental management concerns the species whose continued survival and well-being should primarily be protected. A *biocentric* policy of species preservation holds that we should primarily preserve those endangered species whose individual members have an intrinsic value or have the highest intrinsic value (that is, sentient animals). An *ecocentric* policy of species preservation implies instead that we should primarily preserve those endangered species which contribute to the survival and well-being of the ecosystems. Since something is morally right if it promotes the integrity, stability and beauty of the biotic community, we ought first of all to preserve the endangered species which contribute to the survival and well-being of the ecosystems. In contrast, anthropocentrists maintain – to retain the ecocentrist's terminology – that something is morally right if both now and in the future it promotes the integrity, well-being and beauty of the *human* community. An anthropocentric policy of species preservation thus holds that we should primarily preserve those endangered species which constitute a resource for present and future generations of human beings, that is the species which have the highest instrumental value.

Ecocentrists are worried that anthropocentrists get their priorities wrong when they are forced to choose between the protection of endangered species and the promotion of other human interests such as the building of museums, sports arenas and motorways, or providing for the poor. According to them, the problem is that the anthropocentrists who wish to preserve biological diversity must show that the instrumental values thus achieved are greater than the value which a transformation of the natural areas where these species are to be found (such as productive forest and cultivated land) entails. The preservation of certain endangered species can quite simply be assigned a very low priority when the instrumental value of these species is balanced against other resources which also have an instrumental value for present and future generations of human beings.

But if we accept that these species have an *intrinsic* value, the priorities look quite different. According to the ecocentrists it is because we have injured other species that we have a duty to design our environmental management in such a way that endangered species are preserved and, if need be, rehabilitated. Normally, there is no need for discussion about whether these species have an instrumental value or, given that they have, how far this value is to be weighed against other resources which have a resource value for us as human beings. Similarly, if I injure another human being, I cannot say that I would prefer to invest my money in building a larger house for myself (since that has a high instrumental value for me) rather than pay the hospital costs of the person I have injured. When I have caused another person injury, my instrumental values count for little compared to the person's intrinsic value.

A very important policy question for biocentrists is how we treat the animals we make use of in agriculture. By contrast, for proponents of sustainable development the vital question is whether the land and animals are used in a far-sighted and efficient way so that future generations of human beings can also satisfy their needs. Moreover, some biocentrists maintain that respect for the equal value of animals ought to imply that agriculture is transformed by discontinuing meat production (or at least greatly restricting its scope). In general, non-anthropocentrists question whether it is self-evident that human welfare should be, as the World Commission writes, 'the ultimate goal of all environment and development policies' (World Commission, 1987, p. xiv).

Non-anthropocentrists naturally hold that, as a rule, it is good that proponents of sustainable development pay attention to the issue of intergenerational and intragenerational justice. However, as Robyn Eckersley points out in her comment on the fact that environmental issues and environmental involvement are often dealt with as an aspect of the broader task of distributive justice and democratic planning, 'distributional questions remain crucial questions ... [but] to circumscribe the problem in this way can nonetheless serve to reinforce rather than challenge the prevailing view that the environment is simply a human resource' (Eckersley, 1992, p. 9). The fundamental error which advocates of sustainable development make, according to non-anthropocentrists, is thus that one treats the products of nature simply as a resource for the satisfaction of human needs and interests. Contrary to what the Swedish National Environment Protection Board supposes, it is not unproblematic to base environmental goals purely on what is valuable to human beings (Naturvårdsverket, 1997, p. 13). This is so because nature is not simply a human resource but also has a value in itself and one which we are morally obliged to respect.

An important matter which must be taken up in connection with discussions of policy is to decide what things have an intrinsic value and to determine what consequences are entailed by an acceptance of nature's intrinsic value when it is a matter of how people ought to act and fashion their society. It is worth taking seriously that 'in the face of accelerated environmental degradation and species extinction, environmental philosophers are now asking: are we humans the only beings of [intrinsic] value in the world? Does the world exist only for our benefit?'

(Eckersley, 1992, p. 2). It remains to be seen whether Callicott is right in claiming that such a fundamental change of values will have as great a practical importance within the environmental sphere as the general acceptance of the intrinsic value of all human beings has had within the social sphere (Callicott, 1995b, p. 24). However, as we have seen, it does have practical importance.

Such an environmental discussion and the associated research is worth noting and encouraging because we can already perceive in Sweden and elsewhere – above all among young people – the seeds of just such a shift in values. In the mid-1980s, a survey was carried out at the Department of Theology of Uppsala University into human values. Among the questions which interviewees were asked were the following: 'Ought we to have greater respect for human beings than for other living beings?' Only 37 per cent of those asked replied 'yes' to this question whereas 44 per cent answered 'no', with the remaining 19 per cent being doubtful (Jeffner, 1988). In an investigation carried out some years later, a random sample of people were asked to choose between two points of view: (a) 'Human beings have a higher value than all other living things. Animals have a lower value than human beings', and (b) 'Human beings and animals have the same value'. The results showed that 27 per cent chose standpoint (a) as against 66 per cent who chose standpoint (b), with 7 per cent remaining uncertain (Jeffner, 1992). Anders Jeffner commented on the result as follows: 'What is evident in all the investigations is a tendency within an important part of the population not to assign to human beings a unique place in the scale of values. It would appear that this tendency becomes more accentuated the further down one comes in age-group' (Jeffner, 1992, p. 4).

Similar questions were posed in the so-called EVSSG-study (The European Value System Study Group) which was carried out in 1990. Of the one thousand Swedes who participated in the study, 58 per cent held that 'human beings and animals have the same value', while 44 per cent maintained that 'all life is equally important: it is equally important to save an endangered species as it is to save human life'. In accordance with these values, 63 per cent held that 'nature has an intrinsic value', whereas only 37 per cent believed that 'nature is valuable only through being useful to human beings' (Pettersson, 1992, pp. 64f).

We must naturally be clear about the fact that, because people say that they value something in a certain way, it does not follow automatically that they are also willing in practice to act in accordance with this value judgment. Jeffner points out that the studies also show that when people are forced to choose between saving a human being or an animal which in some sense is valuable or unique, they choose to save the human being. Jeffner's comment on this is that the view that human beings and animals have the same value 'seems to function more as a reminder that we have a responsibility for animals and that we ought not to expose them to unnecessary suffering' (Jeffner, 1992, p. 14). In other words, although the interviewees theoretically espoused some form of strong biocentrism or animal rights biocentrism, in practice they came down on the side of weak biocentrism.

Nor are ecocentric views entirely foreign to Swedes. In another recent investigation, Nils Uddenberg describes the test subjects in the following way:

The interviewees' moral philosophy can best be described as ecocentric ... All organisms, human beings not excepted, were thought of as being dependent on one another and mutually participating in maintaining 'the balance of nature'. Actions which contributed to preserving the ecosystems were thought of as praiseworthy whereas actions which instead injured them were to be condemned. The various organisms derived their justication from being parts of the organic wholes making up the ecosystems. (Uddenberg, 1995, p. 161)

Although in his analysis Uddenberg does not distinguish between what I call 'biocentrism' and 'ecocentrism', his description of the interviewees' environmental ethics shows that they do not find it at all strange to ascribe moral significance to ecosystems and even a greater significance than that assigned to certain specific parts making up the ecosystems. There is therefore empirical support that a shift in values from a purely anthropocentric ethic to a biocentric or ecocentric ethic is taking place in modern Sweden. People in general are not opposed to these alternative standpoints in environmental ethics and indeed many are even prepared to accept them. (The same is probably true about many other European countries.) This is as good a reason as any why decision makers and environmental researchers must not ignore the ethical dimension of environmental issues.

It is appropriate to make a recommendation. Let us recall Andrew Kadak's discussion of the ethical guidelines which ought to constitute the starting point for the treatment and storing of nuclear waste. In his presentation of the conclusions of the working group, he mentions that they also agreed on the form that an intergenerational decision-making process (that is, a decision-making process where the choices we make also have direct consequences for future generations of human beings) should take. One of these guidelines is the following: such a process must be 'capable of dealing with the many values upon which the decisions are based' (Kadak, 1997, p. 50). In other words, a lesson which decision makers can and ought to derive from this study, is that it is important for them to try and specify explicitly the values on which their proposals and decisions are based, and why.

In conclusion, it is my opinion that the discussion which has taken place is sufficiently comprehensive to show that anthropocentrism, biocentrism and ecocentrism generate different views about the direction of current environmental policy making and management, and that lack of unity at the ethical or normative level cannot therefore be ignored. I hope, moreover, that it has become clear what the nature of environmental ethics is, which questions of this type are dealt with in academic studies, and why environmental ethics is relevant for an analysis and solution of environmental problems. In my view the study can provide decision makers at all levels with some of the knowledge of ethical theory which they require to be able to reflect consciously about what significance their own and other people's moral judgments and ethical principles have for environmental problems. It is hoped that the book can give people in general conceptual tools which will allow them to discover and criticize the often hidden, unclearly formulated, or even sometimes contradictory ethical principles on which current environment policy making and management are based.

Bibliography

Anderberg, Thomas (1994), *Den mänskliga naturen: En essä om miljö och moral*, Värnamo: Norstedts.

Ariansen, Per (1993), *Miljöfilosofi*, Nora: Nya Doxa.

Ashmore, Robert B. (1987), *Building a Moral System*, Englewood Cliffs, NJ: Prentice-Hall.

Attfield, Robin (1983), *The Ethics of Environmental Concern*, Oxford: Blackwell.

Barbour, Ian (1993), *Ethics in an Age of Technology*, San Francisco: HarperCollins.

Barry, Brian (1989), *Democracy, Power and Justice*, Oxford: Clarendon Press.

Beauchamp, Tom L. and James F. Childress (1989), *Principles of Biomedical Ethics*, 3rd edn, Oxford: Oxford University Press.

Brennan, Andrew (1988), *Thinking about nature*, Athens, GA: University of Georgia Press.

Brown, Noel J. and Pierre Quiblier (eds), (1994), *Ethics and Agenda: Moral Implications of a Global Consensus,* New York: United Nations Publications.

Callicott, J. Baird (1989a), 'Introduction: the real work', *In Defense of the Land Ethic*, Albany: SUNY Press.

——— (1989b), 'Animal liberation: A triangular affair', *In Defense of the Land Ethic*, Albany: SUNY Press.

——— (1989c), 'Review of Tom Regan: The case for animal rights', *In Defense of the Land Ethic*, Albany: SUNY Press.

——— (1989d), 'Animal liberation and environmental ethics: back together again', *In Defense of the Land Ethic*, Albany: SUNY Press.

——— (1989e), 'The conceptual foundations of the land ethic', *In Defense of the Land Ethic*, Albany: SUNY Press.

——— (1989f), 'On the intrinsic value of nonhuman species', *In Defense of the Land Ethic*, Albany: SUNY Press.

——— (1994), *Earth's insights. A Multicultural Survey of Ecological Ethics from the Mediterranean Basin to the Australian Outback*, Berkeley: University of California Press.

——— (1995a), 'Environmental ethics: overview', in Warren Thomas Reich (ed.), *Encyclopedia of Bioethics*, rev. edn, New York: Simon & Schuster Macmillan.

——— (1995b), 'Environmental philosophy is environmental activism: the most radical and effective kind', in Don E. Marietta and Lester Embree (eds), *Environmental Philosophy and Environmental Activism*, Boston: Rowman & Littlefield.

Commoner, Barry (1971), *The Closing Circle: Nature, Man, and Technology*, New York: Knopf.

Des Jardins, Joseph R. (1997), *Environmental Ethics*, 2nd edn, Belmont: Wadsworth.

de-Shalit, Avner (1995), *Why Posterity Matters*, London: Routledge.

Devall, Bill and George Sessions (1994), 'Deep ecology', in Donald Van De Veer and Christine Pierce (eds), *The Environmental Ethics and Policy Book*, Belmont, Wadsworth.

Dobson, Andrew (1997), *Green Political Thought*, 2nd edn, London: Routledge.

Eckersley, Robyn (1992), *Environmentalism and Political Theory*, New York: UCL Press.

Ehrenfeld, David (1978), *The Arrogance of Humanism*, Oxford: Oxford University Press.

Elliot, Robert (1995), 'Introduction', in Robert Elliot (ed.), *Environmental Ethics*, Oxford: Oxford University Press.

Engel, J. Ronald (1990), 'Introduction: The ethics of sustainable development', in J. Ronald Engel and Joan Gibb Engel (eds), *Ethics of Environment and Development*, London: Belhaven Press.

Feinberg, Joel (1974), 'The rights of animals and unborn generations', William T. Blackstone (ed.), *Philosophy and Environmental Crisis*, Athens, GA: University of Georgia Press.

Ferré, Frederick and Peter Hartel (eds) (1994), *Ethics and Environmental Policy: Theory Meets Practice*, Athens, GA: University of Georgia Press.

Ferry, Luc (1995), *The New Ecological Order* (originally published in French, 1992), Chicago: University of Chicago Press.

Gillespie, Alexander (1997), *International Environmental Law, Policy and Ethics*, Oxford: Clarendon Press.

Goldsmith, Edward (1972), *A Blueprint for Survival*, London: Green Books.

Grenholm, Carl-Henric (1997), 'Etik och djurförsök', *Årsbok 1997 för Föreningen lärare i Religionskunskap*.

Guthrie, R.D. (1995), 'Anthropocentrism', in James P. Sterba (ed.), *Earth Ethics*, Englewood Cliffs, NJ: Prentice-Hall.

Hargrove, Eugene C. (1989), *Foundations of Environmental Ethics*, Englewood Cliffs, NJ: Prentice-Hall.

Irvine, S. and A. Ponton (1988), *A Green Manifesto: policies for a green future*, London: Macdonald Optima.

Jeffner, Anders (1988), 'Människovärde och människovärdering', Department of Theology, Uppsala University.

———(1992), '*Djur och människa. Argumentbilder och strukturer i allmänt spridda värderingssystem*', (Rapport från ett HSFR-projekt), Department of Theology, Uppsala University.

Kadak, Andrew C. (1997), 'An intergenerational approach to high-level waste disposal', *Nuclear News*, July.

Leopold, Aldo (1949), *A Sand County Almanac and Sketches Here and There*, London: Oxford University Press.

Marietta, Don E. (1995), *For People and the Planet: Holism and humanism in environmental ethics*, Philadelphia: Temple University Press.

Marietta, Don E. and Lester Embree (eds) (1995), *Environmental Philosophy and Environmental Activism*, Boston: Rowman & Littlefield.

Merchant, Carolyn (1980), *The Death of Nature*, San Francisco: Harper & Row.

Miljövårdsberedningen (1992), Vår *uppgift efter Rio: Svensk handlingsplan inför 2000-talet*, SOU 1992: 104, Stockholm: Allmänna Förlaget.

Murphy, N. and J. Wm. McClendon, Jr (1989), 'Distinguishing modern and postmodern theologies', *Modern Theology*, 5.

Næss, Arne (1984), 'A defence of the deep ecology movement', *Environmental ethics*, 6.

—— (1989), *Ecology, Community and Lifestyle*, Cambridge: Cambridge University Press, (a revised edition translated into English of *Økologi, samfunn og livsstil*, Oslo: Universitetsforlaget, 1976).

—— (1997), 'Sustainable Development and the Deep Ecology Movement', in Susan Baker et al. (eds.) *The Politics of Sustainable Development*, London: Routledge.

Nash, Roderick (1988), *The Rights of Nature: a History of Environmental Ethics*, Madison, WI, University of Wisconsin Press.

Naturresurs- och miljökommitténs rapport (1982), *Ekologisk grundsyn: Bidrag till en diskussion om ett begrepp*, Stockholm.

Naturvårdsverket (1993), *Ett miljöanpassat samhälle, Naturvårdsverkets aktionsprogram: MILJÖ '93*, Solna: Naturvårdsverkets förlag.

—— (1997), *Ren luft och gröna skogar. Förslag till nationella miljömål 1997*, Stockholm: Naturvårdsverkets förlag.

Nordin, Sören (1991), *Naturkontraktet. Om naturumgängets idéhistoria*, Stockholm: Carlssons.

Norton, Bryan, G. (1987), *Why Preserve Natural Variety?*, Princeton: Princeton University Press.

—— (1991), *Toward Unity Among Environmentalists*, Oxford: Oxford University Press.

—— (1995), 'Future generations, obligations to', in Warren Thomas Reich (ed.) *Encyclopedia of Bioethics*, rev. edn, New York: Simon & Schuster Macmillan.

Nozick, Robert (1974), *Anarchy, State and Utopia*, Basic Books.

O'Neill, John (1993), *Ecology, Policy and Politics*, London: Routledge.

Passmore, John (1974), *Man's Responsibility for Nature: Ecological Problems and Western Traditions*, New York: Charles Scribner's Sons.

Persson, Torsten (1994), *Miljökunskap*, Lund: Studentlittertur.

Pettersson, Torleif (1992), 'Välfärd, värderingsförändringar och folkrörelseengagemang', in Sigbert Axelson and Torleif Pettersson (eds), *Mot denna framtid. Folkrörelser och folk om framtiden*, Stockholm: Carlssons.

Pinchot, Gifford (1914), *The Training of a Forester*, Philadelphia: Lippincott.

Regan, Tom (1983), *The Case for Animal Rights*, Berkeley: University of California Press.

Regeringens proposition (1992/93), *Med sikte på hållbar utveckling*, 180, Stockholm.

—— (1992/93), *Om riktlinjer för ett kretsloppsanpassad samhällsutveckling*, 180, Stockholm.

Rollin, Bernard, E. (1995), 'Environmental ethics and international justice', in James P. Sterba (ed.), *Earth Ethics*, Englewood Cliffs, NJ: Prentice-Hall.

Rolston, III, Holmes (1988), *Environmental Ethics*, Philadelphia: Temple University Press.

——(1994a), *Conserving Natural Value*, New York: Columbia University Press.

——(1994b), 'Winning and Losing in Environmental Ethics', in Frederick Ferre and Peter Hartel (eds) *Ethics and Environmental Policy*, Athens, GA: University of Georgia Press.

——(1997), 'Feeding people versus saving nature?', in Roger S. Gottlieb (ed.), *The Ecological Community*, London: Routledge.

Ruckelshaus, William D. (1994), 'Toward a sustainable world', in Donald Van De Veer and Christine Pierce (eds), *The Environmental Ethics and Policy Book*, Belmont, Wadsworth.

Sagoff, Mark (1988), *The Economy of the Earth*, Cambridge: Cambridge University Press.

Schweitzer, Albert (1949), *Out of my Life and Thought: An Autobiography*, New York: Holt, Rinehart & Winston.

Serageldin, Ismail and Richard Barrett (eds) (1996), 'Ethics and Spiritual Values', *Promoting Environmentally Sustainable Development*, Washington.

Sörlin, Sverker (1991), *Naturkontraktet*, Stockholm: Carlssons Bokförlag.

Statens offentliga utredningar (1997), *Agenda 21 i Sverige. Fem år efter Rio – resultat och framtid*, 105, Stockholm.

Stenmark, Mikael (1997), 'Environmental ethics and sustainable development', in Lars Rydén (ed.), *Foundations of Sustainable Development. Ethics, Law and the Physical Limits*, Uppsala University, The Baltic University Program.

—— (1999), 'Science and ideology', in Carl-Henric Grenholm and Gert Helgesson (eds), *Ideology in Science and Economics, Studies in Ethics and Economics*, 6, Uppsala: reprocentralen Ekonomikum.

Sterba, J.P. (1981), 'The Welfare Rights of Distant People and Future Generations: Moral Side-Constraints on Social Policy', *Social Theory and Practice*, 7.

Stevenson, Leslie and Henry Byerly (1995), *The Many Faces of Science,* Boulder: Westview Press.

Sundqvist, Göran (1996), 'Miljöexperterna: om vetenskapens auktoritet i miljöarbetet', in Lars J. Lundgren (ed.), *Att veta och att göra. Om kunskap och handling inom miljövården*, Stockholm: Naturvårdsverkets förlag.

Swedish Council for Planning and Coordination of Research (1994), *Milijöetik* (Environmental Ethics), Stockholm: Forskningstådsnämnden.

Swedish National Environment Protection Board (1993), *Ett miljöanpassat samhälle* (A Sustainable Society), Solna: Naturvårdsverkets förlag.

Taylor, Paul (1983), 'In Defense of Biocentrism', *Environmental Ethics, 5.*

——(1986), *Respect for Nature: A Theory of Environmental Ethics*, Princeton: Princeton University Press.

Tranöy, Knut Erik (1993), *Medicinsk etik i vår tid*, Lund: Studentlitteratur.

Uddenberg, Nils (1995), *Det stora sammanhanget. Moderna svenskars syn på människans plats i naturen*, Nora: Nya Doxa.

United Nations (1992), *Convention on Biological Diversity*, Rio de Janeiro.

United Nations (1992), *Agenda 21*, New York: United Nations Publications.

United Nations (1992), *Rio Declaration*, New York: United Nations Publications.

VanDeVeer, Donald and Christine Pierce (eds) (1994), *The Environmental Ethics and Policy Book*, Belmont, Wadsworth.

Världsstrategin för miljövård (1993), *Omsorg om jorden – en strategi för överlevnad*, Smedjebacken: Naturskyddsföreningen Förlag AB.

Wandén, Stig (1992), *Etik och miljö*, Stockholm: Norstedts juridik.

——— (1993), *Ideologiska kontroverser i miljövården*, Solna: Naturvårdsverkets förlag.

———(1997), *Miljö, livsstil och samhälle*, Stockholm: Nerenius & Santérus Förlag.

Wilson, Edward (1992), *The Diversity of Life*, Cambridge, MA: Harvard University Press.

Worster, Donald (1985), *Nature's Economy*, Cambridge: Cambridge University Press.

The World Commission on Environment and Development (1987), *Our Common Future*, Oxford: Oxford University Press.

Glossary

Anthropocentrism
The view that human beings alone have an intrinsic value or have moral standing.

Basic interest
An interest which, if unsatisfied, can injure an organism and threaten its welfare.

Biocentrism
The view that living beings alone have an intrinsic value or have moral standing.

Ecocentrism
The view that species, ecosystems, the land or the biotic community as a whole in addition to all living creatures have an intrinsic value or have moral standing.

Ecological holism
The view that the biosphere constitutes an interrelated and organic whole.

Environmental ethics
The systematic and critical study of the moral judgments and attitudes which (consciously or unconsciously) guide the way human beings behave towards nature.

Ethical holism
The view that ecological wholes (such as species and ecosystems) as well as individuals have moral standing.

Hierarchical view of nature
The view that forms of life on earth can be divided into higher and lower value categories.

Homologous principle
The principle that we have an obligation not to cause animals more suffering than that which they are exposed to (on average) in the state of wilderness.

Human ethics
The systematic and critical study of the moral judgments and attitudes which (consciously or unconsciously) guide our behaviour towards other human beings.

Inherent worth
The value which something has independent of human evaluation.

Instrumental value
The value which something has as a means to realizing something else which possesses an intrinsic value.

Intergenerational justice
The justice that should obtain between human generations existing at different points in time.

Intragenerational justice
The justice that should obtain between human generations alive at the same time.

Intrinsic value
The value which something has independent of its utility to others, that is, its non-instrumental value.

Methodological holism
The view that we should attend to a phenomenon as an organic whole rather than to its individual parts.

Minimal principle of intergenerational justice
The principle that we have a moral obligation to utilize or consume natural resources in such a way that we do not threaten the life opportunities of distant generations of human beings.

Moral agent
A being deemed capable of treating others in a morally right or wrong way.

Moral standing
Someone or something is said to have moral standing if it can be treated in a morally right or morally wrong way.

Naturalistic fallacy
The fallacy of deducing from the fact that something *is* such-and-such that it *ought* to be so.

Non-anthropocentrism
The view that non-human living beings or other natural objects have an intrinsic value or have moral standing.

Non-basic interest
An interest which an organism may (consciously or unconsciously) try to satisfy but one such that its non-satisfaction does not endanger the welfare of the organism.

Preservation principle with respect to natural ecosystems
The principle that we have a duty in cultivating wilderness to leave room for the original ecosystem and its inhabitants.

Principle of efficiency and far-sightedness
The principle that our use of natural resources ought to be efficient and far-sighted.

Principle of self-defence
The principle that we have a moral right to protect ourselves against other living organisms which threaten our existence.

Principle of species impartiality
The principle that we should treat all living beings as though they had equal value in the sense that irrespective of the species to which they belong, they should be ascribed equal weight and respect by a moral agent.

Principle of wildlife preservation
The principle that we have a duty to leave remaining areas of wilderness in the world untouched.

Principle of wildlife restoration
The principle that we have a duty to try to rehabilitate those areas of nature which from an ecological point of view can still be restored to natural wilderness.

Principle prohibiting needless suffering
The principle that we have a duty to avoid causing unnecessary or meaningless suffering to animals.

Rule of distributive justice
The principle that, in a situation where our basic interests inevitably conflict with the basic interests of other living beings, we have a duty to attach equal weight to the interests of both parties.

Rule of non-interference
The rule that we have a duty not to limit or violate the freedom of other living beings.

Rule of non-maleficence
The rule that we have a duty not to cause other living beings injury or suffering.

Rule of restitutive justice
The rule that we have a duty to compensate other living beings when we have treated them in a morally unacceptable way.

Static principle of intergenerational justice
The principle that we have a moral duty to bequeath to the next generation the same number and types of natural resources which we inherited from earlier generations.

Strong principle of intergenerational justice
The principle that we have a moral duty to use natural resources in such a way that future generations of human beings can be expected to enjoy a quality of life equal to that of our own.

Sustainable development
Development which satisfies the needs of present and future generations of human beings without threatening the productive potential of the supporting ecosystems or violating basic human rights.

Utility principle with respect to animals
The principle that it is morally acceptable for us to make use of (sentient or higher) animals to satisfy our own basic needs as long as we do not cause them unnecessary suffering or threaten the continued existence of the species.

Utility principle with respect to plants
The principle that it is morally acceptable for us to make use of plants (and insects) to satisfy our own needs as long as the value of the plants does not exceed the value which human beings obtain by making use of the plants and provided that we do not cause unnecessary damage or threaten the continued existence of the species.

View of nature
The view of an individual, group or society about the constitution and structure of nature.

Weak principle of intergenerational justice
The principle that we have a moral duty to use natural resources in such a way that future generations and not simply present generations of human beings will be able to satisfy their basic needs.

Index